MV RANGITATA

PREZZA

PREZZA
MY STORY: PULLING NO PUNCHES

John Prescott

with Hunter Davies

headline
review

Contents

Some Thanks

There are many people in politics I'd like to thank for their help and advice over the years, though I'd like to make it clear that they are not responsible in any way for this book.

I have been fortunate in having some wonderful political advisers, before and after we came into government. Unlike most political teams, they never did any leaking. They have included Rodney Bickerstaffe, Rosie Winterton, Dick Caborn, Alan Meale and Ian McCartney.

I would also like to thank members of my personal staff who made my job bearable, particularly Joan Hammell, Joe Irvin, Ian McKenzie, Mick Halloran, Mike Craven, David Taylor, Joyce Matheson, Tony Sophoclides, Sue Haylock, Steve Hardwick, Della Georgeson, Sue Phillips and Nick Hope.

I also had good advice from Alastair Campbell, plus my old mate Dennis Skinner, and my PPSs John Heppell, Phil Hope, Paul Clarke and David Watts.

Thanks also to a fabulous Civil Service who gave me much support, in particular my private office led by Geoff Jacobs, Peter Unwin, David Prout, Peter Betts and Philip Cox. And also to the cabinet girls led by Claire Sumner and Katherine Rimmer who helped me not to make too much of a fool of myself when I stood in for the prime minister and did Prime Minister's Questions fourteen times.

Outside politics, I'll always be grateful to all the people at Ruskin College, particularly the late Raphael Samuel, John and Vi Hughes, and also Professor John Saville of Hull University, who encouraged me when others, until then, hadn't seen much to encourage. And for comradeship, I'll never forget the friends I made at sea, especially my fellow stewards on the *Britannic*.

Then in my personal life, I must thank my sons Johnathan and David, our new addition Paul, and all my family, but most of all Pauline. She's had a lot to put up with, God knows, but she's supported me through thick and thin and shown the maturity and wisdom that sometimes I lacked.

We are both eternally grateful to those personal friends who have been about when it was necessary, at difficult times, and gave us their full friendship and support, especially Frank and Janet Brown, Ernie and Sally Bamforth and Laurie Holloway and his late wife Marion.

Finally, grateful thanks to Hunter Davies for getting it all out of me, knocking it into shape, and making sense of it all.

Prologue
Late Summer: 2007

It's been very strange, being out of office. Since I resigned as deputy prime minister, in June when Tony gave up being prime minister, I've been going round in a bit of a daze. I've felt sort of displaced, not knowing what to do with myself, where I fit in.

Tony has told me he's been feeling much the same. Apparently he doesn't know how to do texting. People had done it for him. I always made most of my own calls, and I do have a mobile phone, but no, I haven't yet got to grips with texting.

I've just given up my security team, which I've had since, let me think . . . 1997. I had three Special Branch officers, taking it in shifts, and a driver, Alan Hall, a good friend and great behind the wheel. I never had any major threat to my life during those ten years, but there was always the possibility, especially when I was deputising for Tony and acting as prime minister. Oh, of course – I did once have an object thrown at me, but I dealt with that myself, and there was an occasion when our house in Hull was attacked by Greenpeace, which was disappointing when you think how I always supported them. They got on the roof, which was pretty frightening for Pauline.

I could have asked for the security people to stay with me a bit longer, as I gather John Reid and others have done. The whole team was great, and made it so much easier to carry out my official duties, but I wanted shot of that sort of thing. Pauline misses them in some ways. They became our friends.

It's nice to go to places on our own, though, such as the cinema or a restaurant, without having to worry about other people. We were always having to think ahead, make arrangements. The security officers had to know what time and where we were going. Now we can just go out where we want, without any plans.

But it's taking me time to get to grips with a different lifestyle. And different travel arrangements. I was saying this to Michael Howard when I met him by chance in the House. He said hadn't I heard of a Freedom Pass? This gives free travel to people over sixty, by bus and Tube, all over London. I pointed out to him that he and the Tories had voted against it. I've got one, but one morning, a little while back, it didn't work for me on the Tube. Then I realised I couldn't use it before nine, which is why pensioners are known as Twirlies. The drivers and ticket inspectors say to them, 'Too early.' I got that joke from Jack Jones. I had to pay cash and was amazed it cost four pounds. I thought it was a mistake. Although it is cheaper with an Oyster card.

I'm driving myself all the time now as Pauline doesn't drive. And I've just been done for speeding – 35 in a 30 m.p.h. zone. I didn't see the signs. All these years, I've never had to look at road signs. Perhaps I should have a refresher at a driving school – that's what Humberside Police offer as an alternative to a fine. The first time I drove myself to King's Cross, to catch a train to Hull, I managed to park OK – but then, somehow, I locked the car with the keys still inside. I must admit that for ten years, being delivered door to door, it was nice not to worry about driving.

As soon as I gave up being DPM, I had to move to a different office in the House of Commons, on a different floor, miles away, which meant sorting all my files, chucking stuff out. At the same time Pauline and I had to move out of Admiralty House, from the apartment I've had for ten years in government. It's been taken over by Lord Malloch Brown. And I've given up Dorneywood, my official country home. Yes, it's been quite a shock to the system all round. No wonder I'm feeling like a displaced person.

I'm now looking for a London place to live. I'm continuing as an MP, till the next election, so I need a London base. I'm leaving it to one of my sons to find something suitable for us, arrange it all. I'll have to get a mortgage, of course, which at the age of sixty-nine won't be easy.

I've been a bit grumpier than usual, or so my family say. My sons maintain that talking to me has been like walking on eggshells. They've given me a mug with 'Mr Grumpy' on it. I use it all the time for my tea.

I've also felt tired and weak, but that's because I'm still getting over a bout of pneumonia I had in June when Tony and I were in the throes of resigning. It suddenly knocked me flat and I was rushed into University College Hospital, London.

I'd last been in that hospital fifteen years earlier when I'd got injured in a taxi that crashed outside the hospital. This time, I couldn't believe it was the same place. As a result of the public finance initiative, it's all new and wonderful, so light and spacious with excellent staff.

While I was in hospital Gordon Brown rang, asking how I was.

'It's a PFI hospital, the sort I used to be against for the Health Service,' I said. 'You were right to support them, and I was wrong.' When I came out, I gave a little party at Admiralty House for the staff who had looked after me. I invited Alan Johnson and he came along to meet everyone. He'd just been made secretary of state for Health.

Afterwards, I had a short holiday in the Lake District, staying at Scale Hill in Loweswater, where I started working on this book. As I was walking to the lake each day, I was reminded of all those years ago when I went to the Lake District with my secondary modern school, back in the 1950s.

I went to Whitehaven one day and was surprised, going round their brilliant harbour, to see my name. I got quite a shock. I'd forgotten I'd opened their multi-million-pound lock gates, back in 1998. There was a lock-keeper high up in a glass box so I waved at him. He waved back. I waved again. He came to the window and stuck his head out. I shouted, 'I'm John Prescott. I opened this.'

He invited me up to his box and we had a good chat. He'd only been there a short while, so wasn't around when I opened it, but he told me about the huge success and increase in traffic, trade and regeneration since the new gates opened.

My book, by the way, I've already decided it's going to be a personal memoir, my life and thoughts, not a definitive political record of every meeting I ever attended or public speeches I made. I hope it might counter some of the contorted images of me developed by the press.

I plan to follow it with a political book, on Labour's record and the influence of Old Labour on the Blair government, but I think further time is needed and fuller reflection. Meanwhile, this is the story of my 'stormy voyage through life'. So far.

I suppose the biggest problem I have at present is that I haven't got a routine. Before now I've always had a structure, even when I wasn't doing very much with my life.

And for almost the last forty years, my routine has centred around Parliament. Which is strange, I suppose, as I never had any ambitions to be a politician . . .

CHAPTER ONE

My Father
and Other Childhood Stories

My father was a character. Good, on the whole, his heart in the right place, an old-fashioned socialist but, hell, he could get up to some tricks, stunts and capers. He led my mother a merry dance, made her very unhappy at times, though she was just as strong a character as he was. He would never pay for anything, if he could possibly avoid it. It led to him falling out with his own family, which was why, when I was growing up, I had little to do with them. But I saw a lot of my mother's family. Apparently my old feller had had a row with his brothers when his grand-father died. My dad was the only one of the family who refused to pay a penny towards the funeral, so they never spoke to him again. I'm sure there was a lot more to it than that, there usually is, but that was the story I heard when I was growing up.

His full name was John Herbert Prescott, always known as Bert, and he came from Liverpool where he was born in 1911. His grandad had been a printer and his dad worked for Pickfords, the removals firm. The family had originally lived at Anfield, near the football stadium, but they'd moved out to Hoylake when Bert was young. Bert had been a sickly child, weakened by rickets, so they thought the sea air and bathing would help. After school, he joined the railway, starting as a porter. That was how he first spotted my mother, Phyllis Parrish. He noticed her on the platform one day, liked the look of her. When he saw her again at a local hop, he asked her for a dance. She was a maid, working in a big house nearby.

Phyllis came from a long line of Welsh miners, active in the trade-union movement. Her dad, William – my grand-father – was a union branch official for fifty years. She grew up in Chirk, on the Welsh borders. She remembered being taken round as a little girl knocking on doors at election time – general, local or union. One of the things they tried to do was get people in Chirk to read the *Daily Herald*. That was the paper all good working-class socialists took. An old photograph of William once appeared on the front page in 1947, at the time when the mines were nationalised. The caption under his picture read, 'We fought for this.' It was just by chance they used it to illustrate the article, but the family were always very proud of it.

My parents got married on 25 November 1937, at the Presbyterian church in Hoylake. Bert was twenty-six and Phyllis was nineteen. They moved to Prestatyn in North Wales, where Bert had been promoted to signalman. They took some cheap digs at first, right near the beach, but the rent shot up in the summer, the holiday season, so they moved to a bungalow at 10 Norton Avenue, which was about a mile from the signal box.

My mother used to visit him there, which was not allowed – you weren't supposed to entertain women in a signal box. Once they were almost caught by a railway inspector who arrived unannounced.

'Prescott, you've had a woman in here,' the inspector said.

'Can you see a woman, sir?' asked my dad.

And luckily he didn't. My mother was outside, dangling from a window-sill. That was one of my dad's favourite stories.

It was at Norton Avenue that I was born on 31 May 1938. So, yes, I'm Welsh. Most people never realise it because I lost my Welsh accent early in life. I did go back to the house in 1987, when I was helping to support the local Labour candidate, now MP, David Hanson, but I couldn't recognise anything. I was a bit surprised, though, that there wasn't a big blue plaque on the door. I blame the Tories.

I was christened John Leslie Prescott, John after my father's first name and Leslie because my mother always had a fancy for Leslie Howard, a romantic film star of the 1930s.

The moment the war started in 1939 my father was called up as he'd been in the Territorial Army (TA). By that time my mother was pregnant with Ray, my brother, who is eighteen months younger than me.

Bert's first job in the army was rounding up other TA members to get them into the regular army, which he thought was a pretty cushy number, but then he found himself in the 60th Anti-Tank Regiment. After training at Aldershot, they were sent to France, landing at Calais, as part of the British Expeditionary Force, which was to link up with the French and stop Hitler's advance. That was the theory, but Hitler's panzer divisions cut through them and the British forces were forced back to Dunkirk.

My dad had become a quartermaster sergeant and was in charge of five vehicles that delivered food and supplies to the front-line troops. By May 1940 the British soldiers had only four days' supplies left. They were coming under heavy fire, forced to retreat. My dad's company never reached Dunkirk. They got cut off near Rouen, being bombed and shot at all the time. In June, while he was sheltering in some woods, he was shot in the knee. He was taken to Le Havre, where he waited to be evacuated, so he hoped. They put him in a casino on the seafront, which had been turned into a temporary hospital.

He managed to write a letter to my mother, while he was in this hospital, with some details about what had happened but not giving too much away.

It was written on 5 June 1940, in pencil, on notepaper headed 'Church of Scotland Huts'. The address reads 'PQM8, 239, 10/L. A/A, BEF'. I've no idea what those letters meant, apart from the BEF bit – British Expeditionary Force.

Dear Phyllis,

Whilst thinking of John on the 30th May, his birthday, and wrote to that effect, but letter was never posted owing to me meeting with an accident in camp. I have now been moved to a hospital where I have been for a couple of days, but I am a lot better now.

I am expecting to be over in England to a hospital convalescent and this is the best news I have written you yet. Letter writing strictly censored so unable to tell you any more. Don't worry about the fire in the house. I will have sufficient money to cover it . . .

Fondest love to you, John and Ray –

Bert

I don't know anything about the fire, but it shows that letters from my mother must have been getting through to him. He had remembered my birthday – but he was a day out.

What he didn't reveal – or perhaps it hadn't happened while he was writing that letter – was that he had to have his leg amputated. Later on, when we were older, he used to tell us how he was given a choice: have it cut off just below the knee, which meant the rest of his leg might get gangrene, or have it all cut off and be safer. He opted for just below the knee.

There were lots of other dramas, such as being put on a boat, which then got blown up by the Germans, but eventually he made it home.

Meanwhile Phyllis and her two young kids had not heard a word for over six weeks. By now Bert was presumed dead, as he was not among any of those who had escaped at Dunkirk. It was the Red Cross who traced him – lying in a hospital in Warwick.

When he got a bit stronger, he was invalided out of the army and returned to us. We were living with my mother's mother at Upton, near Chester. Bert signed on at the labour exchange, hobbling on crutches, and was given a temporary job checking the disability claims of servicemen and their dependants.

He was still technically employed by the railway, which offered him a position in Yorkshire as a railway controller. When I was about three, we had to move and I lost my Welsh accent for good. I can't remember anything much about Wales. Only what I got told later on.

My dad found himself in a place called Brinsworth, just outside Rotherham, a heavily industrial area. He was there on his own for about a year until he was given a house in a railway terrace in Ellis Street where the air was thick with the soot and grime from the adjoining railway yards. It must have been a huge shock to my mother, moving from the leafy suburb of Upton in rural Cheshire. She used to say that her first impression of it was 'hell on earth'. She had three children by then – me, Ray and newborn Dawn.

This was in 1941 so my earliest memories in life are all to do with being in Brinsworth during wartime. I can vaguely remember rushing around to pick up bits of silver paper from the streets after a bombing raid. The Germans would drop this silvery paper stuff to confuse the radar systems, which were meant to spot them. Then the ack-ack guns would try to shoot them down. Seems strange, dropping silver paper, but that's what I was told. We also looked out for bits of shrapnel. All the kids in the area collected the silver paper, shrapnel and anything else as souvenirs.

I don't remember being scared of the bombs, or of the Germans. It was quite exciting, really, for boys of my age. Being at war was all we'd ever known.

When I started at primary school there was a big air-raid shelter in the playground, and when a bell rang, we had to rush inside it. When I joined the Cubs and then the Scouts, the Scout hut was right next to an ack-ack gun post. We were fascinated by it. I don't remember any bombs falling on Brinsworth, but the planes were always flying overhead.

We all had gas masks, and put them on when there was a raid. My second sister, Vivien, was born in 1944 and I remember her as a baby, with a funny little gas mask that looked like a space helmet.

My dad's stump had a big stocking over it, which came in handy at Christmas as my mother used the old ones as our Christmas stockings. A piece of fruit, if we had any, always seemed to be stuck at the very bottom. Everything was rationed, of course. We had no sweets, but then no one else did. Our house was lit by gas, as it didn't have any electricity, and we had an outside toilet and a tin bath.

If someone was lucky enough to have an apple, you'd beg them for the core. There was no sense of anyone being rich or poor. We were all the same, having to live on the same rations, but I remember how amazed I was when my mother bought me a pair of football boots. I didn't know how she'd got the money, or got hold of the boots. Even at the time, I was so grateful.

For a while we had a Polish lodger. He'd served in the British Army and I think had been injured. All I can remember about him was that he told me how to keep warm in heavy snow. He said you had to rub your hands in it, then roll in it. That way you wouldn't feel the cold as much.

My mother made our clothes as she was a very good seamstress. In fact she trained as a needlework teacher. She made me a brown suit, which I didn't like very much as it was itchy. She'd got hold of some army surplus material which was very rough and coarse.

Like all kids of the time, I'd never seen a banana in my life. When they arrived in the local Co-op, I ate it with the skin on. It tasted horrible.

I ran away from home when I was about eight. I'd had a row with my mother over something and been sent to my bedroom, so I decided I'd make her sorry. I thought I was dead clever by leaving my footprints on the soil in the front garden. This was to make it look as if I'd jumped down from the upstairs window. I hadn't. I'd sneaked down the stairs quietly when I thought no one was about. I'm not sure what difference I thought it would have made if everyone had thought I'd jumped. I stayed out for a few hours, then began to feel hungry.

I crept back quietly and got into our backyard. My mother was there, talking to a neighbour. I crouched down, so she couldn't see me. As I listened, I heard her say, 'Oh, yes, John's run away, but he'll be back for his tea . . .'

All of us were sent to Sunday School on Sunday afternoons. We weren't a particularly religious family, though I was baptised, but it gave my parents a break, I suppose, on their own with the kids out; it was the traditional opportunity for the respectable working-class mum and dad to have time together.

The radio was the big thing during the war and afterwards. My parents loved Donald Peers singing 'In a Shady Nook (By a Babbling Brook)' and laughed at Albert Modley. I loved *Dick Barton – Special Agent*, and used to rush in from playing each evening to listen to him.

I started at Brinsworth Infants, then went into the Juniors. I was never very good at lessons, or very interested, just sort of average, but I wasn't a troublemaker. My mother used to say I was a shy little boy, but I don't remember feeling shy at the time or thinking I was out of things. I'm probably more shy now, which some people will find hard to believe. In snowball fights I was often the leader – then I'd change sides because I'd want the underdogs to win. I took part in most of the school plays, such as a Dick Barton piece in which I was a villain. Then I was Grumpy in *Snow White and the Seven Dwarfs*. Early typecasting, perhaps.

When I was about nine, I was out playing in some field with Ray. We'd pinched a box of matches from home and were experimenting with them, trying to strike them. The grass was very dry and suddenly we'd set fire to the field. The fire brigade was sent for and then my dad arrived. He marched me to the police station where I got a right telling-off.

My dad was very active in local union matters and a local councillor; eventually he became chairman of the council. He was often away on union business. Our summer holidays, when we had any, were always to places like Scarborough or Bridlington where a union conference was being held. We'd stay in the hotel with him, and that would be our holiday. He'd get an allowance from the union for his expenses, usually sent to him in advance. My mother always tried to get hold of the envelope when it was due, because she knew what would happen. He'd put the money on a horse, lose it, and we wouldn't get a holiday. He loved the horses.

When he went to race meetings, he always tried to talk his way in without paying. He once tagged on behind a party of blind people. When it came to him, they could see he wasn't blind and that he didn't have a pass. But he told them he was with the group to write down their bets. They let him in.

He did once win a thousand pounds on the Tote and bought a television – we were the first people in our street to have one. Although you wouldn't necessarily have thought that looking at the aerials that had sprouted up – but those people were just pretending they had sets. The street came to our house to watch the Coronation in 1953, bringing their flasks and sandwiches. Another time, with some winnings, he bought himself a greyhound, which he was convinced would make him a lot of money. He hobbled along, exercising it round the local streets with the dog's trainer, who wore a flat cap and an old silk scarf tied round his neck. My mother found the whole thing very embarrassing. He had to sell the dog in the end as it was useless. He often lost most of his wages on the horses. People would come to the door, demanding money, and he'd fob them off with a promise to pay them sixpence a week.

Outside the house, people loved him, he was all charm

and high good humour, would do anything for anyone, but inside, he was very different. He and my mother were always having rows, which scared us kids.

He became a Justice of the Peace, which he was very proud of, and managed to get himself on the committee that granted licences to pubs and other premises such as clubs, where he was lavishly treated and made sure he enjoyed himself. That took him out of the house even more.

When my mother complained that he was never at home, never helped in the house and never gave her enough money for herself and four children, he used to say, 'You have 'em, I keep 'em.' Meaning it was her job to look after them – while his was to go out and earn.

I used to get embarrassed by him, especially when he tried to get us into places for nothing. His usual trick was to request a wheelchair, pretending he couldn't walk, then come on all pathetic and ask if entry was free for war veterans. It often worked.

He once took me and Ray to a Butlins holiday camp on a day visit. It had lots of attractions, which you had to pay for unless you were a resident. He managed to talk his way in by saying we were staying there, but unfortunately he'd left his badge in his chalet. He'd show it to them later.

We used all the facilities, had a brilliant time, but then he realised he wouldn't be able to get out without his badge. He found a back entrance and pushed us through it, only to find it led on to a wild part of the beach. We had to work our way across the mud flats rather quickly as the sea was coming in. We were soon soaking wet and filthy. It had been agony for him, of course, hobbling on his artificial leg, just to avoid paying the half-crown entrance fee. My mother was furious with him when we got home, our clothes ruined.

He was a funny mixture: his meanness and fiddles upset me, but on the other hand he was a committed socialist and believed in fairness and equality for the workers. We had some good discussions on socialism. I remember, when I was quite young, asking him why the railways had been nationalised. He explained that it made a pound of sugar cheaper. If you had lots of private railway companies, and you were sending a pound of sugar across the country, each of the companies that carried it would charge you, which would put the price up. But if all the railways were owned by one public body, there would be just one charge.

As I got older I used to call him a *Daily Express* socialist – a right-wing socialist. Just to annoy him. In fact, he was a natural rebel, willing to argue with anyone, very independent, always falling out with his Labour Party colleagues and other union officials. He once stood against the official union candidate in a local union election and got in, which didn't make him popular with his union.

He was quick-witted, always had an answer – or, more likely, a lie if he was being asked to pay for something. In his union and council work, he did a lot of good. He cared for the disabled, helped the poor, fought people's causes.

I'm not sure why I didn't argue with him, unlike my brother. Perhaps as the eldest I felt I had to keep the peace between my mother and father, keep the family together. That was my aim.

But he didn't do anything bad to us. He wasn't a tyrant.

He didn't abuse or beat us or even shout at us. And when he was around, he could be good fun, playing games, wrestling with us when we were little.

I would say I had a very happy, normal childhood, just like millions of others, growing up during the war. We weren't really poor, although we couldn't pay the rent now and again. We didn't go without food or have bare feet or keep coals in the bath or even wear clogs. It was just that my dad was a bad husband, who neglected his wife and children, especially his daughters. At times, he made my mother very unhappy. He was also a bit of a Jack-the-lad with women, but of course as kids we didn't know anything about that. Not till later.

I might not have liked his fiddles, but some of them make me laugh now. Later, when he went abroad on holiday he would always call for a wheelchair, get himself pushed through Customs by an official, having concealed contraband, like whisky or cigarettes, in a hole in his artificial leg. I wouldn't have done that.

For some reason, I grew up very moralistic, someone who thought he knew right from wrong. Perhaps it was my mother's influence, or because as I got older, I saw myself as head of the family, with my dad hardly ever there. I tried to set a good example.

But I didn't hate him. I liked both my parents. She was my mum. He was my dad. So that was it.

CHAPTER TWO

1948–1953

11-plus
and Family Dramas

When I was ten, we left Yorkshire and moved back to Cheshire. My dad had got a new job, still with the railway. Before we left Brinsworth, I'd sat the 11-plus exam, which everyone took in the 1940s and 1950s. These little tests determined how clever you were, what sort of school you'd go to and, basically, what sort of life you would have. I hadn't heard the result before we left Yorkshire.

We moved into a brand-new semi-detached house in a cul-de-sac, 29 Pine Gardens, Upton, just outside Chester.

It was a lovely house with a big garden and we all liked playing in it. I don't really know how the old feller had wangled it as it cost £1,200. The British Legion, apparently, had helped with the mortgage and he got preferential treatment as a war veteran with four children. So, in a sense, you could say we'd moved socially as well as geographically, from working-class industrial Yorkshire to middle-class, home-owning suburbia in leafy Cheshire.

But that wasn't how it seemed to me. For a start, I arrived with a strong Yorkshire accent. When I went to the local shop to order the *Daily Herald* they couldn't understand a bleedin' word I was saying. But class awareness really set in when I got the result of my 11-plus exam. I'd failed. I'd already started at the local primary school and found that the class I was in was splitting up, between those who were going to the boys' grammar school in Chester, or the girls' high school, and those who were doomed to go to a secondary modern. I didn't understand it at the time, or realise that 80 per cent of us, of the entire nation's eleven-year-olds, had been branded failures. But I sensed that some sort of social and intellectual division had taken place for reasons unknown to me. Perhaps that was when I got the chip on my shoulder.

I'd become friendly with a girl in my class at the village school in Upton, my first sweetheart, you might say. She passed the 11-plus and I didn't. That felt pretty humiliating. Even worse, I wrote her a letter, a love letter, or a kid's version of one – and she sent it back with the spelling corrected. One of the words I'd got wrong was 'love'. That seemed to sum it up. I was an inferior person, a failure.

Aggression, so they say, may be the result of how a person was branded earlier in life.

I've often wondered how I would have been different, or life would have been different for me, if I had passed and gone to the grammar school. Perhaps if I'd been in Cheshire when I sat the exam, not Yorkshire, living in my nice semi in a nice area at a nice school, I might have passed. It was a better primary school in any case, and I believe that a bigger proportion of people got through in that area of Cheshire than they did from where I grew up in Yorkshire.

That was another unfair feature of the system. It wasn't just that you could become a second-class citizen at the age of eleven, but it depended on where you lived. The number of grammar-school places varied from town to town. Some places even had a tripartite system, with a grammar, a secondary technical in the middle and a secondary modern. In theory, you should have been able to move between them, but you rarely did. You were selected at eleven and that was it: you were stuck.

I found myself at Grange Secondary Modern School in Ellesmere Port, just across the Mersey from Liverpool. It was about twelve miles away, even though we lived only a mile outside Chester. The problem was that we were in the county of Cheshire. If you failed to get into a Chester grammar, the county boys in our area were sent to Ellesmere Port. They provided a school bus, which went from Upton, but I had to be up at seven each morning to catch it.

I felt stigmatised, going to that secondary modern, when so many of my friends from primary school and neighbours were going the other way, on the short journey to a posh school in Chester. But when I got to my school, the roles were reversed: Ellesmere Port was a tough working-class area and the local lads looked down on us lot from Upton as stuck-up Cheshire snobs. We weren't, it just seemed so to them. Class, eh? What a nonsense it is.

I remember going to a Scout camp and the real middle-class kids were sent boxes of chocolate and biscuits by their parents – while my mum sent me four scones. Their mums had gone out and bought treats for them from a shop but mine had had to bake the scones herself. I felt ashamed. I know – you don't have to say it. It was silly. Today, the mum baking scones would be valued more highly than the one going out and buying stuff, but that wasn't how I saw it at that time. That was how my mind worked, imagining slights and division. The chip on my shoulder got bigger. The thing is, in Yorkshire I'd never had any of these feelings. Everyone had seemed the same.

My dad had promised me that I'd get a bike if I passed the 11-plus so, of course, I didn't get one. I don't think in fact he would ever have bought me one. It was all talk. If he'd had any money, it would have gone on a horse. Ray failed the 11-plus too, and went to the same school, but in his second year he was transferred to a secondary technical school, which was thought to be better. Nobody offered that chance to me. Obviously they didn't think I was up to it. My sister Dawn passed her 11-plus, the first in the family to manage it.

I wasn't unhappy at Ellesmere Port. We had a uniform, red blazer with a badge, and it was a good school of its kind, but you didn't sit any outside exams and everyone left at fifteen. There was an A and a B class and I was in the A class all the way through, but it didn't mean much. I still wasn't very good at lessons, because I wasn't really interested, although there was an English teacher I liked, Les George, not that many people today would think he did me much good.

I've never been able to spell properly or understand English grammar. And I still can't. I don't know a noun from a pronoun. I used to take refuge in saying complicated words as quickly as possible. When I was writing something and got stuck trying to spell a long word, I'd end it in a squiggle. That way, so I thought, no one would notice I couldn't pronounce or spell them. I'm still a bit like that. I'm not proud of it. I wish I could spell properly and had had a good grounding in English.

Because I found English hard, I didn't do much reading. It wasn't the teacher's fault. He once gave me a book to read, *Swallows and Amazons*, I think it was called. I quite enjoyed it, but it was a struggle to get through it.

This was after I'd been on a school outing to the Lake District. I didn't want to go at first. I said, 'What's the Lake District? Never heard of it.' They said it was lakes and mountains and fields, and we'd do a lot of walking. I said, 'Why would I want to walk round fields?'

They said, 'Oh, you'll love it,' so I agreed to go. I suppose the trip was subsidised by the school.

And I did love it. We stayed at a youth hostel in Borrowdale and it was brilliant. In those days, in the 1950s, you were in bunks in dormitories and had to do jobs like sweeping the floor. We washed under a cold tap or in a stream, which was bloody freezing. We climbed some mountain beginning with 'Sca'. I've loved the Lake District ever since – and believe that all people need access to open spaces.

I liked playing football, but I wasn't any good at it, unfortunately, so I took up boxing. There was a boxing club at school and we fought against other schools. I thought at the time I was pretty good at it. A few years later, when I was about seventeen and we were on holiday at Butlins, there was a boxing competition and I decided to enter. I was up against this bloke who had all the gear, proper boxing boots and shorts, giving professional snorts while I was in my swimming trunks and pumps. He arrived with this gorgeous girl, who sat down beside him at the ringside. I was still staring at her when he hit me, bam bam. That was it. I never got up.

At Ellesmere Port, I took part in plays and shows. In one I was dressed as a toff, with a top hat and a white silk scarf, while another lad was a labourer, digging a hole in the road. It was a just a little sketch, with some quite funny dialogue, that one of the teachers must have written. Strange to think now I was given that role. Perhaps it was because I came from Upton.

For a while I quite liked woodwork, but then I made a mess of some joints. I couldn't get whatever I was making to stick together, so I just left it, all in pieces, and it never got finished. When my brother arrived in the same woodwork class a year later, the teacher pointed to my bits of wood, still lying there. 'I hope you'll do better than your brother, Prescott.'

I was much the same in most subjects. Once I got

behind, did something wrong or badly, I lost interest. I felt I was a failure, so what was the point?

I haven't retained any school reports. God knows what happened to them. I presume my mother must have had them, but perhaps they were so bad she couldn't be bothered keeping them. Or they've got lost.

But I have three exercise books from 1952, when I was fourteen and in my last year at Grange. One is for maths and another for algebra. My work looks all right. I see I got quite a few 'Good' comments and seven out of ten. The other is my scripture exercise book. My handwriting is much better than I remember it. Very clear and neat. It's got much worse since.

But the spelling's a bit shaky. 'Ezekeel imaged he saw and heard God and the skys opening.' At the end I'd put, 'I don't believe in God.' The teacher had written: 'Who is your God?' I didn't know then. And I still don't.

I had no idea whatsoever what I wanted to do in life. I never had a fantasy of being an engine driver or a pilot or a footballer, none of the usual schoolboy things. I didn't think about the future. I took each day as it came and never worried about tomorrow.

Eaton Hall was nearby, being used for officer training. I hated the way they talked and dressed, in their white macs, Daks trousers, brown brogues. Officer class – not my class. I remember thinking, I'm never going into the army, whatever happens, I don't want to be bossed around by people like them. It was, of course, a strong possibility that I would have to as National Service was still in operation.

I felt an affinity with the underdog, people who had

failed or were being put down. At school one day I came across three lads who were teasing a girl from our sister school. They'd got her in tears. One of the lads turned out to be my brother Ray. I went over and told them to stop it at once and chased them away. Unbeknown to me, a parent had seen the incident and reported it to the school. I got called out in class and praised, and Ray got the strap. I'd done it instinctively, to help a weaker person.

I wasn't always a total goody, though. Once I was caught stealing. I did a paper round for a local shop and when I was there I often served people, helping out if they were busy. They didn't have a proper till, you just put the money in a drawer. Now and again I'd keep a few pennies, thinking no one would ever find out. But my mum did.

She was hanging up my trousers one day and all this money fell out of the pockets. 'Where did you get it from, John?' So I had to confess. She marched me to the shop and made me give it back. I was friendly with the owner, and he knew I was a good worker, so it wasn't held against me. I never did it again.

When other lads at school were stealing Dinkys from Woolies, I never did. Perhaps because I was scared of being caught. Taking pennies from that shop had seemed easy and safe. That was probably why I did it. But it was pretty stupid and childish.

When I was thirteen, in 1951, my dad entered us for a competition to find the Typical British Family. He'd seen it advertised in the papers. The first prize was a thousand pounds. We did well, got through several rounds, because we seemed such a normal, average, happy family – two boys and two girls. Dad's artificial leg probably helped too.

We reached the final, which was held in Brighton, sponsored by Brighton Corporation, as part of some publicity campaign, and they put on a great show. It was dead exciting for us kids, because we were getting a free holiday. They put us up in the Arnold Hotel, which we thought was the height of luxury. But I thought Brighton beach was a bit strange. It was full of pebbles. I didn't know beaches could be covered with pebbles.

The grand finale took place in the local theatre where Tony Hancock was on the bill. The judges included Jack Train and Anona Winn, big radio stars of the day. We went on stage and had to answer lots of questions. My arm was in a sling that day as I'd broken it in a fight with Ray. Nothing nasty, just larking around. One of the questions we were asked was 'Do your parents argue?' Me and Ray immediately replied, 'Yes, all the time.' We weren't telling family secrets – we just thought it was normal that parents should have arguments. But the other family, who won the competition, said they didn't have any arguments. The dad said he always brought his wife tea and breakfast in bed – which my dad never did – and was a police superintendent. My mother always suspected there was a fiddle going on, that they wanted him to win. It came out, for example, that they had a cheque book. Now that wasn't your typical British family, not in 1951. So we were very disappointed. We felt we'd been cheated, but we'd loved the trip.

On the way home on the train my parents started arguing. When we got to Redhill, my mother said she was getting out and leaving – leaving my dad and leaving us. I started shouting, 'Mum, please don't go, please don't go.' I took all my mother's worries to heart. If she was upset by anything, I'd be in tears too. She actually got off the train and stood on the platform. We all sobbed and pleaded with her – so she got on again, much to our relief.

I don't remember now what the row was about. Perhaps the disappointment of not winning the money. Or perhaps something she'd found out he'd been doing, or not doing.

Around that time, I was coming back from Chester Fair one afternoon. I'd won a salt cellar so I was feeling pretty pleased with myself. I was walking under this bridge, on the way home, when I saw a feller kissing a woman up against a wall. When I got nearer, I realised it was my father. I was so shocked. I threw the salt cellar at him.

I ran on and went to the local police station. I told them what I'd seen – my dad kissing a woman. He was a magistrate and I knew he shouldn't be doing such things. The policeman on duty listened to my story and then he said, 'Don't worry about it, son. I'll run you home. But don't say anything to your mum about it, all right?'

I didn't talk to my dad for months. I ignored him in the house and got very moody generally. My mother knew I was upset about something and eventually asked me what was the matter. So I told her what I'd seen. She just sighed and said, 'I might have guessed.'

Eventually my parents separated and then got divorced, a few years later, after I'd left home. It had been obvious for a long time that their marriage had collapsed, though in 1958 they had a fifth child, Adrian, fourteen years after Viv was born. My mother was forty-five. Adrian was born with a hare-lip and a cleft palate. He had operations till he was twenty-one, which were successful, thanks to the wonderful NHS.

I was asked by my mother to be a witness against my dad in the divorce case. That was what happened in those days. You had to prove guilt, or one person had to admit it. I refused to give evidence against my dad. He was still my dad. He got married again – but that collapsed too. He came home one day and found that his new wife had put his furniture and other possessions on the pavement. He still lived locally, so I often saw him around. My mother also got married again and that worked out fine. I got on well with my stepfather.

My dad continued as a magistrate – for a while anyway. At one point he got involved in some land investment scheme with a partner. He didn't put in any money, as he hadn't got any, but the other person did, then disappeared abroad when it all went wrong. There was an investigation and Dad was told he could never hold public office again so would have to resign as a JP. He refused. For some reason, they couldn't actually strip him of the position, so they stopped sending him any invitations to serve on any magistrates bench. He still called himself a JP. One day, when I met him in the street, he gave me his card, which he'd had printed. It read, 'Herbert Prescott, JP, MGC.' I asked him what the hell MGC stood for. He said, 'Marriage guidance counsellor.'

'Bloody hell,' I said. 'You've got a cheek.'

He said, 'Nobody's got more experience of marriage than I have . . .'

Some time later there was another family row when Dawn got married – and he refused to contribute to her wedding. I was working by then, so I helped out.

CHAPTER THREE

1953–58

Life as a Hollywood Waiter

When I came to leave school at fifteen, my mother had a word with the headmaster. 'He won't amount to much in life,' he told her, 'but he's a decent lad.'

I left school with no qualifications – no certificates of any sort – no aptitudes, no interest in anything. I didn't even show any of the basic manual skills, which would have got me taken on as an apprentice plumber or electrician. Certainly not as a carpenter, with my lousy woodwork. Instead I seemed destined to become some sort of unskilled worker.

Yet I don't remember worrying about this. While I got upset by people who I thought considered themselves superior to me, I had no interest at all in bettering myself. The thought of further education, or trying to get qualifications to help me, that sort of stuff didn't interest me. I suppose I was in a doze, sleep-walking through life. I didn't wake up till much later, the classic late developer.

So when a friend of my dad's said he'd heard of this job going as a hotel porter, I said, 'Yeah, why not?' even though it meant living away from home. Sounded good.

It turned out to be in North Wales. I was given a dinky little suit and told I was now a boy porter on a wage of £2 0s 7d a week.

I'd only been there a few days when a Bentley arrived at the front door. It was my job to run and open the car doors when guests arrived. He was a rich American who was so impressed by my speed and door-opening skills that he gave me half a crown. I handed it back to him. 'It's all part of the service, sir,' I said to him.

When I later told the manageress, she stared at me in amazement. 'When that happens again,' she said, 'if you don't want it, you can give me the money.'

Blokes used to arrive at the back door of the kitchen and open their raincoats to reveal a large salmon hanging there. Money would change hands. I was a bit shocked to hear the fish had been poached. I knew that was illegal. My father might have been a bit of a scallywag, up to various dodges, but I don't think he ever did anything exactly illegal. And my mother certainly wouldn't. I suppose I was naïve and innocent.

After a bit I moved to another little hotel, the Talardy in North Wales, and got promoted to commis chef. It meant doing all the dogsbody work in the kitchen, but it was slightly better money. In this hotel, we had a cocktail barman called George. He was quite a character. One day I saw him wearing a gown, which looked very odd to me. 'Why is a feller wearing a woman's frock?' I asked one of the porters. They all laughed.

Some years later I saw a photograph of George on the front page of some film magazine. He was in a group with Rock Hudson. The penny still didn't drop. No one at the time knew that Rock Hudson, of all people, was gay.

Then later again, I read about a sex change, one of the first – it was all over the newspapers. Everybody was reading about it. The man had become a woman and was now called April Ashley. Then I saw the photographs and immediately recognised George. I could hardly believe my eyes.

Just a year or so ago, Rosie Winterton, then minister of Health, told me that she'd come across someone called April Ashley. 'Oh, I used to know her, or him,' I said. I wrote to her and said, 'Remember me? I was the commis chef at the Talardy Hotel.' She wrote back – and asked me if I could fix her up with a council flat in Chelsea. Chelsea! Hell, we'd all like a council flat in Chelsea.

It was at the Patten Arms, Warrington, another hotel that I worked in, that I got drunk for the first time. There was a Christmas party, for guests and staff, but I was too shy to go. I just carried on working in the kitchen. An American had given all the residents and staff a glass of Drambuie, as his Christmas box, but a lot of people left them. When I went into the dining room to clear up, I drank all the leftovers. I must have knocked back dozens – and then I was violently sick.

As I'd become a commis chef, the hotel decided to send me on a catering course. I didn't ask. They just said I had to go. For two days a week, I went to the Manchester Domestic Science College. I quite enjoyed it. I found the studying not as hard as I'd thought it would be, but of course it was mostly practical, not much more than I was doing at the hotel. I was studying to get my City and Guilds. I was told it would help me get a better-paid job in the hotel industry, which sounded a pretty good idea.

I thought the Warrington hotel at that time was poor, and the wages were a joke. I started protesting, getting the other chefs and porters to complain, and was suspended. The official reason was that I was too disruptive and they were sending me home to calm down.

I suppose I had become a bit argumentative, even when I had nothing much to argue about. My dad was like that. He could start an argument in a phone booth. He was cleverer and quicker than me, and had a better way with words, so when I was young, and living at home, I hadn't answered him back. Or anyone else, really. But once I was on my own, living away from him, I began to get more confidence. Out in the world, working, if I saw something I considered wrong, I spoke out.

So I found myself at home again. To earn some money, I went back to my old job delivering newspapers. It was something to do, I couldn't be idle, and it made me a bit of money. Then, after a couple of months, the hotel took me back.

After two years in the catering trade, by which time I

ones, out in the country. And, of course, I was still only seventeen. Anyway, I got accepted by the union. The fact that my father was a union activist and delegate helped get me my card.

I was told I was being given the job of a boy waiter. You had to work your way up before you got to be a proper steward. Then I found I had to fork out a hundred pounds for my uniform – before I'd even started work or earned a penny. Obviously lads of seventeen like me didn't have that sort of money, so they had a system called 'allotment'. You got given your tuxedo, white shirt, swallow-tail collars, bow tie, black trousers, white waistcoat, all the bits and pieces, then they deducted so much a week from your wages. What a scandal that was. It meant for months and months you hardly earned a penny because you were paying for your uniform.

My first boat was the *Franconia*, the ship Churchill had been on at Yalta when he met US President Franklin D. Roosevelt and Soviet Premier Joseph Stalin in February 1945. When I went on board for the first time, in March 1955, an unofficial strike was in progress, something to do with four Liverpool lads playing skiffle in their bunks. No, not the Beatles, though it was only a year later that they were beginning as the Quarrymen. All over Merseyside, and then Britain, groups of lads were doing the same sort of thing. These four waiters had allegedly upset some first-class passengers with their music, so the management had sacked them.

It wasn't an official strike. The National Union of Seamen, as I soon discovered, didn't go on official strikes. It seemed they were in a cosy sweetheart arrangement with the bosses, which of course I didn't know at the time. So, when any seaman had what he thought was a justifiable complaint, or wanted things changed, they couldn't do much about it. He or she had to put up with it, or leave. But the more active, or more militant if you like, would go on an unofficial strike and try to get the rest of the crew, or at least some of them, to join in. The strikes usually failed – most people caved in and the activists lost their jobs.

I'd got on board, because boy waiters were exempt from the strike, and had passed what I realised later were picket lines. I wandered round the ship, looking for the chief steward, and found myself in the Pig. That's the name for the crew bar. I could hear a meeting going on, so I hung about to see what happened.

I'd arrived in the middle of a violent argument – which turned physical. I couldn't believe my ears or eyes. Some of them turned on a bloke and beat him up so hard that his testicles were damaged for life.

You have to realise the nature of seamen at the time. It was seen as a community thing. They all tended to come from the same Liverpool background, same area, and if you were from that group, you stuck together, whatever happened. Anyone who stepped out of line, or went against the community, got intimidated. The heavies had taken over this particular wildcat strike and were dishing out punishment to any scabs.

There was a feature film at the time, going round the cinemas, *Hell Drivers* with Stanley Baker, which was full of fistfights among working people. That meeting was just like it, though I would never have believed it if I hadn't seen it for myself.

No, it didn't put me off union activities, unofficial or

otherwise. I was appalled by what I saw, but it made me think there must be something wrong going on some- where for people to get so worked up.

I was put in a bunk room with ten other boy waiters – there was hardly room to breathe. They were mostly from Liverpool while I was from Chester, so they looked on me as a bit posh. They followed either Liverpool or Everton, which I didn't, and talked about the Locarno ballroom, which I hadn't heard of. They moved and fought in packs and there was always a leader, trying to sound you out. On the first night I took out my pyjamas to put on before going to bed, a new pair my mum had given me. They didn't half take the piss. What a mistake. None of them wore pyjamas. That was for sissies. They all thought I must be gay.

There were various initiation ceremonies, such as getting your stuff chucked out of your locker, being hit with a burning rope, all to test you, work out how hard you were. I survived all that. I gave as good as I got in any verbal battles and I was always willing to stand up for myself physically.

As soon as we set off, I was seasick: I'd never been on a boat before. I felt as if I was choking. I eventually got to sleep – but then the next morning I slept in.

One of the jobs I'd been given was to take the chief steward his breakfast in his cabin. This was my first time, so I jumped up in a panic, got his breakfast ready and ran down the deck to his cabin. There was a bloke sitting in a gangway, having a quiet smoke. Instead of asking him to move out of the way and let me by, I was in such a hurry I decided to jump over him – and hit my skull on the was seventeen, I decided to branch out a bit, do something more exciting and glamorous. I'd heard about the great life that waiters had on the Cunard liners. Quite a few lived locally because, of course, we weren't far from Liverpool and the docks. All the girls fancied them in their uniforms, so I was told. They got good tips and saw the world. It sounded great.

My father knew a chief steward who said I'd have a good chance of being taken on, with my catering background. They liked people with hotel experience.

First of all I had to be interviewed by Cunard. They gave me some numbers to add up, such as 'What's four, twenty-seven, eleven and forty-three?' I suppose this was to see how good you would be at taking orders from tables and doing bills. They did this about six times – and I got four wrong.

Then I had a medical test. All this meant was they said, 'Drop your trousers and cough.' I passed that, all right. Even though I couldn't add up, they were still willing to take me on. I presumed it was my two years in hotels that mattered most.

Then I had to go to what was called the Pool, down near the pier in Liverpool. Although Cunard said they would give me a job, it was a union closed shop, for everyone working at sea. You had to be vetted by the seamen's union, get their approval and agree to join before you could be officially employed.

It was the most filthy part of Liverpool. All these prostitutes were hanging around outside the building. I'd never seen prostitutes before and didn't know what they were doing. The hotels I'd worked in were mainly little bulkhead. The blood was pouring out and I had to go to the ship's hospital to get it stitched. I still have the scar to this day. But, of course, it gave me a good excuse for being late with the chief steward's breakfast.

The *Franconia* was a cruise liner, some twenty thousand tons with about nine hundred passengers and a crew of around four hundred. We went to Québec on that first trip, down the St Lawrence Seaway, and on the second to New York, which I thought was marvellous.

One of my other jobs was lift boy – standing in the lift, taking the first-class passengers up and down. It was operated by a handle. You had to time it exactly so that when the lift came to a halt, passengers could walk out easily, with no step. If you missed it by an inch, you got a rollicking. If I had any difficult passengers, snotty and superior, I would deliberately stop short so they had to clamber out.

I loved being on the liners, going round the world, seeing places I would never otherwise have seen. In New York, on one voyage, I decided to buy a washing-machine. It was a second-hand one, which I got from the Sally Army and only cost a few dollars. People in England didn't have washing-machines at the time, not in our street anyway, so I thought it would be a brilliant present for my mum. You were allowed to bring things on board and because it was second hand, there was no problem at Customs. My mother was dead thrilled – till she tried to switch it on. The electrics and plugs were American, so it had to be completely rewired.

I also bought myself an 8mm cine camera – silent, of course – which no one I knew had seen before. I took it with me on most voyages – I've still got films of me on board in the 1950s.

Most members of the crew would bring back whisky and vodka, which cost a fortune in England, or the sort of perfumes and Yankee clothes English girls longed for. There was no problem buying the stuff or bringing it on board. Getting it through the docks in Liverpool or Southampton, though, was another matter. I remember returning from my first voyage and noticing that many of our crew were shaking the hands of the dockyard police as they left. I thought how friendly seamen were. It was some time before I realised that each policeman was getting a half-crown slipped into his hand to turn a blind eye.

On board, there was an upstairs–downstairs atmosphere – among the crew as well as the passengers. Passengers had to stick rigidly to their first-, cabin- and tourist-class areas, and so did the crew. And there was a strict hierarchy. The deck officers looked down on the engineers and the engineers considered themselves superior to the stewards.

One of the things I had to do, when I was still a boy waiter, was serve the engineers in their dining room. There was this one who shouted at me, 'Take away this steak, boy, it's overdone.' I slapped it down in front of him. 'Don't talk to me like that,' I said. 'You've come from the Birkenhead shipyards where you were lucky to get a fucking cup of tea in a dirty tin can, so shove it.' I was removed from the engineers' mess and returned to serving tourist class.

After the *Franconia*, I did several voyages on the *Saxonia*. On one, a regular steward missed the boat, because he was drunk, so I was given his duties, looking after certain cabins. I said, 'I'm not doing it unless I get a man's wage,' which I got.

I had to look after a wealthy American woman and her daughter, fetching things back and forward from their cabins and waiting on them at meals. I had to serve them a flambéed *Bombe Jubilee* one evening. I hadn't done it before and burned my arm. Worse, the lady lost her eyebrows and eyelashes. All the head waiter worried about was that we'd lose a tip, but they were very nice about it.

I was eventually promoted to be a full steward. We were known as wingers. I'm not sure why – winging our way round the cabins, lounges and restaurants, perhaps. There was a lot of shipboard jargon. If we did some 'dhobi', we were washing our clothes. 'Scrubbing out' was washing the stairs and decks, which we had to do between our other jobs.

You were never, ever to visit a woman's cabin unless, of course, you were working. That was a terrible crime and you would be up before the captain and fined – ten bob and a day's pay for a first offence. The charge for being caught with a woman passenger fell into the category of 'broaching ship's cargo'.

But of course it went on. Cunard stewards in the 1950s and 1960s were known as the Hollywood Waiters because of their handsome uniforms, and I have to say, we did look pretty smart. We were young and fit too. So, now and again, the inevitable happened when a woman passenger took a fancy to a waiter.

The passengers were mostly women who were emigrating. They were on the voyage of a lifetime, at sea where no one knew them, and they wouldn't be going that way again. It was very romantic, far out on the ocean, on deck on a starlit night, the moon shining. I'm not saying I never broke the rules but I will say I was never up before the captain . . .

On those voyages, I saw some famous people. I was on the *Rangitata* in 1957 when Anthony Eden joined us. He'd resigned as prime minister after the Suez crisis and was wanting to get away from everything. We went to New Zealand, via the Panama Canal, and I was his steward. Then, in 1959, I was on the *Britannic* off Cyprus when Archbishop Makarios and Sir Hugh Foot, who was governor of Cyprus, came on board for secret talks.

Many years later, I met Hugh Foot again, or Lord Caradon as he had become, at a posh government dinner. I found myself sitting next to him. 'We've met before,' I said.

'Hmm,' he replied.

'Yes. I remember you dining at the captain's table on the *Britannic*.'

'Oh, yes,' he said, 'but I'm afraid I don't remember you.'

'That's because I was your waiter.'

He never spoke to me again.

I did a bit of boxing on board. It was something to do and, of course, I'd been in the boxing club at school. They put on contests to amuse the passengers. Ordinary seamen, members of the crew, would be slugging it out against each other. The passengers would sit at tables sipping cocktails while our mates would be hanging out of the lifeboats, cheering us on. Dom Volante, a 1930s featherweight champ, ran the ship's gym on the *Britannic*, even though he was nominally a steward. He organised a lot of the fights.

The rings were usually makeshift affairs on the deck,

and the prizes were fairly modest. I remember winning two bottles of beer and two hours' overtime – and I was presented with my big winnings by Sir Anthony Eden. Another time, after I'd knocked a feller out, I got awarded a proper silver trophy. I later presented it to Les George, the English teacher I'd liked at my old school in Ellesmere Port. It still gets competed for, last time I heard, but for swimming, not boxing.

During my years at sea, I didn't drink on board, even on my hours off, but when we arrived at the end of a voyage, or at some foreign destination after months at sea, I usually went out with the lads and got drunk. I have some snaps from those days, taken by my mates, in places like Panama, all of us looking pretty merry.

In Barcelona they left me behind in this bar, still drunk, I suppose, while they staggered back to the ship. I woke up with my head in a bowl of olives and a priest mopping my brow. I'm suppose to have kissed some stewardess, but I don't remember.

Eventually I got myself back on board. 'Oh, Prescott,' said the chief steward, 'you've returned at last, have you? Well, get working.' I was still hung-over, but had to serve a meal for my passengers. I managed to pour the tea in a big circle, all over the tablecloth, without any going in the cups. Luckily, the chief steward didn't see me.

When you were on those Cunard liners, or P&O or whatever, you usually had a rival ship. If they happened to land in the same port as you, you'd try to get on board and wreck the place. In New Zealand once we went really wild. We arrived in Auckland to find beside us a ship from Glasgow, so a big rival to us from Liverpool.

We got on board and ran amok, letting off fire extinguishers, raiding their bar, trying to steal signs, generally shouting and yelling. Then we ran off again, into the town, and hit the bars. But we overdid it – and ended up in gaol. The local police rounded us up and dumped us in the nick for the night till we'd cooled off. There were no prosecutions, thank God.

In New York I nearly got locked up for insolence. I was queuing up at Immigration to get my Alien Crewman Landing Permit, brought in under a law to hunt out Communists. You needed it to prove you were on shore leave, not looking for work or trying to infiltrate and stay.

'Are you a Communist?' the immigration officer asked me.

'No, I'm a socialist,' I replied. 'But I bet you don't know the difference.'

'Funny, huh?' he said. 'Has there been any incidents of mental instability or lunacy in your immediate family?'

'Yes,' I said.

'What?'

'My auntie,' I replied. 'She married a GI.'

'You wanna go to Ellis Island?' That was a detention centre.

'I thought this was the land of the free.'

'Don't think. Just answer the questions, smartass.'

I replied properly after that. If you got sent to Ellis Island, for any old reason, your ship had to pay a thousand dollars to bail you out.

Yeah, I did have some good times at sea in those early years. I had some good mates, and many of them I still see to this day, and I've still got my Seaman's Discharge Book.

It's like a sort of passport: it records each voyage you'd made and what your engagement was for that trip – boy waiter, steward, whatever. At the end, when you're discharged, they give you a mark for 'Ability' and 'General Conduct'. I see in my book it was always marked 'Very Good'. A bit of a lie, of course, as many captains grew to hate me, but that was the convention at the end of a voyage. You were termed 'Very Good', unless you had done something really serious or criminal.

My discharge book started in March 1955, when I joined the *Franconia* as a boy waiter. My photo at the front, taken when I was seventeen, is still a bit smudged, and the ink has run. That's because when I first got it the chief steward said, 'Go and wash out the saloon.' My discharge book dropped out of my pocket into my scrub-out bucket and got wet.

On my third trip on the *Saxonia*, the discharge book says I joined as a boy waiter but this is crossed out and changed to 'radio steward': I was the steward for the radio officers, and also four passengers. That was the voyage on which I set the American woman's eyebrows on fire. The record shows I'd won the argument when I said I was doing man's work.

After the *Saxonia*, in January 1957, I joined the *Rangitata*, then the *Carinthia*, the *Britannic* – on which I did lots of voyages – followed by the *Mauretania*, the *Transvaal Castle*, the *Amazon* and, my last ship, the *Andes* in 1963.

To me it's a fascinating record of dates and places and ships long gone; of people, too. When I finally left the sea, I got a lot of my mates to sign it. 'Best of luck in the future, John,' one has written while another put, 'John – a good judge of Pernod and Bacardi'. I'm sure he meant it professionally, not personally . . .

When I first started out at sea, I was still trying to keep up with my catering course even though I was travelling all over the world. I was doing it by correspondence, which, of course, was bloody hard when I was in a cabin with ten others. It was hot and noisy and they were all reading *Reveille* or *Titbits* while I was trying to get stuck into catering textbooks.

My saloon boss, Owen Thompson, who was in charge of my group of stewards, heard I was having trouble studying. He managed to arrange a soft number for me – looking after the first-class dining room when it wasn't being used. This was to stop people coming in and stealing the cutlery, which happened all the time, crew and passengers wanting mementoes. I just had to sit in a corner, keeping an eye on things. It was nice and quiet so I could get on with my studying.

I'm not sure why I decided to carry on with my catering course, now I was at sea, when I'd hated any sort of studying at school. It wasn't that Cunard, the merchant navy or the union was encouraging me. None of the other stewards I knew was doing anything similar. I was on my own. But I'd been told I would be able to get a better job back on shore – perhaps I'd even get into hotel management. So I stuck with it for the first year I was at sea until another activity took over my life. When that started, and I got really passionate about it, I had no time for or interest in anything else.

And when I was ashore, I'd found a better leisure activity than reading catering books . . .

CHAPTER FOUR

1957

Enter Pauline

I first met Pauline Tilston in 1957 when I was nineteen and she was eighteen. I knew of her before I started seeing her because she worked in a hair salon, Quaintways, in Lewis's, one of Chester's smart department stores.

I'd been going out with another girl until I went on a long voyage to New Zealand. When I came back, she'd not only dropped me for an American but married him. That's what happens when you're a seaman. You can be quite a glamorous figure – at least when you're on shore, with money in your pocket and American clothes or records to give to the girls – but soon forgotten when you leave on another voyage. I remember bringing home a pagoda umbrella. They were all the rage in Chester because no one could get them in England. Oh, we were very popular, we Cunard Yanks. Everyone called us that. I enjoyed the status, swaggering around the town, but I wasn't quite as extrovert as some of the others.

One of my pals, when he was at home, used to walk around in sunglasses, a big white jacket, chewing gum and pretending he really was a Yank. You'd see him in the middle of Chester, carrying a guidebook to the city. But when we all went off to sea again, well, we were usually soon forgotten.

That evening, not long after I'd come back from New Zealand, I spotted Pauline standing at the bus stop. I went across, we chatted, and I asked her if she'd like to go the pictures. She said yes, so we made a date. We were both on the rebound, so it was fortunate timing. Can't remember what the film was, but I know she talked all the way through it and I was a bit embarrassed.

Her uncle, Fred Tilston, had been a local boxer before the war, known as 'Tilly'. Pauline got called that by her girlfriends but I usually called her Paul. Her father had been a bricklayer, and a union man, but he had died when Pauline was fourteen. Her mother had gone out to work in a local laundry. She had one brother, Peter, but he had developed TB and was in a sanatorium.

Pauline was stunning, always immaculate, and everyone fancied her. When we first got together, I used to wind her up by saying, 'You know, you remind me of a film star, now who is it . . . ?'

She would preen herself, thinking I was about to say Elizabeth Taylor – everyone said she looked like her. Then I'd pause. 'I've got it – Joyce Grenfell . . .'

I knew she'd had a baby. It wasn't public knowledge, but one of the girls at the salon had told me. When she was fifteen and a half she'd met this American serviceman from a local base. There were lots of US bases around Chester at the time, and had been since the war. This bloke was twenty-one and married, though Pauline didn't know that when she met him. They'd been going out for some time when Pauline discovered she was pregnant. Her mother went to the base, but the security people on duty denied all knowledge of him. Said she must have the wrong name or wrong barracks. Very soon afterwards, they shipped him back to the States. Pauline wrote to him, to say she was pregnant, but he never replied. That was the last she heard of him.

She gave birth to a little boy, in January 1956, when she was sixteen, in a Church of England home, run by nuns. After three months, they tried to get her to have him adopted, but she didn't want that. She couldn't really look after him, as she was out working all day, and so was her mother, so the baby went into a nursery at Matlock. It meant a long train ride when Pauline visited him.

He then fell ill with suspected meningitis. Luckily, it wasn't. When he recovered, they said he was becoming institutionalised. He'd woken up one day and called one of the nurses 'Mummy'. So he was fostered.

I saw him once because I went with Pauline, when we

were first courting, to visit him in hospital. It wasn't a secret among her close friends, and it didn't bother me in the slightest, but in the 1950s it was a matter of great shame for an unmarried girl to have a baby. Neighbours would all go, 'Tut tut, how dreadful, lowering the tone of the neighbourhood,' so you tried to hide it. The family would send the girl away to have the baby in another part of the country. That was the usual way. Then the baby was immediately adopted and the girl went home, as if nothing had happened, to get on with her life. So, Pauline was unusual in trying to struggle on, despite her circumstances.

When the child was about three, Pauline realised she couldn't carry on any longer. It was becoming impossible for her. A very nice family, in their forties, with no children, had been fostering the little boy for twelve months and wanted to adopt him. She thinks they were living somewhere near Stoke or Wolverhampton. He loved being with them, and they loved him. It seemed obvious they would be able to give him a better chance in life than Pauline could offer at the time. Also the nuns were pressuring her to let him go, so she agreed.

Of course, she felt terribly guilty about what had happened. But she had been very young and naïve when she'd fallen pregnant.

She found it very hard, thinking that she'd never hear of Paul again. That was the name she'd given him. She didn't know the parents, or exactly where they lived or even if they continued to call him Paul. Every New Year was a difficult time for her, thinking of his birthday.

*

Pauline's mother seemed to quite like me, even though I was a seaman and away a lot. She appeared to think I was quite stable, as I continued to go out with her daughter.

When on shore I'd go round to her house and Pauline would make me a meal. One evening she'd made me a curry and I said, 'I don't eat curry.' In those days I looked upon it as fancy foreign food. So she made me two boiled eggs, putting them in cold water to boil. My mother always used hot. I said to her, 'Christ, can't you even boil an egg properly?' She smashed the eggs over my head, then ran upstairs and locked herself in the bathroom. That was the first time, but not the last, I was hit on the head with an egg.

We used to do a lot of dancing, at jazz clubs and local hops. Oh, aye, we were great little boppers. In the early days I probably didn't realise how bright she was, or give her enough credit. I saw her as a great beauty, and I knew she was very tidy and kept her mother's house perfect. So I didn't tell her, because I thought I'd bore her, about all the new stuff I was getting into. She certainly had style, but when I first met her, I underestimated her intelligence.

I was like the typical seaman brought up in that culture. So when I began to go to more and more union meetings, turning up late at her house or for our dates, she'd get fed up. But we stuck at it, loved going out with each other, being with each other, and our relationship developed.

One night I organised a posh dinner at the hotel in Warrington, the one where they'd sent me home for arguing. The French chef was a good friend of mine, and he laid on a special dinner for us. I was excited and had a bit to drink, and on the train home I stupidly smashed the bulb in the carriage, just to make it darker and more romantic. Then I proposed and handed over the ring to her. Which, of course, she'd chosen anyway. It was an antique one we'd bought in Chester. So me popping the question wasn't exactly a surprise.

After we were officially engaged, we went to London for the weekend. I booked us into the Strand Palace Hotel, two rooms, and had to pay for both. One was in her name and one in mine. I deliberately kept the two separate bills, in case her mum asked.

I don't think my mother, Phyllis, was so keen on Pauline. She knew about the baby, because she knew the girls at Quaintways, and I think she held it against her, as many people did in those days.

One day I went to my mother and said, 'Mum, I've broken off my engagement to Pauline.'

'Oh, John,' she said, 'I'm so pleased.'

'No, I haven't,' I said. 'I was just seeing how you'd react. Now I know what you really think.'

It might sound like a nasty trick, but it's always been part of my character to find out the truth.

CHAPTER FIVE

Wildcat Strikes and Marriage

It was because of the union that I didn't go on to take part two of my catering course. It took over my life and my thoughts and I had no spare time for my books.

The National Union of Seamen (NUS) was allowed to operate a closed shop, and dictate who worked in the industry. In return for that, they kept in with the owners, allowing them to get away with poor pay and lousy conditions. That was how I saw it. It was a cosy little relationship, but I thought it was a disgrace. They never seemed to side with the men or fight their cause or improve their conditions. At the top there were all these self-satisfied, self-serving officials, who'd lost contact with ordinary seamen.

I'd seen for myself how seamen were exploited. We'd do a seventy-hour week and hardly get paid for overtime. When you did get a few hours off, you couldn't do anything with it, could you, stuck in the middle of the Atlantic?

At ports up and down the country, there were more and more wildcat strikes, which the union condemned. I have to admit that some of the more militant were trying to bring down the Government, hold the country to ransom, not just fight the union and the ship-owners. They included Communists, anarchists and, on the Right, the international religious movement Moral Re-Armament. But I was never any of those. From the beginning, I saw myself as an industrial militant not a political militant.

My enemy was my own union. I figured the way to reform them was to work with them, try to improve things from the inside, use official channels. Which, of course, didn't make me very popular with the real militants. And the union didn't like me either. They wanted timid, obedient members, doing what they were told, not upsetting the owners or the status quo.

On my various voyages, once I started shooting my mouth off, I found myself first an unofficial, then an official shop steward. When the men had a complaint, or I thought something was wrong, I'd lead a delegation to the captain and try to get justice. That meant I made myself unpopular with captains, and the ship-owners, and soon I was finding it hard to get jobs. When I discovered

I was banned from Cunard and P&O liners I tried elsewhere and the same thing happened. One captain even tried to remove me from a ship in New York. When that happened, they had to put you on another ship or fly you home. It was illegal to dump a seaman in some foreign port.

The militants saw me as selling out when I didn't join in their wildcat actions. When I was with a crew who knew me, they understood that I was working with the union to improve things. They knew I was against our union leaders. But when I joined up with a new crew, they thought I was siding with the union against wildcat strikes and the militants would call me a fucking bastard.

One of the things I was working for was one man, one vote. The union had a system at the time of one extra vote for every five years' service. So the older men, who didn't approve of me, could have, say, four votes each while the young waiters, my mates, had only one. There always seemed to be some sort of fiddle going on so the older members had all the power and influence and kept things as they were.

On one ship I thought I'd counter this by getting people to request proxy votes in advance of a forthcoming union election, even though I knew a lot of them wouldn't be bothered to use the proxy in the actual election, not if they were on shore. I'd read the union's constitution carefully, and it appeared to allow for proxy votes, but no one had ever asked for them. I handed in a huge bundle of requests. The union couldn't say they were illegal, because they weren't, so they had to consider them. And endlessly delayed making a decision – until suddenly the election had been called and it was over, too late for proxy votes. They were devious bastards.

In 1960, a series of wildcat strikes took place all over the country. It started with a breakaway group in Liverpool, who had called everyone out after four lads had been 'logged for insolence', and spread nationally.

The original reason seamen's strikes had been made illegal, under various Merchant Shipping Acts, was because it was thought shipping was vital to the security and safety of the whole country. We'd just been in a war when our merchant navy had proved vitally important. So, like the police, seamen were not allowed to strike. Of course the union had gone along with this, not fought to alter the law as they should have done.

It became a huge strike, with thousands out and ships tied up in docks for weeks. On the *Queen Mary*, passengers offered to serve their own meals after the stewards walked out at Southampton.

I was out on strike as well, even though I didn't agree with some of the militants and their tactics to form a new union: I still believed it was best to work from within.

I helped to organise what was called the National Seamen's Reform Movement. This was not aimed at overthrowing the Government but at reforming our own union, getting rid of the people who were blocking all the things I wanted done. I saw it as a way of making clear that we were not trying to replace the union but change it. I helped persuade some of the strike leaders to join it. The chairman was Paddy Neary, who had been sent to prison in Southampton for picketing in contempt of a court order.

The Reform Movement had discussions with the union and the employers and it was agreed we would all go back to work with the promise of negotiations for better pay and conditions and no victimisation of the strikers. This seemed reasonable to me, most of the strikers having gone back, but not in Liverpool. When the lads rejected the policy, I was asked to address them the next day, to try and get them to accept the settlement.

The meeting took place in the open air, on what had been a bombsite, near the pier head. We put it to the local strikers, some two thousand of them, that they should go back to work. That was when I gave my first big public speech. I'd addressed small meetings on board ships but nothing like this. First I discussed it with my dad. After all, he had long experience of union affairs. He advised me against it. He said there would be too many people there to handle. I was too young, only twenty-two, and had no experience of such a big open-air event. I should start with something smaller. But I decided to do it anyway. I believed in what we had agreed and wanted them to understand the reasons, and that we had to stay nationally united.

In the morning there were smaller meetings, then the big one at three in the afternoon. Quite a lot of the men had been to the pub and arrived steamed up, very angry. There were shouts of 'Sell-out' as I started to explain, as best I could, the reasons for going back, followed by lots of booing and jeering.

I could understand their reaction. They'd risked a lot by going out on a strike they believed in. Now I was asking them to go back. The first time I called for a show of hands, only five hundred put them up. I carried on and got it up to a thousand. In the end, I had a majority. The motion was carried and they went back. It was a close-run thing, but it confirmed to me that it was the way to work. Doing it from within the union was the best chance of improving every seaman's lot.

I went back to sea, as no one was being victimised, but the problem rumbled on. I was on the *Britannic* when a telegram arrived for me from Paddy Neary, telling me the terms now being offered were unacceptable and the strike would be back on. It was addressed to 'John Prescott, Convenor of the *Britannic*'.

The captain called me to his cabin. He was absolutely furious that he had discovered a rebel on board plotting strike action. He was ranting away as if I'd been planning an insurrection, as if I wanted to take over his ship, as happened in the movie *Battleship Potemkin*. I hit back, saying someone had committed an offence.

'Oh, yes?' he said.

'Interfering with the Royal Mail and intercepting messages is illegal,' I replied.

That got him. But, of course, my card was marked.

During that trip, while I was in New York, I was walking down one of the streets off Broadway and I noticed a theatre showing *The Quare Fellow*, the play by Brendan Behan. As I was going past, who should come out of the stage door but Behan himself. I walked over to him and said, 'Thanks for your solidarity.'

I knew he had sent a letter of support to Paddy Neary in prison, with some books and five pounds. He said the screws would probably steal the money but they wouldn't take the books as they couldn't read.

He took me for a drink to a pub, but he stuck to milk – unusual for him, of course. I was just an ordinary seaman, meeting him by chance in the street, so I was most impressed by his interest and kindness. I had on me the telegram Paddy Neary had sent me, so I asked him to sign it. He wrote, 'To Good Old Johnny – a lightning strike is a good strike but an unofficial lightning strike is even better.' I'm sure I've still got it somewhere.

The second strike lasted seven weeks and collapsed with great bitterness in Liverpool. I had previously argued that we must unite nationally and recognise that all but Liverpool had gone back. This still held true in my opinion and when back on shore I once again tried to address the men and put it to a vote, but on this occasion I was denied and the mike grabbed out of my hands. I resigned from the strike committee and the strike itself collapsed not long afterwards, with no agreement. The men drifted back to the ships and this time there was the inevitable victimisation of those who had been out.

The company swapped the crews around on the ships, which led to tensions and arguments between many seamen on board. I found myself back on the *Britannic* with a mix of crews that I did not know.

On the ship I was threatened by someone: he said he was going to get me. I said, 'Fine, I'll see you on the after-deck.' I knew he'd turn up with his mates, so I got myself a big piece of timber and put some pepper in my pocket. I waited for him and, sure enough, he arrived mob-handed. There was a nasty atmosphere for a while, and it looked as if it might turn violent, but I managed to keep them talking. In the end, he agreed I was fighting to improve our lot and reform our union.

If you stood up to their physical intimidation, made it clear you wouldn't be cowed, then the heavies usually backed off. But there was a poor fellow on one ship who felt so threatened he went to the toilet and cut his throat.

At home, Pauline would sometimes come to union meetings with me, when they were in clubs or pubs. Sometimes we'd have get-togethers at her house. I'd invite colleagues over to discuss union matters. She wouldn't contribute as she wasn't interested in all the detail, only in supporting me and our struggle.

One day I was late home after a big march through Liverpool. When I got in I found a handwritten note from her. It began, 'Darling', 'Dear', but both words had been crossed out. Instead she'd put, 'John, so glad you're back from your march and that you could make it. Well, I've just gone on a march, so you can bloody wait for me.' It was signed, 'Love Pauline', but she'd crossed out 'Love'. Anyway, she did come back and I apologised.

We got married on 11 November 1961 at Upton Parish Church, Chester. All my friends from sea, the Hollywood Waiters, were there, dressed by Moss Bros. Pauline's stepfather wore an ordinary suit. I provided all the drink for the reception, which I'd brought back duty free from my voyages and saved up.

My brother Ray was best man. He lost the ring, so there was a bit of a crisis over that. Then by mistake he sent away the wedding cars. So Pauline and I had to walk into Chester in our wedding clothes, looking for a taxi.

We had our honeymoon in Ibiza. We had to get there

on a boat from Majorca, filled with pigs and chickens. I felt a bit guilty later on that I'd been to a Fascist country.

We managed to buy a semi, just a few doors down from my mother's house, at 20 Pine Gardens, Upton. We got a good mortgage and didn't have to put down much of a deposit. Pauline financed it, thanks to the employee shares she held in Lewis's, where she was still working.

My prospects when we married weren't good. I was twenty-three and had been six years at sea. I had no qualifications, except some catering ones. I still loved going to sea but my union work meant I was a marked man. The employers were determined to get rid of me, so I had longer and longer periods out of work.

On one occasion, my dad, the JP with the headed notepaper, wrote to Cunard to complain. He said they could not victimise or sack me for union activities as that was against the law.

They eventually wrote back to him. My trouble, they said, was not my union work but being 'indifferent to discipline'. Bloody cheek.

CHAPTER SIX

1961–65

Dreaming Spires

It probably surprised a lot of people when I applied to study at Ruskin College, Oxford. Such a thing had never been part of my plans or my daydreams, mainly because I didn't know that the place existed. So, I was as surprised as everyone else when it was first suggested to me – and not least by where the suggestion came from.

My ambition, if I had one, was to be a full-time official with the National Union of Seamen. I still wanted to change the structure of the union, get rid of the dead wood and improve conditions for all seamen. I fancied that I could do a much better, fairer job than the people who were currently running the union, such as Bill Hogarth, the general secretary.

Meanwhile I was still at sea, though continually suspended for my union activities. On ships, as an unofficial union convener, I would always take the men's grievances to the captain, whether or not I had been asked to.

On the *Mauretania* I organised a meeting at midnight in one of the passenger restaurants and had posters printed on board, using the back of the first-class menus. When we got to New York, the captain had contacted the owners and called me before him. He said he wanted me off the ship, so I was being discharged. All my shipmates rallied round and walked off with me. The ship couldn't sail and they had a very tight turnaround time. The captain had to give in. I was allowed back on board but, of course, my card was marked again.

On the Royal Mail liner *Andes*, the air-conditioning in the crew's quarters packed up and it was unbearable in our bunks, hellishly hot. The lads were sleeping on the decks, under makeshift awnings. 'Are you going to do something about it?' they were asking me. I got a thermometer and took readings in our quarters, then went to see the captain. I was accused of fomenting a mutiny, when all I wanted was better conditions. But the air-conditioning was eventually repaired.

On shore, when I was out of work for weeks and sometimes months, I would still be involved in union affairs and meetings. The more I was out of work, the more I put my energies into the union – and I think that was how the idea came up that I should try for Ruskin. It was the union bosses who suggested it. They wanted me out of their hair. One man told me about a union scholarship I could apply for, which would pay all my fees. I'd be away studying for two years – and not bothering them. That was clearly their thinking.

Various good friends said, yeah, it was a good idea, it would help me a lot. I'd learn more about things like economics and also the union movement, which would make me a better trade unionist. I'd be better able to argue with the union hierarchy and the ship owners.

Ruskin was founded in 1899 and is a union-affiliated college, meant for people like me, mature students with no academic qualifications, late developers who missed out on the normal education process for whatever reason. Walter Vrooman, one of the founders, said that 'the purpose of Ruskin is to take windbags out of the movement, open them up, fill them full of sand and send them back'. I think I've got that quote right. It probably did apply to me.

To get the union scholarship to Ruskin you had to write an essay of two thousand words. The title was 'The future of the unions'. I had not written anything for some years, apart from table orders, 'steak and chips' or whatever, or union posters. I'd long since given up the catering correspondence course, which did not involve essays anyway.

I wrote the essay while still at sea, staying up till two or three in the morning. Then when I got home I decided to seek proper advice. I went to the Seafarers' College in Balham and showed my essay to a Professor Hope. I wanted him to tell me what he thought of it.

'From what I can read of it, you haven't got a chance in hell,' he said. He was a very dour Scotsman.

I was furious so, back home in Chester, I worked on it again. I also went on a week-long Workers' Educational Association (WEA) course in Chester, during the summer of 1962, trying to get the hang of what lectures and studying might mean.

I sweated on that essay for months, then my mum got a neighbour from a couple of doors down – Mrs Robinson – to type it out for me. To my surprise, I was accepted. I'd get union funding to attend Ruskin for two years.

It so happened it was the annual union conference and, of course, I was going to it, hoping to get a chance to speak. When I did, I stood up and argued against the union bosses. I said that Bill Hogarth was not doing his job: he should be fighting the owners, not selling out. Bill Hogarth had been a union official since 1942. For some years he'd been acting general secretary. Then in 1962, aged fifty-one, he'd finally got the top job.

Well, when he left the platform, the first thing he said was, 'Who is this bloody man?' When he was told I'd just won the union scholarship to Ruskin, he got them to take it off me. And they did. So I had no funding.

By this time, I had a child as well as a wife to support. Johnathan was born on 5 April 1963 – just in time for the tax bonus. We argued and argued about his name. I wanted to call him John, after me, which is a working-class tradition with your first son. Pauline wanted Jonathan. We compromised on Johnathan. According to him, it's the worst deal I ever brokered.

The only thing I could do to support my family was go back to sea, which is what I planned to do.

Meanwhile, I'd still got a place at Ruskin, in theory,

although I didn't know how long they would keep it open for me, but I couldn't go unless I got the funding. So I applied to my local council in Cheshire. You had to put down what you intended to do after you had completed your studies. I wrote, 'Union official.' Cheshire was a strong Tory council – and rejected my application.

I was helped by my old teacher from Ellesmere Port, Mr George, who'd continued to encourage me and follow my progress, long after I'd left school. He said, 'Don't put down union official. Say you want to be a schoolteacher.' He helped me get references, from other teachers and a vicar, all saying I was good teacher material.

This time I was awarded the grant – but by then, at the end of the summer with the new term about to start, I'd lost my place at Ruskin. They'd filled it for that year.

I went down to Southampton and signed on for a second voyage on the *Andes*. But when I got on board, the senior catering officer said, 'Come here, Prescott. You're not joining this ship, you're bloody trouble.'

On 11 September 1963, when I'd just got back to Chester and was wondering what the hell I was going to do, not just for then but the rest of my life, I got a telegram saying Ruskin could offer me a place for the academic year that was just starting. Someone had dropped out. If I'd gone on that voyage, and been on the high seas for three months, I could never have taken it. So that was fortunate, in among all the bad luck.

At the age of twenty-five, married with one child, I went off to Oxford to become a full-time student. Pauline was all for it. She said she would look after the house and family and support me in any way she could. She never once objected. She could see I wanted to do it and that it would help my ambition to become a union official.

It might seem strange, to some people, that she was prepared to go along with a two-year absence but since we'd met, I'd been going off for long stretches at sea, sometimes six months at a time. At least for the next two years I'd be in England, not on the other side of the globe, and I'd get proper vacations – that was one of the new words I soon learned to use.

It was funny, in those first weeks at Ruskin, getting to know my fellow students, noticing the difference between the white-collar union people, such as Clive Jenkins, who went on to be chairman of the TUC's general council, and those like me from blue-collar, industrial unions, seamen and miners. We turned up for the first lecture in our best suits, white shirts and ties while the clerical types immediately started appearing in revolutionary green and Che Guevara berets. Later, we all dressed casually. I even grew a beard.

I got into an argument with one and he called me a 'lumpen proletarian'. I'd never heard that phrase before. It took me about three months to discover what it meant – I read the same words in a textbook. I hadn't realised till then it was an insult.

My mind was in a whirl, those first few months, confused by what was happening, what I was learning, what it was all about. One of my tutors from those days, Mr Tredder, whom I looked upon as very right wing, said it was OK me generating all that heat, but I wasn't boiling any kettles, just letting off steam. I had to focus it. He was right, of course. One of Ruskin's aims is to make people like me less revolutionary and more effective.

My first essay, which had to be two thousand words long, was entitled 'Power tends to corrupt, and absolute power corrupts absolutely'. Lord Acton's famous phrase, not that I knew who he was at the time. I was immediately in a total panic. In the tutorial group, most of the others had seemed quite confident, compared with me, so when I got back to my room, I just sat there, thinking, What do I do now? What the hell have I let myself in for?

I talked to some other people down the corridor – and found most of them were in a panic as well. Everyone was saying, 'Bloody hell!' We'd been big fish in our little pools, among our fellow workers in our factories or mines or ships, but now we felt lost. It was a bit reassuring to realise we were all in the same boat. One bloke, a bus driver, had seemed confident in the tutorial, but packed his bags and left. We never saw him again.

I cobbled together that essay somehow, but it didn't get much easier from there. When I had the mock exams at the end of that first year, I still felt it was all way above me and I'd never cope. There was a paper on statistics and they handed me a slide rule, which I'd never seen before. There were references to things like logarithms, which were totally new to me. I handed back the paper without writing a word, and walked out. The invigilator chased me down the street, asking me to come back, but I wouldn't.

When I got back to my room I found a note on the back of an old envelope from my tutor, Raphael Samuel: 'John

– why not take the paper anyway? Do it in your own time over the weekend? Main thing is just the practice of *writing*, not the time – Best wishes, Raphael.' It had never occurred to me you could do that. I've still got his note today.

I struggled for about a week, reading up on logarithms, and eventually managed to get the hang of them, roughly. Then I discovered that the slide rule meant you didn't need to know the theory of logarithms. You used it instead.

I found talking in tutorials not too bad, arguing my case, but writing essays was never easy, though it got a bit better as I gained more experience.

For the first year I lived in a college hall of residence at Headington, and then in Walton Street, where the college was, but still in college accommodation. We were considered a proper part of Oxford University and allowed to use all its facilities, such as the Bodleian Library. We sat our exams in the Examination Schools building, like normal undergraduates, and had to wear big white dicky-bow ties like they did.

When we set off the first time from Ruskin, going to the Schools, the housekeeper lined us up and gave us each a red rose for our buttonholes. That was another Oxford tradition when taking exams.

But I didn't take part in any university life, apart from going to the Bodleian. I never joined the Oxford Union, though I could have done. I felt it was theirs, not mine. I never even wore a Ruskin scarf, which some students did. I never visited any of the famous colleges. The only other one I went into was Nuffield for lectures on industrial relations. They had people like Kenneth Wedderburn and

William McCarthy, both now Lords, who were excellent, real experts.

I felt no connection with normal Oxford students, getting pissed, staying up all night. I was there to study, to learn, not doss around. I wanted to prepare myself to be a good union official, equipped with the right intellectual tools. I didn't want to feel inferior any more when I came up against grammar- or public-school-educated people. Of course, I soon realised that they weren't actually cleverer than me. They just spoke better.

In the vacations, I was still throwing myself into union or Labour Party activities. I'd joined the Party in 1956 when I was seventeen and did local door-to-door stuff or sent out leaflets at general elections. My first real experience of party-political work came in 1964 when I was about to begin my second year at Ruskin. I got myself appointed as the Labour Party agent in Chester, my home town. It was a Tory stronghold, so we hadn't a chance, which was why someone like me with no experience was allowed to do the job. I told Ruskin about it, saying it would be just a few weeks in the summer. They said OK, as long as I was back by October for the new term.

The Labour candidate was Anthony Blond, an old Etonian publisher. He appeared to be very fruity with this deep posh voice, although he wasn't very old. I thought, Bloody hell, what chance have we now? He arrived in a pink Lincoln Continental covered with Labour stickers in which he toured the constituency. Meanwhile, I dashed after him on an old scooter. He was well off, I gathered, because his family made knickers for Marks & Spencer, so he told me. He

73

brought Vanessa Redgrave to Chester to speak for him. When we went into the council estates, he would insist on peering through people's letterboxes. I don't know what he was looking for. Probably never seen the inside of a council house before. He lost, but not by too much – he got sixteen thousand votes to the Tories' twenty-three thousand. We had a good time at that election and I was very sorry to read of Anthony's death in March 2008.

Nationally, Labour got in, if only just, by five seats, and Harold Wilson became prime minister. I got through my exams and was awarded my diploma in politics and economics. After two years at Oxford, I went home to Chester.

A lot of marriages collapsed while people were at Ruskin. Blokes arrived married but were divorced by the time they left. They felt their lives were different: they had moved on intellectually and culturally, and felt increasingly remote from the wives they had left behind who had not moved on or experienced any changes. I never felt that. OK, you could say that intellectually and culturally I hadn't actually changed because I hadn't swallowed the Oxford life; my accent and attitudes to life had remained the same. But I think the real reason was that before Ruskin I'd never discussed politics and suchlike with Pauline anyway, so being there had made no difference. I had, of course, learned a lot, or so I thought – hoped.

The two years I spent at Ruskin were probably my happiest time ever. It was the beginning of such a huge change in my life, and I'll always be grateful for what happened there.

*

A few months ago I was contacted by the present principal of Ruskin, Professor Audrey Mullender. She'd read I was working on my life story and, by chance, had recently come across my student files. Did I want them, or should she throw them out?

I wrote back and said I'd love to have them, not knowing what they contained. I was amazed at how detailed they were, how every little scrap had been retained, from bills paid to private reports on my progress. They'd also kept all the letters to do with my application, the messing around when they had offered me a place and the union had taken away my scholarship so it looked as if I wouldn't get in. I hadn't known how hard Ruskin had worked on my behalf to get me there.

They'd even kept my entrance essay, which I have in front of me now. Its full title was: 'What do you consider should be done to re-organise the structure of the British Union Movement to make it better fitted to meet modern industrial conditions?' It's a bit heavy going, full of lists and facts, but beautifully typed. My conclusion was that the structure of the union movement 'has tended to become outdated, but not the social function'. Still true, I suppose.

I wrote Ruskin a long letter from sea, boasting that I would be sending them references from '2 MPs, 4 mayors, 4 city councillors, 5 union officials, 1 vicar, 1 director of education, 2 magistrates and a magistrates' clerk'. Impressive, eh?

However, from the files they sent me, they appear to have kept only two. One is from Mr George, who was now headmaster of Christleton County High School in Chester.

He said I'd been a 'boy of excellent character and distinctive personality and although not at the time the hardest worker, he has developed into a man of ability and sound common sense with obvious gifts of leadership. I am sure he will prove to be a hardworking student.'

The other is from an official of the National Union of Seamen in Southampton. He writes that I am 'honest and sincere' but then he gets the boot in. He describes me as 'a lad with the right ideas but in the wrong company'. Typical of an NUS top official. The union was always out to get me. I'm surprised Ruskin didn't hold that against me. To me it was a nasty smear, because he didn't explain what he meant by the 'wrong company'. All I'd done was criticise their union structure.

The most interesting stuff, to me now, are the internal reports. At Ruskin, my essays were marked and given back, of course. Usually with the spellings corrected. So I knew roughly how I was getting on. And I did pass my exams at the end. But during those two years we were never given any progress reports, on how we were actually doing, or what the college thought of us.

What I didn't know then was that every tutor and lecturer had to produce a written report on every student, which was kept private. They needed them, apparently, to report every year to your education authority, or whoever was giving you your grant, to confirm that you were studying properly, doing well, not just pissing away the money.

What surprises me now is how *well* they thought I was doing – yet I was never aware of it at the time. I was enjoying Ruskin, but in my mind I was always struggling, finding it hard academically. These reports show that they considered me a B-plus student, sometimes getting A. Forty-odd years later, that does cheer me up.

Of course most of them drew attention to my problems with the English language. In my spring term report for 1965, my economics tutor, Henry Smith, who was also the vice principal, writes that 'Mr Prescott has a mind like knitting that the cat has played with: pull one bit straight and you tighten up the tangle elsewhere'. But he does say that orally I grasped things very clearly. He also says I was 'worried stiff and doing his best, so he ought to be encouraged'.

Another says I am 'pathologically sensitive to criticism'. Very true.

But the overall feeling of all these internal reports was positive: that I was a good student, working hard, should do well, despite my problems with exams and writing essays.

In a letter in 1965 to the Cheshire education authority, the principal of the college, Billy Hughes, gave me an excellent overall report: 'A hard-working student of sound natural intelligence, whose progress is still somewhat hampered by weaknesses in the organisation and expression of his written work. Potentially he is above average in perception.'

I left Ruskin in 1965, not knowing how highly they had rated me, and found myself back home in Chester, out of work.

My union wouldn't have me. Hogarth was still in power and still against me, and I was blocked from getting any full-time position. One or two people on the union executive had promised there would be a job for me after I'd finished at Ruskin, but Hogarth was determined it wouldn't happen. He took me aside one day and said, 'Listen, John, you come into this union, and I'll make sure you won't last . . .'

That was how the union worked, the sort of pressure they could bring to bear on any member they didn't like. Naturally, it was done behind the scenes, with a nod and a wink. They'd encourage the employers to sack someone they didn't approve of, making it clear that they wouldn't protest if it happened. So you'd had it. Neither side would help you. That's what had happened to me, over and over again.

One of the tricks they used to pull, when I first started, was to contact the Government about any activists they didn't like when they were out of work. In other words, he's left the sea, so send him his call-up papers for National Service. That was a real threat. Toe the line, or you'd be off to the army.

I got a temporary job, for a few weeks, with the General and Municipal Workers' Union, under Dave Basnett, the national officer. My job was to recruit new members, so I went round some factories, with Eric Smith, son of the general secretary of the woodworkers' union, trying to get people to join. At a Liquorice Allsorts factory in the Midlands I persuaded the bosses to let me have a meeting inside the factory gates under an awning – but only if it rained. I put 'if raining' in tiny print and 'management permission granted' in very large print, so the meeting looked much more official than it was. At a pickle factory in Leeds I put up a notice that claimed the owners had said 'unions do a good job'. The owners protested, and the union got a writ saying that the statement wasn't true.

I did quite well, though, recruited lots of new members. Then I discovered the local union officers didn't actually want any more members, but I was offered a permanent job.

But all the time I still wanted to work for my own union, the National Union of Seamen. I couldn't think of any other job I was suited for. The sea was what I knew best, and seamen the people I cared about most. That was why I'd gone to Ruskin, to make myself better qualified to work in my own union.

Although the NUS still wouldn't give me a position, there was one loophole. I could work for them if I was in full-time education. It was Raphael Samuel, my tutor at Ruskin, who suggested I should apply to Hull University to read for a degree. At Hull, the well-known socialist economic historian John Saville made it possible and was a great influence on me.

There was a big connection at the time between Hull University and Ruskin, with lots of left-wing people in both places, so Ruskin often sent students there. Raphael said I didn't have to go through UCCA, the university clearing system, or whatever it was called at the time. He could fix it for me. He came back and said there was a vacancy, if I wanted it.

It would keep me active in the union, but did I want to go to university at the age of twenty-seven? While at Ruskin I had still been going to sea during some of my vacations, to make a bit of money to help my family and to keep my hand in.

So the alternative to going to Hull was to go back full time to being a steward, as the money wasn't bad, plus all the tips. If, of course, they'd have me. There weren't many liners now that I hadn't been banned from. The truth was, neither the ship-owners nor the union wanted me. So there seemed no future there.

I thought about it for some time and discussed it with Pauline. If I went to Hull, I'd be going for sideways reasons, just as I'd gone to Ruskin. But university would at least allow me to continue with union and Labour Party activities. Moreover, the union's national executive committee was moving to the Left and great changes were expected.

But the main problem was, where would university lead? Ruskin hadn't really helped me, career wise. Would a proper degree help me any more? After all, I didn't want to be a bloody university professor. I just wanted to be a union official.

CHAPTER SEVEN

To Hull and Back

I was walking past the University Library in Hull one day in 1965, not long after I'd arrived, when I saw Philip Larkin coming towards me. I knew he was the university librarian and a poet. At Ruskin I had been introduced to Ted Hughes's poetry and Larkin's, and I quite liked it. For a while, I used to read a bit of poetry, or try to.

I decided to go to up him. 'Excuse me,' I said. 'Do you do seminars?' I thought I might go along, if he did.

He looked down his nose at me – and walked on.

I was reading politics and economics under John Saville, and I was still having problems with technical things like statistics, which people doing economics have normally learned about at school. But it wasn't just lack of education that held me back: I found it hard to ask people for help. I suppose I was scared I would be condescended to and looked down on as thick – or lumpen.

For my first year I was in a student house, then in my second Pauline and Johnathan, now aged three, joined me. I was going to be away for three years, longer than at Ruskin, and we wanted to keep the family together this time.

Pauline never objected to me continuing to be a student. She was still totally supportive. She had worked as a hairdresser to keep us going financially, right up to the moment she gave birth to Johnathan. After that, she still did hairdressing from home. For a while we took in lodgers, to get extra money. I had a good grant from Cheshire as a mature student – and having Johnathan meant they gave me a bit extra – but it was still a struggle. Pauline managed it all, did the bills and balancing. I could never have done what I did without her.

We sold the house at Upton, Chester, and bought a three-bedroom semi at Cottingham, a nice village just outside Hull. Quite a few of my mates from Ruskin, mature trade-union people like me, had come with me to Hull and we used to congregate at our house and discuss how we were going to change the world. Pauline would make us coffee, then fall asleep while we talked and argued, waking up to make us more coffee.

There was this pub in Hull where it was known that the

landlord was banning 'criminals, queers and women'. He even had a little notice up, saying so. We were outraged, thinking this was terrible. One of my mates thought up this plot where we would take Pauline along to the pub to provoke a reaction. The plan was that when she got chucked out, we would start a demonstration outside, picketing the pub so the landlord wouldn't have any customers. They all thought this was a brilliant idea and put it to Pauline. She said no. She didn't want to. But they found a woman student who was willing to do it. She got chucked out and they picketed his pub. It ended with the company making the bloke take down his notice.

I think Pauline probably did feel a bit inferior, among all those university people – but that's what places like universities do to the working classes: they make them feel inferior. But the working classes also do it to themselves. They think they're not up to it.

Mind you, some of us did suspect it might be true. We had to do a weekly essay. Early on in the first term the tutor said he was going to put the names on the board of people who couldn't spell: he wanted to see them afterwards. My name went up, along with that of a mate of mine, Jim McConville, another seaman. We trooped along on this very wet day to the tutor's study. He was in his early twenties, but looked much younger, like a little lad. I was twenty-eight and McConville was thirty – he was wearing big seafaring boots and oilskins. We tramped into the tutor's little room and towered over him.

'Oh,' he said. 'I thought you were two of those who'd just come from grammar school and should have known better . . .'

As he spoke, he had our essays in front of him and I could see that both of them were covered with his pencil marks – spelling corrections plus comments in the margins. While he was still talking to us, he was surreptitiously rubbing out most of the pencil.

'Right, then,' he said, 'sorry, and thanks . . .' And he handed us back our essays. Today, McConville is a professor.

When the subjects were practical, about current labour relations, we could do good essays, as we knew what things were like on the ground. It was on the theoretical and history side that we fell down.

I didn't take part in the university's students' union activities. I was more interested in local politics. I joined a group called Humberside Voice, which was a left-wing, Labour-supporting action group.

In January 1966 there happened to be a by-election in Hull North because the sitting Labour MP had died. It was suggested I should put myself forward as a possible candidate, but I didn't. Instead I threw myself into campaigning for a Labour victory, going round the docks and canvassing for votes among the seamen and dockyard workers.

One of the independent candidates in the by-election was Richard Gott, the *Guardian* journalist. It seemed he might be attracting quite a few supporters from the Left. Lots of Labour voters at the time were turning against Harold Wilson, the prime minister, saying he should be exerting pressure on the Americans to pull out of Vietnam. Humberside Voice members were torn, wondering if they could still support Labour, but I didn't have any doubts. I was solid Labour.

Our man was Kevin McNamara and he got in, with a

big swing to Labour. Gott polled only something like 250 votes.

Wilson was finding it hard to govern as his general election victory in October 1964 had given him such a thin majority, so in March 1966 he sprang another general election, which people hadn't expected. Maybe our excellent result in the recent Hull by-election had encouraged him. This time I did find myself put forward as a Labour candidate, but not in Hull.

What happened was that my union, and other unions, said they would like me to stand, and they would support me. Obviously, at my age, with my lack of experience, I was never going to be offered a half-decent seat, only a no-hoper. The National Union of Seamen wrote to the hopeless constituencies, where Labour didn't stand a chance – and they were all dead keen to have me. With union support, it meant the local Party would only have to find a small part of the election expenses as the unions would pay 80 per cent. So, I had quite a choice. I did think about Blackpool North but I chose Southport as the trains from Hull were better.

I went before the selection committee. I remember one of the other candidates was called Goldwater, like Barry Goldwater, the American presidential candidate. I was selected as the official Labour candidate, and after the meeting, an old Amalgamated Engineering Union (AEU) shop steward came up to me, moaning that his union had tried to force him to vote for me. He'd refused. He said he wasn't going to let anyone tell him how to vote.

Pauline and Johnathan came with me and we lived in a hotel in Southport for about a month. I didn't tell the university, or ask their permission. I just did it. I didn't want them put in the position of having to decide whether I could or not. The local paper carried a headline saying, 'Seaman Selected', and in my election leaflet I stated I'd travelled to most parts of the world, working for large steamship companies. The Tories made a big thing of it, asking if I had a parrot on my shoulder, so at public meetings, I usually started by addressing a make-believe parrot with 'Pieces of eight!'

But just after I arrived I made one terrible mistake by telling the local paper, the *Southport Visitor*, that I'd do a series of articles on Labour Party policy. I even agreed to write three a week – I must have been mad. There were only certain areas of policy I knew about, such as the sea. A local ex-MP came to support me and I said to him, 'Will you do me an article on our defence policy?' He said he didn't know what it was. I realised then that some MPs had a set piece, which they would trot out all over the place as they went round.

One of the people sent to speak on my behalf was Lord Longford. I didn't know him, or ask him. I was just told one day he was being sent up by the Labour Party. I got a lift with him in his car and we had a long discussion about abortion. I was for it but he, of course, was against it, as a Catholic. He was a nice enough bloke, not aggressive, so there was no row, but he wasn't exactly my type.

I remember one Sunday going to church for a constituency election service with Pauline. The vicar started a long sermon in which he got on to 'the rich man in his castle, the poor man at his gate'. I got a bit of paper out and started making notes.

'What are you doing, John?' whispered Pauline. 'Stop rustling.'

'I'm making notes,' I muttered. 'I'm going to ask him questions afterwards. If he's made a political speech, I'm going to ask him political questions.' Pauline was dead worried, thinking I was really going to but I was just winding her up.

I haven't been in a church many times in my grown-up life. I'm an agnostic. I did go into Durham Cathedral once, when I was at the Durham miners' gala. The Bishop was speaking, and he was supposed to be very controversial. But I fell asleep – and unfortunately started snoring.

Another time I went into a church in Chester because I was feeling rotten and shivery, mainly because I had a nasty boil on my neck. I was warming myself by their heater and an old woman came up to me. 'I can see, son, you've got a boil. The best thing to do is get some soot from the chimney and some milk. That'll fix it.'

So I went home, got some soot, mixed it with some milk and drank it. And it didn't do any bloody good. Forty years later I was telling Joan Hammell, my chief of staff, this story. 'You stupid fool, John,' she said. 'You don't drink it. You use it as a poultice.'

While I was away canvassing in Southport, I still had to hand in a weekly essay at Hull. One week I couldn't manage it as I had no time, so I copied a mate's. He had a different tutor so I thought no one would find out. What I didn't know was that my tutor had fallen sick and this other tutor had taken over his work and marked all his essays that week. He found that two of them were identical. I got a telegram asking for an explanation. So I had to confess. I got a bit of a bollocking and had to write the essay again.

In that general election, Wilson was boasting that he would take on the unions, crush the militants and stop all these wildcat strikes once and for all. He warned that the next lot to raise their heads above the picket line and go on unofficial strikes would be for it. The election slogan was 'You Know Labour Government Works!', which was pushing it a bit as Labour had only been in power for five hundred days. Now I look at my leaflet again, I see that one of the things I listed that the next Labour government would do was: 'Steps will be taken by using TV and Radio to establish the University of the Air.' That did come to pass, but its name changed to the Open University.

Pauline canvassed with me, looking stunning, as she always did, and Johnathan. She had a Jackie Kennedy hairstyle at the time and Johnathan was so blond. I didn't win, of course. We got twelve thousand votes while the Tories romped home with twenty-two thousand, but I did improve our position, by increasing our share of the vote. Sir Ian Percival got in again. He was later the Tory solicitor general. Not long ago, I heard that he had been reminiscing about me and said I 'had fought a good, honest campaign'. Quite flattering. Not that I ever take much notice of what Tories think.

All in all, it was an interesting experience, for someone of twenty-seven, but I had assumed it would just be a short interlude in my life. Then I had to go back to Hull, to my studies and other concerns.

*

I got very involved in the official seamen's strike of 1966. The Reform Movement had managed to force through some changes, and secure some important positions, but Hogarth was still the general secretary, my sworn enemy. In 1965, though, the union's executive had swung to the Left, led by Jo Kenny and Jim Slater, who later became general secretary. I was active all over the country, rushing up and down to union meetings, addressing the strikers in dockyards and factories. One of the places I went to on my industrial tour was the Jaguar factory at Coventry.

I was exhausted by all the meetings and travelling. I remember arriving back at Hull railway station at four o'clock one morning, then having to take my first-year exams a few hours later. On the train I'd been trying to study Stonier and Hague – they did a book on basic economics – but kept falling asleep.

I got to the examination room and looked at the first paper. I thought of all my mates, still on the picket lines, and I wondered what the hell I was doing there. I should be fighting with them, I thought. So I walked out. Without writing a line.

I went to John Saville and apologised. I said I'd let him down. He'd got me into Hull and supported me all year, done so much for me, but I was afraid it wasn't for me, after all. I was packing it in. He said, 'Go home and sleep on it. Don't do anything hasty.'

So I went home and went to bed. When I woke up, I felt a bit better, so I decided to go back and complete the papers. They let me take the exam, on my own. I failed one paper but they let me resit it in September. This time I managed to pass.

In those days they chucked out a fair number of students for failing an exam – mainly because they had done no work but had just been dossing around. They knew I wasn't spending my days drunk in the union bar but fighting for better conditions for seamen.

Harold Wilson had set up a Royal Commission to look into the trade unions and I wrote part of the NUS submission to it. It included a section on the arts – yes, the arts – saying that unions must pay more attention to them. The working classes went to the theatre at Christmas to see a pantomime, but never in the rest of the year. Why was this? I suggested that the unions could help change working-class perceptions to make theatre and the arts more available and attractive to the workers. I had been involved with getting Barrie Rutter's production of *Animal Farm* by the National Theatre brought to Hull. It was for union guys and their wives.

I was more accepted by the union now, except Hogarth, of course. 'What the hell have the arts to do with us?' he wanted to know, when he heard I was working on their submission for the Royal Commission. He had a draft of the report in front of him and tore out the arts section.

But others were realising my value. Having been at Ruskin and now doing a degree at Hull, I could argue my case a bit better than I had in the past and be of more use to them. And the union was changing, again except for Hogarth.

I had one argument with him, face to face, which ended in him telling me he hoped I'd be chucked out of Hull University and finish up with a job in the docks. If I persisted with my union ambitions he'd send me as an official to Australia and I'd never come back. 'I hope when I get to your age,' I replied, 'I'll be tolerant of younger men demanding a change.'

Perhaps the most important thing I did while I was still a student at Hull, was to work on a pamphlet called *Not Wanted on Voyage – The Seaman's Reply*. It was published by the National Union of Seamen's Hull Dispute Committee and came out in June 1966, price 1/9d.

It was meant as a rival, or different voice, to the recently published Pearson Report, the official government inquiry into the shipping industry. We printed it in the same format and shape. In fact, we overprinted our title and cover on a faded-out print of their official cover. It was only twenty-four pages long, but very dense, with lots of facts and figures, quotes and references and carefully worked-out arguments. My name was on the first page, at the end of the Introduction, J. Prescott, along with Charlie Hodgins, the chairman of our committee. A number of people worked on different sections, particularly Tony Topham, but I pulled it together and was mainly responsible for it.

Our main contention was that the Pearson Report was biased against the seamen. We were going to prove our claim – and we did. We analysed the backgrounds of the authors of the Pearson Report, revealing their vested interests, and exposed the ship-owners and their secret profits. We argued that the power of the international banks lay behind the Government's resistance to the seamen and their just demands. It was a pretty devastating document and had a big effect on national thinking.

Despite all the union work, I somehow managed to

continue with my studies. At the end of my third year, I managed to graduate – with a third.

By then I was better in with the union, thanks to that pamphlet and other work. Things had changed and I sensed more changes were coming. I could see Hogarth going soon and began to think, You never know, I could be general secretary of the seamen's union one day.

I was writing reports, including our evidence to the Government on safety at sea, giving speeches, working on behalf of the union, even though I knew that Special Branch still had me in their sights.

It had been during the 1960 strike that us union activists began to suspect that we were being checked up on. The Government were obsessed with the possibility that Communist agitators were stirring up trouble and it seemed that Special Branch had been instructed to investigate.

In a way, it was part of the romance of being an activist, thinking the police were watching you all the time. We never had definite proof, but I thought it was appalling. The police and the Government's defence was that they were just watching the militants and Communists, as a precaution. But what was wrong with being a Communist? Nothing. It wasn't against the law. So they tapped phones and photographed people at rallies and demonstrations, just in case, or so they said.

I was convinced that Special Branch were watching me, and others, during the seamen's strikes because I'd read in the press names of people at certain meetings, including mine, when I knew the press had not been there. So the police must have been spying on us, infiltrating our meetings, or they had an informer – in fact, they had a lot of them, people inside the union who would tell them bits and pieces, in return presumably for a few favours.

By the 1966 strike our suspicions were all but confirmed when Harold Wilson announced that he was going to make public the names of the baddies. We suspected that most would be known agitators, but I was told that I was going to be on the list. Wilson was convinced there was a 'tightly knit group of politically motivated men' who were determined to create strikes to bring down the Government and paralyse the country.

I sat in the public gallery of the House of Commons when it was thought Harold Wilson was going to name me among the guilty men, but in the end he didn't. Someone must have realised it would make him look pretty stupid to do so, as I had been a Labour candidate at Southport.

I was outraged by the police tactics and often complained to the Home Office. All they ever said was, 'Where's your proof?' They'd deny it, but I knew they were looking the other way. I was against all this snooping and prying – and vowed if I ever got into any sort of power, I wouldn't condone it.

I was pretty sure that although I hadn't been named in Parliament that day, I was still on the suspicious list. That, coupled with the fact that in 1968 Hogarth and others were still at the top, and I didn't know how long that would last, meant I feared I'd rise no higher in the union.

It was during 1968 that the sitting MP for Hull East, Commander Harry Pursey, announced that he would not be standing at the next election, whenever that would be.

To my surprise, Bill Hogarth said that if I put myself forward to be the Labour candidate, the union would give me their support. This was significant because the NUS was very important in a shipping place like Hull, so they would play a vital part in me winning the nomination. But I knew what was behind NUS thinking. This was another example of them trying to sidetrack me so I'd never become general secretary of the union. It was Hogarth and his cronies' latest plot to offer me a consolation prize and get me out of their hair for good. That's how I saw it anyway. So, should I go for it or not?

CHAPTER EIGHT

1968–70

Standing for Parliament

I suppose I should have been dead keen on the possibility of becoming an MP. I'd been brought up in a very political family – on both sides. Our house had always been used as Labour committee rooms during local and national elections, and my dad was usually standing for the council. MPs would often come to the house. I remember one called Ernest Fernyhough, MP for Jarrow, who was a parliamentary private secretary to Harold Wilson, visiting our house in Chester during some election. From a very young age, me, my brothers and sisters were sent out to distribute Labour Party leaflets.

My mother's family were Welsh miners whose devotion to the Labour Party went back several generations. In their house, Attlee was the hero while Churchill was the baddy. He'd never been forgiven for sending in the troops against the striking miners in Wales.

The very first vaguely political action I ever took, of any sort, apart from giving out leaflets for my dad, was when I was about eighteen and I'd just joined the Labour Party. I'd got it into my head that vasectomy was a very good thing and it seemed stupid that the Government wasn't supporting it. Surely it would help to solve the growing population problem. The whole legal side was a mess, which didn't help. I couldn't understand why it wasn't being sorted out.

I went to see our local MP in Chester, the Tory John Temple, queuing up at his weekly surgery. I don't think he actually understood what vasectomy was any more than I did. I just knew the effect of it. It was a fairly new idea, which was beginning to be mentioned in the newspapers.

Temple was very pleasant, not at all dismissive. He was a gent, a Tory of the old school, and probably quite impressed or amused that a local lad was worrying about such things. He said he would find out. He wrote a letter to the Ministry of Health and eventually got a reply, which stated that the reason the law was unclear was that doctors in effect were prevented from operating on otherwise healthy organs. Some years later it was all sorted and became very popular.

Then came a more practical experience of politics, when I did my stint as an agent in Chester in 1964. But that was a bit of a laugh, really, because we were in a hopeless situation. To liven it up I spent some of our election money on hiring a Chester band, for a few bob. They were called Russ Abbot and the Black Abbots – the bloke who later went on to become a well-known TV comedian – and I got them to perform from the back of a lorry, going round the constituency with the candidate. They played and sang a special Labour Party song. I can't remember the words now, but I pinched the idea, and the song, from Bessie Braddock MP, over in Liverpool, who was using the song in her campaign.

Then, of course, I'd had a previous try at getting into Parliament, standing at Southport in 1966, but again that was done for the experience, rather than the likelihood of winning. Now, if I put myself forward for Hull East, I'd have a good chance.

I hadn't honestly ever planned to be an MP. It had never been my main ambition, either when I was at sea or working for the union. But the more I thought about it, the more I realised that if I got in I might have a better opportunity to improve the conditions of seamen and repeal the old master–servant merchant-shipping legislation.

Hull East was considered a safe Labour seat. Commander Harry Pursey had held it since 1945 and had a majority of twenty-three thousand. But, of course, there was keen competition for the Labour nomination. The others on the shortlist were pretty good, including Tom Ponsonby, who later became Labour's chief whip in the Lords. There was also a CND person, then Harry

Woodford, a local railway man who had the support of the National Union of Railwaymen, and Alex Clarke, a local solicitor. As well as the NUS, I also got support from Jack Jones of the Transport and General Workers' Union, with whom I'd had discussions on changes to the NUS. He said it was a company union – i.e. corrupt.

It was the unions' support that swung it, and in November 1968 I was adopted as the Labour candidate for Hull East. I then asked Harry Woodford, whom I'd defeated, if he'd be my agent as I thought he was so good. And he was. He has proved to be a most loyal friend for over forty years, running my election campaigns, giving me good advice and allowing me to have an active campaigning role in the Party.

I had told Pauline that if any reporter ever rang her about anything at all, to say, 'No comment.' Don't tell them a thing. They rang her at home with the news I had been selected and got a quote out of her, which appeared in the *Hull Daily Mail*: 'I'm so proud,' she said. 'He was only a waiter, when I first met him.' I was annoyed that she'd been caught out, but it was funny.

There were two years to go before the possibility of a general election so I carried on working for the union, though for a long time they wouldn't give me a proper position, even though I was doing so much for them – giving evidence to the Royal Commission, writing pamphlets.

There were two people on the union executive, Jim Slater and Jo Kenny, who'd made sure my work was openly recorded by being minuted in a meeting. They had recommended that I should be given a job on graduating from Hull. Hogarth had always refused, but when I found the minute I took it to him. Hogarth looked at it and said, 'I'll find a job for you, don't worry, on the buses in Hull . . .'

But he was forced in the end to give me something and I became a minor union official in Hull, on not much money. So I did that during the day, while in the evenings I went out canvassing for the forthcoming election.

There were still a lot of wildcat strikes, among the seamen and other workers, and Wilson was again threatening all sorts to stamp them out. For instance, he proposed his *In Place of Strife* legislation in 1969, which was meant to reduce the power of the unions but it was withdrawn. A result of this was that the seamen were the only group of workers with a penal clause in our legislation.

I got called into the assistant general secretary's office one day. There were three men there, asking questions. They were holding photographs of picketing seamen. They were trying to identify particular people. I was certain they were from Special Branch.

I was then asked to step outside. I knew at once what was going on. Some of the union officials and the Special Branch people were Freemasons, and I was sure they were helping each other.

The irony now, all these years later, is that Wilson himself was being secretly investigated by some Special Branch officials who suspected he was really a Russian double agent. The fact that some people thought that was outrageous.

I was interviewed on *Panorama* once, and they were

trying to find out if our union or a group within it was Communist backed, which, of course, was what the police believed. They kept on and on, saying we must be getting money from political parties. I said that ordinary people supported and gave us donations, but there was one party which contributed – not the Communists but the Young Liberals. That floored them. But it was true. The Young Liberals were pretty left wing at one time, back in the days when they had people like Peter Hain.

What's forgotten from this period is that while all union activists were under observation, in the attempt to identify militants and Commies, we were being targeted at the same time by the Right. Moral Re-Armament was watching us as well, trying to influence us, to save us from the Commies. Pauline once got visited by a Moral Re-Armament official who said they had heard that I was a future leader of my union so they were offering help. She showed him the door.

I met Harold Wilson when I was with an NUS delegation who went to see him at 10 Downing Street in 1970, before the general election. It was the first time I'd been there and we were taken into the Cabinet Room. He sat with his pipe, no civil servants, wearing his Trinity House tie to show he was a friend of seamen. He'd just come back from his holidays in the Scilly Isles and boasted about easterly and westerly winds, getting it all bloody wrong.

We wanted the laws changed, outdated penal clauses altered, such as laws that made disobeying orders mutiny, and 'broaching ship's cargo', which I'd known as a Hollywood Waiter was used to dock wages for trivial offences. I knew the Shipping Acts backwards, better than he did, so I spouted away and he couldn't interrupt.

When we'd finished, he said he would set up an investigation, and review legislation then going through. The problem was, as I pointed out, it had already reached the House of Lords. Oh, we hadn't to worry, he assured us, he'd see us right.

I told him it would take time. 'And how do you know,' I said to him, 'you'll still be here?' Meaning, of course, would he still be prime minister at No. 10?

He wasn't so amused by that. 'I don't envisage my plans being upset,' he replied coldly. Two months following, he was out.

The Tory candidate, my opponent in the 1970 general election, turned out to be a young Cambridge graduate and banker, who'd worked at Conservative Central Office, called Norman Lamont. There was a new Tory council in Hull who weren't very popular as they were going to double council rents. All Lamont could do was run a defensive campaign, trying to explain things away. It was easier for me, with the NUS on my side, even though I knew perfectly well that the leaders, like Hogarth, wanted me to get into Parliament so I'd be out of their way.

Pauline was heavily pregnant at the time of the election. In fact our second child was expected on 18 June 1970, which was polling day. Pauline jokes that I used to shove her in the car, drive like mad and shake her about, hoping the baby might be born the day before, which, of course, would have been nice publicity. But it didn't work. David, our second son, was born four days later on

22 June. He was Pauline's third son, but no one knew about that.

Lamont was having a hard time. When he went round the council houses, people spat at him. I found him a decent enough bloke, but he hadn't much chance. I got in easily, with thirty-six thousand votes, twenty-two thousand more than Lamont.

The *Hull Daily Mail* said I had 'Won The Battle Of The Bright Young Men'. They also did a bit about Pauline. 'Perhaps the most excited supporter of Mr Prescott was his raven-haired wife Pauline. Smart and erect in a striking red frock, nobody would have guessed that she was within a few hours of giving birth to her second child.'

A few years later I saw Lamont interviewed on TV and I remember him saying, of that 1970 election, how I'd struck him at the time as 'a glamorous figure, with a Jaguar and a glamorous wife'.

Funny how people retain certain images of you. I don't think I've been called glamorous many times since. I certainly wasn't aware of it at the time. But it's true that I had a Jag, a very old one, bought second hand. I'm not sure if I'd been influenced by Anthony Blond, going round in his flash car as a Labour candidate in Chester. It was more that I'd always wanted a Jag. And why not? Nothing's too good for the workers.

As for Pauline, well, she was glamorous, no question. In my election leaflet photo, she does look like Elizabeth Taylor. I suppose I was still slim and youthful-looking in those days, with probably a few touches of the Hollywood Waiter still lingering. I always did try to look smart in a nice suit.

I was just thirty-two – it was a few days after my birthday – when I got elected to Parliament.

Up to then, all I'd really wanted to be was a full-time union official and eventually to make some changes to the NUS. My experience of real life so far had been my years as a seaman, and based on what I'd seen and heard, I considered my union had grown corrupt, doing too many deals with the ship-owners, and had ceased to care enough about its ordinary members. If I'd been asked at any time in the sixties what my ambition in life was, that's what I would have said.

I'm never sure what people mean by 'ambition'. To me, all it ever meant was I wanted to do my best at whatever job I had. And up to 1970 that meant trying to do my best as a union official. I never saw any position I had as a stepping stone to higher things, a rung up some ladder that I was imagining stretched up before me.

I liked to think I was a grafter, that was what people saw in me, someone who tried hard at whatever he was doing. I didn't think of the future or plan ahead. It could have been the result of that 11-plus failure, having my horizons limited, feeling I was no good so what was the point in having too many aspirations?

I suspect people like Roy Hattersley, or Michael Heseltine, when they were first elected MP, thought, Aye aye, next stop the cabinet, after that prime minister. I can understand that, but I never thought like that because I never knew where I was going. I took chances when they came, when people offered me things or made suggestions, like going to Ruskin, but nothing was ever worked out in advance. Even in my dreams.

CHAPTER NINE

1970–74

MP

I somehow expected I would get a letter from the House of Commons, perhaps on parchment, congratulating me on being elected and telling me what to do, when and where to arrive – but nothing happened. So I asked Kevin McNamara, MP for Hull North, what the procedure was. He said, 'There isn't one. You just turn up.'

So, I put on my best suit and went to London. I wore that suit for almost the whole of the next year. I have a photo of me in it, on the Terrace, which my mum took when she came to visit me in Parliament. On that first day when I arrived, I had to swear an oath to the Queen. I was given a locker and told I could sit in the library and work. Last time I looked inside that locker it was full of copies of a book written by Paul Foot in 1971 about the 1961 Hanratty case. He gave me a pile of them to distribute to MPs. Bit out of date now.

There wasn't security like there is today – searches and X-ray machines. Back in 1970, the police and parliamentary officials prided themselves on recognising you by sight. With new MPs, whom they didn't yet know, they'd have your photo, or your election leaflet, under their desk, which they would refer to till they got to know your face.

I had been to the House of Commons quite a few times before I became an MP. In the previous few years I'd often been down when Shipping Acts were going through, to brief MPs on behalf of the NUS. Then I'd sit in during committees, on the public seats at the back, and listen to what was being said.

And of course, I'd been in the public gallery when I thought Harold Wilson was going to name me as an agitator. On that occasion, I got given a pass by Michael Foot. I remember wandering around, looking for the public gallery, when I happened to bump into Jennie Lee, who in 1929 had been the youngest MP in Parliament and who had later married Nye Bevan. 'Are you supporting us?' I asked her.

'It's very difficult,' she said, hardly pausing, then walked on quickly.

After about three months in the House, I was given an office, but I had to share it with five other MPs,

Tories and Liberals as well as Labour. They included Tom Pendry, Norman Fowler, Kenneth Clarke and later on Cyril Smith. Cyril Smith, the man mountain Liberal MP for Rochdale, was too heavy to get into the lift, so he never used the office. That was handy and gave us more space, such as it was. It was a very, very small office for five people.

I didn't feel any sense of awe and wonderment on becoming an MP. To me, Parliament was just a place of work – and I was there to work, not mess around enjoying myself. I didn't hang around the bars, as some MPs do, and never have. I wasn't aware of the magnificent architecture and the wonderful history. I am more conscious of it today than I ever was in the past. It is only now, when I know I'll soon be leaving the House of Commons, almost forty years later, that I find myself walking down the corridors and thinking about all the people who have gone before and the great historic moments. But not when I arrived.

Back in 1970, I told myself I was there to fight so I didn't worry about any feelings of inferiority I might have had, especially listening to the Tories with their lovely accents and gift of the gab. I remember thinking a lot of the stuff going on was nonsense, all these pointless, piddling questions to ministers. Load of rubbish, I thought. It's just showing-off time. Today, I've rather changed my mind. I realise that what might look like a charade to outsiders serves a purpose. The minister has had to get someone to look up the point being raised and it makes him or her aware of topics they might otherwise not have been interested in.

But my thinking then was, I'm not here to show off. So I didn't worry when I got mocked for my accent or my background by any stuck-up Tories.

One incident got reported in all the press, involving the Tory MP Nicholas Soames, Churchill's grandson. Whenever I got up to speak, he really did shout out things like, 'A whisky and soda for me, Giovanni, and a gin and tonic for my friend.' By then, most MPs knew I'd spent ten years as a steward at sea. And I did go on a lot about the plight of seamen.

The first time it happened, I replied, 'At least I'm here because of my brains, not my father's balls.' That remark was not reported in Hansard. I wonder why.

Then there was the time that Cecil Parkinson, the Tory minister, was mocking me for going on and on about the seamen's union. 'He's always talking about British merchant ships and their decline,' he said. 'I bet he plays with little boats in his bath.'

But I got him with my intervention: 'I'm sure the House is fully aware of what he plays with in his bath.'

By then everyone knew he'd been having an affair with Sara Keays, his secretary. She was a lovely girl. She worked on the same floor as I did at one time.

I gave my maiden speech just a few weeks after I became an MP, on 13 July 1970. By tradition you talk about something to do with your own constituency. I wanted to broaden mine and did a much longer speech than normal, about three thousand words, which I slaved over for ages, writing and rewriting.

I started by praising my predecessor, Commander Pursey, and all his achievements, then moved on to the

Hull docks, one of the biggest in Britain at the time. Then I praised my electors.

> Hull's greatest asset is the people whose warm Yorkshire hospitality and generosity and shrewd judgement of character and appreciation of value are universally renowned. Never was this so amply demonstrated than in the recent general election when the Labour candidate was elected with no evidence of the national swing against the Labour Party. I like to think that this was due to the personal qualities of the candidate, although I am prepared to accept the advent of Hull's first twelve months of rule by a Tory council since before the war in which rents were raised from three pounds to nine pounds a week played no small part . . .

I also attacked the Tory government for the port of Hull's lousy road system and for delaying a decision on the Humber Bridge. I finished with some good old-fashioned socialism, saying that the only solution to the mess in both the docks and shipping was 'to take both industries into public ownership in the interest of the nation . . .'

Kevin McNamara, in his speech, said that I had 'made a notable maiden speech'. Then he added, 'And I say that not only because I have to travel up and down the country with him every week, but because it's true.'

Michael Heseltine, for the Tory government, con-gratulated me. 'It was one of the most remarkable maiden speeches I have heard in the House,' he said. 'I am pleased to have the opportunity of congratulating him. I am sure we shall hear from him on many occasions with equal enjoyment in the near future.'

You're always kind to a maiden speaker, but I liked to think he meant it.

During that first Parliament, from 1970 to 1974, the Tories were in power with a majority of about thirty seats and Edward Heath was prime minister. Harold Wilson was still our leader, even though he'd lost the election. I didn't have much to do with him during my early years in Parliament.

I was mainly concerned with my campaigns. I had been working on some of them for years. Now I was in Parliament, even if we weren't in government, I was determined to see if we could get some of the laws changed, so I got involved with many maritime issues over the next years.

One of the first things I got involved in was flags of convenience. This was a huge tax fiddle by ship-owners and was losing the country millions: they would register the ownership of a ship in a place like Liberia or Panama and therefore not pay British taxes. But it wasn't just the tax avoidance I objected to: they were endangering the safety and health of our seamen, many of whom died, because their rules were lax and working conditions much worse than they would have been if they'd been flying the Red Ensign.

I learned one parliamentary lesson while working on this campaign: your enemies are very often on your own side, not the opposition. I was attacked for the Red Ensign campaign by one of our senior Labour MPs, Jimmy

Johnson – and discovered he was an honorary adviser to the Liberian government. He was getting paid by it and handing out scholarships to Liberian students. I was staggered.

I didn't make much progress with this campaign, until a tanker flying a flag of convenience sank in the Channel. This caused terrible pollution and a huge outcry. I remember thinking how appalling it was that there was more concern about oil on the beach than there had been in the past about the blood of seamen spilt while sailing on unsafe ships. The blood was far easier washed away, it seemed. But at least attention was now being focused on these flags-of-convenience vessels, and I could take advantage of that to try and effect some change. Not that ultimately I was able to make significant improvements until quite some time later. There was considerable resistance. As the Tories were in power, the ship-owners always had lots of influence in Government.

I did better with my campaign for deep-sea divers. North Sea gas exploration was starting up, though it wasn't the huge industry it later became.

I was one of the first MPs to go out to the oil rigs and investigate conditions. I'd been appalled to hear how many divers were dying. I learned to dive, so I could understand what was going on, and found out they were being sent down with inadequate equipment and training. Some of them were diving to depths of two hundred metres and being left there hanging in the water for up to twelve hours, often with no proper decompression chambers. There were few regulations, and a lot of the divers, attracted by the good money, said they were trained when they were not. They'd say they'd once been on a boat and thought that qualified them. One ate a huge chicken lunch before he dived. He was sick under water and his lungs got sucked right out. They had no idea what they were doing and the owners couldn't have cared less.

I discovered that no proper records were being kept of the fatalities because many happened miles out at sea, outside British jurisdiction. The oil rig owners and the Tories denied my figures and said there was nothing to worry about, I was scaremongering.

I went to see the minister in charge, John Davies – one of the early Tory ministers, not an elected MP, who had been brought in from outside. It was clear he didn't know what was going on, so I gave him a brief.

I was helped in my campaign by the *Sunday Times* 'Insight' team. This was when newspapers did proper investigations, on real subjects, not all this nonsense about celebrities. Today when the *Sunday Times* rings me on a so-called story, I say, 'Call that an investigation? It's crap, back in the seventies, your paper did real investigations.'

The *Sunday Times* journalist on the story was David Blundy. A great lad but hopelessly disorganised. He seemed to live in a mess and could never find all his papers, but he was a good journalist. He helped a lot with his coverage. Later he was killed while covering the war in El Salvador.

In the end, I got a Divers Charter passed, so the conditions of North Sea divers were greatly improved.

I worried generally about safety at sea – it had concerned me ever since I'd gone to sea myself. When I was still a student at Hull, and also working for the union, there used to be something called the Silver Cod Award for the trawler captain that caught the most fish in a year. It was a big event locally, because the prime minister of the day would present it personally at a big London do.

I was against this competition because it encouraged owners to send their ships out in terrible weather so they'd catch more fish than the others. Seamen were made to go, whether they wanted to or not. In 1968, three trawlers iced up and sank off Iceland, which highlighted the problem.

We had a giant Silver Cod made out of paper and cardboard, and we toured the streets of Hull with it. We had a big banner that read, 'It's not fish you're buying but men's lives.' We eventually persuaded Harold Wilson to stop presenting the award. After he'd backed out, they soon gave it up. The Silver Cod, the real one, is now in a museum in Hull.

Another drama I got involved with, years later, concerned the loss of the *Gaul*. This was in 1974. The *Gaul* was a Hull trawler that disappeared in the North Sea, near Russia, leaving no trace. It was thought in Hull that it had been torpedoed and sunk with all hands by a Soviet submarine perhaps by mistake – or because it was being used as a British spy ship.

I asked a question in the House: was it true that Royal Navy people were sailing on our merchant ships? The answer was that they were, in civvies, but just to get experience of the merchant navy. That was seen as an admission that something was going on. But they refused to reopen an investigation. Eventually, in 1997, the ship was found by a TV company. I reopened the inquiry and it concluded the ship had gone down in bad weather. The Russians even agreed to an examination of the bodies, and there were no signs of explosive contamination. It had been an accident.

Shipping disasters became something of a constant theme for me. I thought it was very important that they were dealt with properly. In 1980 the bulk carrier *Derbyshire* sank with the loss of thirty-nine crew. The implication was that the crew had been negligent. The ship was located, several years later, very deep down. In 1998 I ordered a formal investigation into the loss. I asked Tony Blair to ask US President Clinton if we could use the diving team that had recently discovered the *Titanic*. He agreed, and an inquiry found the crew had not been negligent. The ship had sunk because of a leaky air vent that had allowed water to flood in during a typhoon.

Then there was the 1989 *Marchioness* disaster, the pleasure boat that sank in the Thames. In the House of Commons, I accused the Tory government of being culpable because they had allowed a dance deck to be created, which meant the captain couldn't see properly. There was a campaign for an inquiry, one of the leaders being Eileen Dallaglio, mother of the famous rugby player; her daughter had died in the disaster. The Tories refused, but a decade on I managed to order an inquiry and the families of those who had died were very grateful to have a conclusion at last. The Department of Transport was required to apologise, which I did on its behalf, to the Commons.

A year into that first term in Parliament, because of the campaigning I was doing, almost all connected with seafaring matters, I found myself becoming front-bench

114

spokesman on shipping specifically. Roy Mason was our shadow minister for Trade, which covered shipping, but he didn't know much about it, so I made most of the relevant speeches. Although I continued officially as a back-bencher, this was a pretty big deal, given my relative lack of experience as an MP. Especially when you consider that back in the seventies, our merchant fleet was huge, our Cunard liners, like the *QE2*, ruled the waves and the North Sea oil rigs were becoming vital to our economy.

In 1972, the chief whip called for me and asked if I'd like to become a Labour member of the British delegation to the Council of Europe. I wasn't quite sure what this was. It had been a forerunner of the Common Market, but was separate from that body. The Council had more members, about forty-six in all. I accepted the position.

Later, in 1975, I became a delegate to the European Parliament – the EEC – which Britain joined in 1973. In 1976 I then became leader of the UK delegation to that parliament. I quite enjoyed both positions. It only meant a few meetings a year in Europe and I usually took Pauline, sometimes the boys too.

We were in Switzerland once, all the delegates, plus their wives and partners, being taken on some sightseeing trip. They had an annual weekend for families. While we were on the coach, my younger son David, then aged about five, said he wanted to sit next to Barbara Castle, who I think was secretary of state for Health at the time. She agreed, and her husband, Ted, gave up his seat. She asked David why he wanted to sit with her. 'Because I've never sat beside a famous person,' said David.

'But your father is famous, David,' replied Barbara.

'Yes, but only in Hull,' said David.

When I first joined the House of Commons, I was told to fix myself up with a pair from the opposite side; the idea is that when one of you has to miss a vital vote for some reason, the other doesn't vote either so your absence is evened out. I was against this system. I thought it encouraged lazy MPs.

I also didn't want to have anything to do with any Tory, as I disliked them all. Officially I was paired with Hugh Dykes, MP for Harrow, who was pro-Europe. But we hardly ever paired. When Tories came up to me and said hello in the House, I would ignore them. Dennis Skinner would usually talk to them, for he's a decent man.

Now and again I had a bit of fun. I played for the House of Commons football team, mainly in charity games against showbusiness elevens. In one game I found myself marking Dave Dee or it might have been Dozy, Beaky, Mick or Tich, one of them anyway, from that famous pop group. I wasn't very good at football, having very little skill, but I could put myself about. A bit like Nobby Stiles. And I was a lot thinner then. Anyway, I tackled this pop star and unfortunately broke his ankle. He was furious. He turned to me and said, 'I'm only doing this for charity.' Diddy David Hamilton, the disc jockey, was in that game. He jumped on my back, made rude gestures. I dumped him on the ground and put mud on his flowing locks – much to the crowd's delight.

We played another charity game against the Penthouse Pets. Our manager that day was Malcolm Allison, who used to be manager of Manchester City. Can't remember the score but it was a good laugh. We also played German MPs, from their House of Commons – and beat them 2–0. No, I didn't score.

It's interesting to see now which MPs were keen members of the parliamentary football team. I've got a programme for a game against a showbiz eleven in 1975, which was apparently the first time ever that the House of Commons fielded a team. It lists me as a defender, Neil Kinnock as goalie or defender. Robert Kilroy Silk and Jonathan Aitken were also in it. We were all in our thirties, then able to run and tackle people.

Every weekend I went home to Hull, to Pauline and the boys. When the boundaries of my constituency, Hull East, changed, we decided to move as I'd always made a point of saying I would live in my constituency.

We found a house in Sutton, once owned by some rich merchant, which had become a Salvation Army home. It was huge, with eight bedrooms and lots of turrets, too big in one sense for us, but as an MP you need a bit of space for Party meetings and visitors. We made an offer and got it for twenty-eight thousand pounds. We sold our other house for twelve thousand – I think that's right. I'm no good on house prices. I let Pauline and the boys sort out such things. We had to get a mortgage, of course. It was a bargain, for such a big house, but this was because it was in what was considered a rather poor area. It was surrounded by council houses, so not many people were after it.

Some time later, the road outside got diverted when they made a bypass. That made it a lot quieter. Some of the local Tories said I'd known about this all the time, but I didn't. It was just luck. We always had lots of friends and Labour people staying so, having once been a homeless commune, the house became a political commune.

In London, I had a rather unusual arrangement. I lived with Dennis Skinner. He and I had become MPs at the same time and one day we got talking. He came up to me and said, 'Have you joined Tribune?' He meant the Tribune group of left-wing MPs. I said no. My reasoning was that although I agreed with nine out of ten things they believed in, I knew when it came to the tenth, I might not. They could rely on me most of the time, but on certain things they might not be able to and they'd call me a sell-out.

Dennis said to me, 'We don't have votes, we have views.' I agreed to join.

Like all new MPs – or, at least, Labour ones from the provinces with no income or private wealth – he was struggling to find somewhere to live in London. He was MP for Bolsover in Derbyshire and, like me, had been to Ruskin.

I was lucky with my accommodation because the NUS had provided me, as a union official, with a flat at their headquarters in Clapham. It was quite big so Dennis moved in. We got on very well and shared for many years. We didn't spend a lot of time at the flat, as we were at the House, and usually ate there, then went home at weekends.

We had one or two differences. I wanted a phone installed straight away, so I could be in touch with Pauline and the boys, my union contacts, or people involved in my various campaigns, but he didn't want one. He didn't want to be bothered in the flat. He loved watching sport on the TV, especially football and snooker. I've never been a huge sports fan. I always wanted to watch current-affairs

'We fought for this.' My grandfather William, centre, on the front page of the *Daily Herald*, when the mines were nationalised. Working-class socialism was in my blood

Above: I'm sure that home-made outfit must have been very itchy

Above left: Dad, Dawn, me, Mum and Ray. Think Dawn must be practising her counting at an early age. Guess that's how she passed the 11-plus

Left: Me, third from left, in the Cubs. Obviously

Left: At the front of the class at PE. I get the feeling there wasn't any central heating when this photo was taken

Below left: Family holidays in the late '40s were spent in the most luxurious of settings. That's me on the left, about to overtake the kid in front. That's how I remember it…

Below: Sitting, far right, in a natty plastic sheet, in the Lake District in 1953 with mates from Grange School. I loved it

Far left: The clean-cut schoolboy

Left: A natural as a toff

In the kitchen of the Patten Arms, Warrington. I'm at the back

Lesson one of my catering course: 'How to pour a cup of tea.' Think I've cracked that one

Off to sea...munching on an apple

Above: Practising for later in life. Boxing on board to entertain the passengers. That's me on the right. Probably wouldn't have included this photo if I'd been on the left

Left: 'Hollywood Waiter'. On board the *Britannic*, 1959

It's a hard life on the ocean waves

Above: Panama

Right: The Bahamas

Below: The West Indies

'Where's Prezza?' Clue: look for the beard. Ruskin College

Graduation from Hull University, 1968

In that jacket and quiff…

…'Liz Taylor' couldn't possibly resist…

…a date at the local dance followed…

…my blue suede shoes weren't stepped on and Pauline and I were engaged…

…and holidaying in London

11 November 1961. My happiest day. Thank you, Pauline, for supporting me through thick and thin and for loving me

Below: Four days after I became an MP, our second son, David, was born

Bottom: Me holding David still and Pauline with a restraining hand on Johnathan. The boys seemed keen to rush off and change. Can't think why

programmes, like *Newsnight*. Over the years we had a few disagreements about the TV.

He didn't approve of me becoming a Labour delegate to the European Parliament – believing that if I was anti-Europe, I should have nothing to do with it. But I've always believed you should try to change things from within, not from without, and after all, the people had voted in a referendum to stay in the EEC.

He's a very decent bloke, is Dennis, still a good friend. Pauline used to refer to us as the Odd Couple.

I often gave Dennis a lift to the House in my Jaguar. Which raised a few eyebrows. There was a short spell when I had a Rover. It was rubbish: the electrics were always breaking down. I went back to the Jaguar.

My Jags have always been second hand, bought for a couple of thousand or so. I usually get my brother Ray, who's clever that way, to inspect them. Even today, I still have an old Jag and I've never paid more than seven thousand for any of them. They don't hold their value as well as Mercedes, so you can get a good one for not much. As a kid, I loved the look of a Jag and promised myself I'd get one, if I ever could. I love driving them – perfect for the long journey from Hull to London. I need comfort when I'm driving.

People have always made remarks about my Jag, about someone like me, from my background, driving such a car, but I could never see the problem. It is, after all, a British-made car. Many of those mocking me have usually been driving foreign vehicles.

I remember Austin Mitchell, MP for Grimsby, saying to me one day, 'How do you drive a Jaguar, John?'

'Easy,' I said. 'Put the key in the ignition and away you go. How do you drive yours?'

He was one of those with a foreign car at that time.

CHAPTER TEN

1974–79

Cod War

During the October 1974 general election campaign, a vicar in my constituency, the Reverend Jack Reed, attacked me from his pulpit one Sunday, saying in his sermon that I represented the jackboot of trade unionism and that people should not vote for me. He said God had told him not to vote for Prescott.

I rang his bishop and asked, was it true that it was God's view that people shouldn't vote for Prescott? I didn't want to attack the Church, I said, I just wanted to get to the truth. The bishop sighed, and said there was nothing he could do about the vicar.

Reed kept repeating it, so I challenged him to debate with me on the radio, to which he agreed. They also got the Tory candidate, Stephen Dorrell – later a Tory minister. I said to the vicar, 'Are you still saying that God has told you not to vote for me?' He said that was how he interpreted it. 'Well, that's all above my head,' I said, 'at least eight feet above my head,' meaning somewhere in heaven, 'but it's not in this world anyway.'

I then asked if it was true that he had said all politicians were corrupt. He said that money comes first in our present-day society and that commercial values were now so great that politicians got corrupted by them.

I said to him, 'What about that youth centre that's been closed in your parish?' I'd managed to do a smart bit of research and found out about it, which he hadn't expected. His parish had closed this youth centre and were now renting it out for storage at a commercial rent. He had to agree I'd got the story right and that was the position. So I'd got him there. All he could say in reply was that the Church always had to have money. Huh.

Labour got back into power – but only just, which was why there were two general elections in 1974, in February and October. I got a big majority in each, over twenty-three thousand, but after the first election Labour only had a majority of four over the Tories, so it was tough going. Wilson had returned as prime minister but he was just hanging on so in October he called a second general election. This time we won with a slightly bigger majority over them, forty plus, which made things a bit easier.

122

I was made parliamentary private secretary to Peter Shore, who was secretary of state for Trade. In theory, this is the first rung on the ministerial ladder. You don't get paid. You carry the minister's bags and briefs and do the donkey work, but you learn a lot about the inner workings of government. I suppose it was a surprise that someone like Peter Shore should ask me, as he was such a quiet, restrained, academic type. I admired him greatly as he had been the architect of Labour's 1964 manifesto, which had brought us to power.

When he first asked me, I didn't fancy the job. He had three PPSs, including Nigel Spearing and Bryan Gould. I said I preferred to be free to campaign for changes in the shipping industry and I presumed I wouldn't be able to do that as a PPS. He said, 'Don't worry, you'll still be free to say what you believe in.' I then asked if I would have any influence on policy. He said of course I would. So I said I'd take the job.

One of the things I got involved in was a new maritime authority, bringing all the various coastal bodies – police, security, harbour agencies and others – into one separate organisation. This seemed sensible to me, but those inside the Department of Trade were against it, fearing they would lose some of their authority. I spoke in favour of the new body, in various committees and at Conferences, and got told off by the Department. They complained to Peter that I wasn't toeing the government line. He called me in and told me quietly that he wasn't really bothered. Yeah, he was a great bloke, Peter Shore, a real gentleman.

Very recently, under the thirty-year rule, I discovered

that the permanent secretary had actually taken his complaint about me to the prime minister. But the PM had said nothing to me at the time.

I held the PPS job for two years, but I can't say that the Government was always happy with me. On 21 July 1975, Wilson sent a letter to the Department complaining about my behaviour. I'd supported an amendment to the Defence White Paper, along with several other PPSs. The letter warned that 'Mr Prescott should be informed that it is incumbent on him as a Parliamentary Private Secretary to support the Government . . . and to avoid diversionary preliminary votes.' I was furious about the whole thing, and still voted for the amendment.

Then, some months later, just before Peter and I went to Russia on a trade delegation, Peter told me that Wilson had taken me off the visit. I stormed into the PM's office at the House of Commons. Wilson sat there looking at me, smoking his pipe. 'Why have you taken me off the trip?' I asked him. He said it was because I had voted against the Government when there had been a three-line whip. As a PPS, he said, I was not allowed to do that.

'When I took the job,' I said, 'nobody told me I could never vote against the Government. If I'd known that, I would never have agreed.' Anyway, as it was clear I was getting the sack unless I went along with what he said, I told him, 'You can stick your PPS,' and walked out.

This whole business of being a PPS was cloudy at the time. We all know a government minister has to toe the party line. It's called the payroll vote. As a minister, you get paid extra and are involved in the decision-making process, so you have to vote the way you're told. But a PPS is not paid extra. So it seemed to me at the time that you should be able to vote with your conscience. The position really wasn't clear. Today there's no choice. A PPS is considered an unpaid member of the Government and has to vote with it.

Soon after the bust-up, I was coming back to London from Hull on the train with Peter, who had been speaking in my constituency. He said he would like me to continue as one of his advisers on shipping, even though I was no longer his PPS. And he made it clear I would be free to speak my mind.

As we were travelling together, I said, 'Do you have a field marshal's baton in your rucksack? Are you really considering standing for the Labour leadership, if Wilson gives up or gets pushed out?' He said he might. Why was I asking?

'Well,' I replied, 'I admire you a lot, but apart from being against the Common Market, I don't really know what you stand for.' He just smiled.

Anyway, that was me, out of my first government appointment, after only two years.

While I was a PPS I got involved in a strike involving women workers. They had taken over a typewriter factory, run by Imperial Typewriters, a US-owned company, who were threatening to close it down. I think they realised that electric typewriters were going to take over from manuals. They didn't need the capacity in the UK.

I got a telegram in the House from the women strikers, saying, 'Taken plant over, come and see us.' The whips said I hadn't to go, but I said, 'Get lost. I'm going to see what their grievances are and try to help.'

The whips responded that I had to stay and take part in some vital vote or fix up a pairing. 'Sod you,' I said. I was always in rows with them about pairings. I didn't like it when some Tory or Labour MP got a pairing because he was a barrister and was appearing in some case – in other words, swanning off to make some money. I thought it was disgusting: I was in the House of Commons to work. I did not believe that MPs should have an outside job.

In fact, one of my campaigns was to stop MPs taking on jobs outside Parliament. By January 1975 I was trying to get it established that an MP should have no outside occupation and that a register should be set up to record everything they earned outside. I wrote to Harold Wilson about it, when he was still prime minister.

There had been the John Stonehouse scandal in 1974 – the Labour MP who faked his own drowning – when it was disclosed just how many business affairs and outside interests he had, which presumably surprised even Wilson.

We got paid well enough as MPs, with expenses, so there was and is no need for it. In Wilson's reply to me, he said we should wait for a Select Committee to report, before considering it. But nothing happened. It took some years for the legislation to be passed setting up a register of MPs' interests, but we got there in the end.

Anyway, the woman strikers had been out for seven weeks, so it was becoming urgent. The thing about women workers is that it takes a lot to upset them. They put up with most things in life and in the workplace, more than men would, but when they finally break and go on strike, they are far stronger and more resolute than men. Seven weeks was a long time to be out. I was most impressed. I gave them a bit of advice, but the strike eventually collapsed. I still get a Christmas card each year from one of their leaders, Ethel Langley. She always signs herself the 'typewriter lass'.

By early 1976 the so-called Cod War had broken out. Iceland had declared a two-hundred-mile exclusion zone round their country and threatened to cut the nets of any foreign trawlers caught inside, including any British ones. Britain claimed it was illegal and James Callaghan, who was then foreign secretary, said we would send in gunboats.

In Hull, our local fishermen were worried about their jobs, naturally enough. Two out of the three Hull MPs backed the British reaction – but I didn't. I thought the Icelandic government had a case. I knew more about the law of the sea, Iceland's history and attitudes, and what was currently happening in the North Sea than most MPs who just automatically sided with our Government. I believed Iceland had rights on their side as well.

International sea law had traditionally given countries the right to the two hundred miles around their shore, the so-called continental shelf. We had given up our exclusive rights when we'd joined the Common Market, as its members shared in all the rights. But here was the anomaly. We had somehow retained exclusive rights to oil exploration around our shores yet not for the fish. I thought it was a bit hypocritical of Britain to maintain our oil was on our continental shelf but to threaten Iceland with gunboats when they said the fish on their continental shelf was exclusively theirs. I made a speech at the Hull Co-op meeting on International Co-op Day, supporting Iceland's case and calling for 'jaw jaw, not war war'.

I then decided to go to Iceland to investigate. I went on my own, unofficially, not as a government spokesman, because by this time we had broken off diplomatic relations with Iceland. We were dealing diplomatically at third hand, through the Norwegian ambassador to Iceland, who said he was forever getting a right bollocking from James Callaghan, as foreign secretary, and the Foreign and Commonwealth Office. I was never a fan of Callaghan. Nice enough bloke, but too right-wing for me. And his background was Royal Navy, not merchant navy like me.

Roy Hattersley was the minister under Callaghan and he attacked me for going to Iceland, saying I was therefore not supporting our own fishermen. Luckily, our fishermen gave me the benefit of the doubt because they knew how hard I had always worked on their behalf.

Behind the immediate diplomatic row was the future of fishing. I knew that the seas were being overfished by all nations. The big factory ships were hoovering up everything, leaving parts of the seas empty. Some sensible compromise agreements had to be reached. I maintained we had to negotiate with the Icelanders, not threaten them.

So, I went to Iceland and met the prime minister and other government ministers. They laid on a special meal and said they had a local delicacy for me. It was put in front of me, wrapped in silver paper. I opened it and the smell was awful. They said it was rotting shark, a great delicacy. I joked I was there for cod, not stinking shark, which caused some amusement.

There was huge coverage in the British press about the Cod War from the very beginning. The tabloids got steamed up about someone they termed the Mad Axeman – a captain of an Icelandic boat who was cutting the nets of any British fishing-boat that invaded the two-hundred-mile zone. I was against such tactics, as they were dangerous, but I was also against Britain threatening to send gunboats.

It was arranged I should meet him. When I saw him for the first time, I thought, Oh, no, this is gonna look bad back at home. A BBC TV crew had arrived to film my meeting. He was huge, this so-called Axeman, with a massive beard and a big black trench coat and silk scarf. He looked like a German U-boat commander. He gave me a big salute as I went on board. Luckily I was able to have a talk with him about the dangers to all our seafarers and this was filmed by the BBC.

In my meetings with the Icelandic government, I discovered that their home secretary was making all the war-like noises, not the prime minister himself, but he had to keep in with him as the Government was a coalition and the home secretary was from another party. You often find out there are undercurrents and differences between your so-called enemies, once you properly investigate things on the ground. You shouldn't accept everything that the papers, or your own Government, are saying.

My belief was that we had to negotiate, otherwise there was a real danger that people on each side would get killed. We had to agree something on the lines of there being no total fishing exclusion zone, but each country could only take whatever tonnage of fish was internationally agreed. I put this to the Icelanders. They said they would discuss it in their parliament, and let me know.

Back home, I got a call from the Iceland PM's office saying they had accepted what they were calling the 'Prescott Deal'. I was very pleased so I went to tell Fred Peart, the minister of Agriculture, Fisheries and Food. The thing about Fred was that you had to catch him sober. I went to his room but he wasn't there. I knew he'd be in the bar – and there he was, supping away.

I shouted at him: 'This is about bloody lives and you're sitting here getting pissed!' And I stormed out.

The following Sunday, at home in Hull, I was told that Jim Callaghan wanted to see me the next day. When I got there, I was told he had gone to meet with Andrei Gromyko, the Russian foreign secretary, but Roy Hattersley was there to deal with me. He said Jim wasn't very happy with me and handed me a telegram they were sending in secret in a diplomatic bag to Iceland, Washington, Oslo and all our officials in NATO posts. It was headlined 'Icelandic Fishers – Rumoured Intervention by Mr John Prescott, MP'. In a nutshell, I was being disowned. Among other things, it stated that 'there is no truth in the story that Prescott has authority to act on my [Callaghan's] behalf'.

I still thought British policy was insane, putting the lives of our trawlermen at risk. Some sort of negotiation had to be achieved, especially as we were soon to be renegotiating our fishing rights with the EEC. 'John, you can't trust the Icelanders,' Roy Hattersley told me. I said if

I had to choose between my Icelandic contact and him, I'd trust him as far as I could throw him.

But I was told to stop it and shut up because a leadership election was suddenly coming up.

It was a week of big drama because on 16 March 1976, the day after Callaghan had sent that telegram, Wilson had amazed everyone by resigning. Callaghan was wanting to take over as leader. They didn't want further diversions.

I'd been invited to appear on a *Panorama* programme about the Cod War and Callaghan's record as foreign secretary and to be interviewed by Peter Jay, Callaghan's son-in-law. I refused, and decided to keep quiet and not make any more comments for the next forty-eight hours during the vote for leader.

Callaghan became prime minister on 5 April 1976. I voted for Peter Shore.

In due course, Anthony Crosland became foreign secretary in place of Callaghan. I went to see him, told him about the deal I had agreed with the Icelanders. He didn't seem to know much about it. I said it must be lying in some drawer in the Foreign Office, covered with dust. See if anyone can find it. He was MP for Grimsby and more aware of the realities of fishing than 'Farmer' Jim Callaghan had been.

He asked if I considered the Icelanders would still agree to my deal. I said I thought they would, so he decided to start new negotiations.

In the end a deal was done, based on a limited number of fishing trips, which was the principle I had been working on. So it ended happily. Roy Hattersley later had the courtesy to say that my deal was the right one.

*

Early in September 1976, I was coming back from a meeting of the European Parliament when I read in the London *Evening Standard* about some riots at Hull prison, in my constituency. The prisoners had gone on the roofs and refused to come down, complaining about the conditions and the vicious treatment by some prison officers. They'd set fire to one of the wings, wrecked various buildings, going on an 'orgy of destruction', so the papers said – about £750,000 worth of damage. It was the worst mutiny in any British gaol since the Dartmoor riots in the 1930s.

The ringleaders were encamped on the roof, throwing missiles at the police and prison officers, flying flags and banners and singing. Eventually they said they would only come down if 'Three Just Men' looked into their grievances; one of those named was me and another was Dick Pooley of the prison reform group.

I went up to visit the gaol, one of the first people allowed in after the riot, and it was as if a huge ball of hate had rolled through there; blind anger had made them lash out at everything. I started my own investigation into exactly what had happened, interviewing people from both sides. I came to the conclusion that the terrible conditions and overcrowding had created a volatile situation which had been whipped up by some prison officers during their industrial dispute. I was told that when the prisoners had come down from the roof, some of the officers had set the dogs on them, then assaulted and beaten them, which was appalling. I could hardly believe it, but I was convinced it had happened.

I'd got my report ready by the end of the year, all 20,000 words of it. I knew that when I presented it to Merlyn Rees, the home secretary, his civil servants would just laugh it out of court and nothing would be done – and they'd rubbish it by picking on little things like the grammar. So I got Jim Mitchell, news editor of the *Hull Daily Mail*, to go through it and correct any mistakes. In it, I had a description of some writing on a wall, which the inmates had done to publicise their complaints, such as lack of conjugal rights and exercise time. Jim pointed out that there was a word for writing on a wall – 'graffiti'.

My report was made public – and, of course, the prison officers jumped on it, saying it was 'incomplete and subjective'. They said the prisoners at Hull enjoyed conditions second to none. I defended my conclusions regarding the behaviour of some of the officers and maintained that the dehumanising conditions were the root of the trouble and, without changes, there could be further riots. One of my recommendations was an amnesty, letting people out early to reduce the prison population.

A Home Office inquiry found that there was no single cause for the riots, rejecting my report, but in 1977, some of the inmates pressed charges that they had been assaulted by some officers after they had surrendered. And so began a new series of investigations by Humberside Police. It went on for months and ended in a trial at York Crown Court in 1979. Eight prison officers were sentenced for up to nine months each for conspiring to beat and assault inmates at Hull prison. So, my findings had been proved right, after all.

During the riots, there had been one incident that had amused me. While the prisoners had been on the roof, rioting and refusing to come down, they had deliberately sent a huge chimney crashing through the roof of the prison chapel. The chaplain happened to be the Reverend Jack Reed, the cleric who had said people should not vote for me. It turned out the prisoners hadn't thought much of him either . . .

With all the campaigning I was doing, rushing around, I was feeling absolutely exhausted. In those days, you were only allowed money for half a secretary unless, of course, you had private means. Most Tories could usually pay for a full secretary, or get their business or wealthy cronies to pay for it. I'd been struggling with very little help to keep all these campaigns going, plus having been a PPS, and working in Europe as well.

One evening in London in 1976, after a dinner given by Humberside County Council, I felt so tired I could hardly eat. I was sitting opposite Anthony Crosland, who was there as MP for Grimsby, the next constituency across the Humber. 'Are you all right, John'? he asked me. Apparently I looked awful. I went to the toilet and sat there crying. It was uncontrollable. It just all came out. After ten minutes or so, I managed to pull myself together and got back to the dinner.

It was a strange incident. I wasn't depressed. I wasn't worried about something. It wasn't mental. I might get moody and bad tempered, shout and swear at people. I've always done that – and not always been proud of it. But I'm not a depressive sort of person. I don't bottle things up.

I let it all out. So it was a bit of a shock to find myself in floods of tears. But, no, I didn't seek medical or psychological help. I never even thought of it. I knew, or at least felt, that the only cause was sheer exhaustion, with doing too much. Since then, I've only once broken down and cried. But that was for another reason.

Afterwards Anthony Crosland sent for me and said I should take things easier, not work as hard. My union decided to allocate some money to help with my shipping campaigns and I was able at last to afford a full-time secretary.

Crosland probably thought, that evening, that I was having a heart-attack, which I wasn't, luckily. But, alas, the following year he suffered a fatal stroke while working late. I was a big fan of Crosland and his wife Susan. And he seemed to quite like me. When I first entered the House in 1970, Tony was quoted as saying that he thought, 'Prescott will go far – if he calms down.'

CHAPTER ELEVEN

1980s

A Wink from
Mrs Thatcher

I never realised at the time that my brief spell as a PPS would be my last experience of any sort of government post, however humble, for more than twenty years.

After Callaghan had taken over from Wilson in 1976, there was a Lib–Lab pact which ran from 1977 to 1978. We were then thrashed in the general election of 1979 when Margaret Thatcher came in. She would half smile at me when I was speaking from the front bench. Really, that was my definite impression. And even a wink on one occasion. Quite flirtatious, I suppose.

It all began when I went to see her at No. 10 with a delegation of fishermen from Hull in 1980. There was another fishing crisis on and she agreed to see us. She took us into the Cabinet Room and sat there while I delivered my spiel. I did most of the talking, being an MP and a front-bench spokesman. I knew it all anyway, had lived it all my working life, hadn't I?

She listened in silence, then suddenly pulled me up on a minor factual point. Can't remember what it was now, which rather weakens the story, but I realised at once I'd made a slip. I was stunned. How did she know that? Christ, I was thinking, she's not only been well briefed by someone, but she's taken in every point. I couldn't really deny the mistake, blunder on and bluff my way out of it, so I stopped, corrected myself, smiled, then ploughed on. After that, she just smiled back all the time I was talking.

That was the smile she used to give me when I was spouting away on the front bench, a sort of conspiratorial smile. She didn't have to say anything, just give a slight nod and that quick smile, meaning, 'Don't forget, I caught you out once. Don't get too cocky.' Politicians aren't as confident as we like to make out. We all suffer shades of doubt. Well, most of us. I can think of one exception – Robin Cook. But we'll come to him later.

I didn't like Mrs Thatcher's policies or admire her. She was a Tory, wasn't she, one who never backed down, not like Heath. She promised harmony but brought discord. I disliked her more than the other Tories. I hated her for stopping free school milk when she was Education secretary – the 'milk snatcher' – and later for what she did to the miners and their communities and her total indifference to mass unemployment. To us on the Left of the Party, she was the devil incarnate. But all the same, I have to admit that, as a politician, she was a thorough professional. A woman to be careful with.

After that 1979 election, I had a set-to with Jim Callaghan. In some debate he'd brought up the subject again of our nuclear deterrent, putting the multilateral case, against our unilateral Party policy. It was one of the topics that had divided Labour for years, along with the problem of the militants and the unions. I was never in CND, unlike most of my fellow Labour MPs from the Left. I felt if we didn't have the bomb, we might get flattened by someone who did. What would we do in our defence? Run up a white flag?

Anyway, I felt it was a mistake to go on about that subject again. I was in the tea room, eating a tuna salad, when Callaghan came past.

'Hey, Jim,' I shouted after him, 'going to cost us another election, are you?'

It was a pretty cheeky thing to say to our dear leader. But we didn't have a shouting match, though that was how it got reported. In fact, nothing should have been reported. What happens in the tea room, or the bars, is supposed to be confidential, but I know some Tory bastard leaked it to the papers and as usual it got blown up out of all proportion.

Oh, there was another tea-room storm in a teacup a few years later. I was sitting there one day, next to the door in the Terrace café, eating chicken and chips this time, and that Tory MP Neil Hamilton – the one who came to grief over alleged outside payments – came in from the Terrace. It was bloody freezing, so I asked him to close the door, which he ignored. I then said, 'Listen, son, close that bloody door.'

That was all. No argument ensued. I didn't threaten him in any way, but the tabloids got hold of it – I wonder how – and in their version I was supposed to have lashed at him with a bowie knife or similar. It painted a picture of me as a mad, aggressive thug. Once a paper does that, totally exaggerates some minor incident, all the others pick it up – and you're lumbered. That's your image from then on.

I realise now that it was from that period, with those blown-up tea-room stories, that I got branded as some sort of uneducated yob. It was an image that, I suppose, never left me.

The broadsheets are just as bad. One makes a mocking remark about my grammar and they all copy each other. The implication is that bad grammar equals low intelligence. An image gets established and nothing can shake it. It's the herd mentality. Journalists follow the pack, so people who have never met you, never heard you speak, know nothing about your work, your campaigns, or what you have done, make the same old stupid, clichéd, boring, typecast comments about you. That's one reason why I began to hate the press.

So I rarely had drinks or lunch with any political journalist. On a campaign, like the North Sea one to help divers, I might talk to serious investigative reporters, like

David Blundy, helping them get the story straight, but I never met journalists just for a drink. All they want is gossip and I've never dealt in that. I kept away from the press lobby – which means the parliamentary and political reporters – the exceptions being Michael White of the *Guardian* and Colin Brown of the *Independent* and one or two others. I suppose that's part of the reason why most papers were always having a go at me. It was payback time for not helping them when they asked me for parliamentary chit chat and stories.

Callaghan remained as Labour leader for a short time after our 1979 election defeat. One day in August 1980 he sent for me. I thought I was in for a lecture. Then I thought, perhaps he wants my advice on some maritime issue. It was neither of those things. To my total surprise he said he wanted to put me forward as a European commissioner, in place of Roy Jenkins. The job would last five years and over that time, in salaries and expenses, I would expect to earn £400,000, plus a pension. It was an amazing sum. Even today it sounds pretty huge.

I was flattered, of course, but I said to him it didn't fit in with my views on the European Treaty. I was a sceptic, and I was worried about the establishment of a federal Europe. He said that was the sort of person they wanted to present Britain's case.

If I became a commissioner, he said, I'd have to give up being an MP. So I said to Jim, 'You're asking me to cut my throat.' He told me to think about it anyway.

No, I didn't suspect he was trying to get rid of me from the House. And I don't think he was. I took it as a genuine offer, that he seriously thought I would do the job well. Although we'd never really got on, I think he recognised how much work I'd done during the seventies, with the Council of Europe and then the EEC.

I rang Pauline and told her – and, of course, mentioned the money. That week she'd been thinking about buying a Brueghel print from WH Smith for seven pounds but had been holding back.

'Does this mean, John, I'll be able to buy that print?'

'Listen, love,' I said, 'if I take this job, we can buy the original – tax free.'

But she agreed with me that it would mean giving up all I had been fighting for for so long, all the campaigns. At the age of forty-two, I felt it was far too early to leave Parliament when there was so much to do – even though it looked as if we might be out of office for a long time. So I turned it down.

It got into the local papers, as someone had leaked it. I discovered that Jim had discussed it with the Tories and they had been in agreement. So it would have gone through. I would have become a European commissioner. And the papers would have said, 'Oh, yeah, another junket, Prescott swanning off to spend our money again . . .'

In 1980, Michael Foot took over as our leader. Footy is a lovely man. I voted for him, but I was voting with the heart not the head. I don't think he really wanted to stand, but Neil Kinnock and Norman Buchan, the long-standing Scottish MP, pushed for him. They wanted someone from the Left to take over, after having had the right-wing Jim Callaghan. That was the general thinking in the Party.

142

The alternative was Denis Healey – and he scared the life out of us. Nobody on the Left wanted him to get in.

On reflection, we were wrong, as we very soon discovered. Foot was not a party leader. I also realised that Denis Healey was not as robustly against the Left as we'd all imagined. I later told him I'd made a mistake, that I should have voted for him. He was very intelligent and liked by the general public. I think now he would have had a better chance than Foot of doing well in the next general election. But, all the same, I don't think he would have won it.

Michael Foot was one of those people who was marred by his public image. That picture of him at the Cenotaph on Remembrance Day in what the papers said was a scruffy reefer jacket was the main image people had of him. That was certainly an occasion for a smart suit and a tie if ever there was one, out of respect and propriety. Foot just didn't think about things like clothes.

I remember once when he addressed a meeting of the the Parliamentary Labour Party. He was on the platform, raised about six feet above the audience. I was in the front row and I noticed that he had huge holes in his socks. They were big enough to put his hands through.

But he is a wonderful man. He had been right about the dangers of Fascism, and was a brilliant writer and editor of *Tribune* magazine. He was always identified purely with the Left of the Party – and that doesn't always win votes, as Tony Blair realised pretty early on. I consider it a great privilege to have known Michael and had him as a guest in my home.

*

In 1979, still under Callaghan, I had been made shadow spokesman for Transport, my first official front-bench appointment, a job I continued under Footy. I was second to Albert Booth. I did most of the work, as number twos usually do, in the engine room. I was fighting hard to stop Thatcher privatising the buses and the railways, but I could see the problems. There just wasn't the public cash to improve public transport the way there should have been. Transport also covered the sea, so I was still concerned with maritime problems, even when in 1981 I was moved on to be shadow spokesman for Regional Affairs and Devolution.

In 1983, there was big uproar when it was revealed that nuclear waste was being dumped in our seas, killing fish, polluting the water, endangering us all. Greenpeace was up in arms and organising demonstrations. I was concerned, of course, by the pollution of the seas and our fishermen losing their livelihood.

I agreed to take part in an NUS and Greenpeace protest, a typical gimmicky event to attract attention to the problem. They wanted me to swim down the Thames.

I've always been quite a good swimmer. In 1979 I swam ten miles in nine and a half hours on a sponsored swim, raising money for a spina bifida charity. It almost finished me off, but luckily the charity had a couple of Bunny girls to help me out of the water.

For the Thames protest, I had to swim two miles down the Thames to the House of Commons – in frogman's gear with a mask, oxygen and wetsuit. I'm not that daft. One gulp of the Thames and you'd be a goner. I had dived, when I was campaigning for divers, so I knew roughly what it was like. Hellish. And I don't think it did my ears any good. But I quite liked the notion of a long swim. It reminded me of Chairman Mao swimming down the Yangtse. I'll wait till the tide goes out, with the rest of the crap, then reach the House of Commons. That was a phrase I used when the story first came out.

The idea was to swim from Battersea Bridge and arrive at the Palace of Westminster, climb out of the water and go up the steps on to the Terrace of the House of Commons, carrying a message for Mrs Thatcher, which I'd deliver to her at No. 10. It was a petition signed by lots of trade-union leaders and other public figures, pointing out that she had signed a communiqué against nuclear dumping in the Pacific, but here she was, allowing it to happen on our doorstep in the Atlantic.

I realised I needed permission to land at the House, so I went to see the Speaker, Bernard Weatherill. He said, no, I couldn't use the steps, not for a political purpose. I tried to explain it wasn't political but environmental. Above me as we argued there was a painting of King Charles on the same steps, coming to arrest some rebel MP. I said that was political. If he could use them, why couldn't I? That didn't impress him.

I tried using sea law, because he wouldn't know much about it. I said that under the rules of the sea, you always have to give safe access to anyone coming out of the sea, especially if they were in danger, as I might well be, swimming in that polluted river. If I was refused landing rights, I might be in further danger. If the police pushed me off the steps, I'd be caught in the tide and swept out to sea.

It was finally agreed that I would arrive at the steps –

but would not be allowed to walk up them and into Parliament. A boat would be moored there and I'd step into that, so I'd be safe, then move off again.

We got a telegram beforehand from Spike Milligan, saying he was delighted we were taking an interest in the environment, which would affect our children in years to come. He said I deserved a medal for what I was doing – but I should have a typhoid shot before I attempted it.

So I did the swim, in my wetsuit, two miles down the Thames, which took me about an hour. It was December and freezing cold. I was accompanied by demonstrators in little boats with banners saying 'Stop Nuclear Dumping at Sea' and Greenpeace people with oil cans marked 'Radioactive Waste'.

At the steps of Parliament, I climbed out of the water, then was taken in a boat to a landing stage on Westminster Bridge. From there I walked to 10 Downing Street, still in my wetsuit, to deliver the petition to Mrs Thatcher. It made a great series of photos – but, of course, it had a very serious purpose.

What I didn't know at the time was that some Greenpeace demonstrators had been planning to use me as a Trojan Horse to get into the Palace of Westminster. If I'd been able to go up the steps, they were going to follow me, climb over me and storm into the House, carrying their banners.

A few weeks later, they did get into the House, but by another route. This time they climbed the clock tower of Big Ben and hung one of their banners on it.

I wasn't quite as, er, hefty in those days, and was pretty fit, even though I'd had a terrible accident. It happened not long before the opening of the Humber Bridge. There was private access across the bridge, though it hadn't been officially opened. I had invited some Dutch MEPs to see it, and visit Hull, which I told them was the fishing centre of the world. We were going across the empty bridge but the driver didn't see a concrete block lying in his path – and we hit it at 70 m.p.h. I wasn't wearing a seat-belt, which was pretty stupid as I'd spoken in the House in favour of the law to make wearing them compulsory. I landed on the gear lever and broke my back. It took me weeks to recover fully.

Fortunately I was back on my feet sufficiently to get involved in the grand opening. Once I'd sorted it out, that is. The budget allocated for the opening ceremony was two thousand pounds – not nearly enough to do anything decent. I said, 'Give it to me and I'll double it.'

I organised a special gramophone record, all about Hull and its wonders. I got Alan Plater, the playwright, who came from Hull, to write some of it, and John Alderton, the actor, also from Hull, to take part. We had songs about Hull Kingston Rovers and other topics. It was a souvenir record, but meant to be fun. More than four thousand copies were sold and we made enough for a really good do.

The big drama in the mid-1980s was the miners' strike. It started in March 1984 and lasted almost a year. Kinnock had taken over as leader from Foot, after we'd lost another general election in 1983. He was determined to show he could be tough on the miners – though not as tough as Mrs Thatcher. She had been ashamed at how Heath had bowed to pressure from them. Kinnock, like Wilson, feared that

147

militant union agitators were ruining the possibility of Labour ever getting elected. And he seemed to hate Arthur Scargill, leader of the National Union of Mineworkers.

I refused to condemn the striking miners. I remember how during all the seamen's strikes we'd always had support from the miners. It had been vital at the time, so I wasn't going to turn against them now. I believed they had a case but, of course, as always, some sort of conciliation had to be reached.

So, I joined them on the picket lines, understanding their grievances. My aim was to reach some sort of agreement from the inside but then, of course, it just dragged on and on. It was a tragedy for the mining community, which never recovered.

Personally, I didn't like Scargill. I thought his ego had taken over. In my view it was 'me me me' in so much of what he was doing and saying. I was also suspicious of any union leader who wouldn't allow one member, one vote. I didn't like that. All in all, it was a terrible time for the miners, the trade unions, the Labour Party and the country.

In 1983, I moved from Regional Affairs back to Transport as shadow minister. Then a year later, I became shadow minister for Employment. I began work on the huge task of trying somehow to come up with ideas for cutting unemployment, which was running at around 15 per cent in the mid-1980s, which meant three million people were on the dole.

When I'd been shadow spokesman for Regional Affairs and Devolution, I'd produced a pamphlet, *Alternative Regional Strategy*, which outlined how, when we got into power, we aimed to reverse the growing inequalities between the regions and reduce mass unemployment. I now began work on an Employment pamphlet, which took a great deal of research and discussion and involved a lot of people. Labour was determined to fight the next election on a return to full employment. This pamphlet tried to spell out where the jobs could come from. It was called *Planning for Full Employment* and was published in 1985. It was followed by *Real Needs – Local Jobs* in 1987, which looked at what could realistically be achieved in a two-year period.

It meant months and months of work for a lot of people, so I decided to give a party, as a thank-you to all those who had helped. I hired a Thames pleasure boat and invited some MPs, trade unionists, Party workers, researchers and anyone else who had been involved or interested in the pamphlet. The idea was to have a short sail down the Thames, with some food and a few drinks.

That same day, by chance, a deputation of unemployed people came down from the north to Westminster. A lot were on bikes, as an ironic rebuke to Norman Tebbit who had been telling the three million unemployed that what they had to do was get on their bikes. Our pamphlet was aimed at helping the unemployed, so I invited some of them to join us on the boat, as our guests.

It was all going well, everyone tucking into the chicken and chips, till this woman stormed up to me. 'Why is there no vegetarian food? Just like you fucking politicians.'

I was taken aback, but also pretty furious at her attitude, so I gave her a robust reply. She was one of the guests, invited at the last moment out of the kindness of our hearts, and here she was moaning on. Clare Short was there and tried to intervene, but this woman went on having a go at me.

'Any more of your abuse,' I told her, 'and I'll throw you and your bike in the river.'

That didn't help matters, of course, but I was livid.

The party ended up on the Terrace of the House of Commons, with all the MPs and Party workers – plus some of the bikers who had managed to hang on.

I left early and had gone home, so I had no idea what happened afterwards. But the Press Association had a story about some woman dangling by her bra strap over the river. It got written up in other papers with headlines like 'Ship of Shame' as if the party had degenerated into some sort of orgy – which I had organised. It was all total crap. There was no woman in her underwear. Typical of the press.

CHAPTER TWELVE

The Beautiful People Arrive

In 1983, the year I got elected into the shadow cabinet, two new young MPs arrived – Gordon Brown and Tony Blair. In that same new intake were Clare Short and Chris Smith. You could say, now, things looked hopeful, but they didn't at the time. We'd got stuffed in the 1983 election, with only 209 Labour MPs, almost half the number the Tories had. Our share of the vote was just 27.6 per cent with the Liberal–SDP lot catching us up on 25.4 per cent.

I'd met Gordon a year or two earlier when Michael

Foot, as leader, had asked me to work on getting agreement for devolution. I was preparing the *Alternative Regional Strategy* pamphlet and went to Scotland to meet some of our Labour activists up there. Gordon was also working on a devolution pamphlet, from the Scottish point of view. Like me, he was a supporter of devolution.

He was on the Scottish Labour Party Council, but wasn't yet a full-time politician. I think he was still working as a journalist and editor for Scottish TV, though his day job never came up in any conversation we had. He was just one of a group of Scottish Labour people I was meeting. He didn't strike me any more than the rest of them. Just one of our Scottish guys. Though, thinking back, he seemed a bit more dour than the others, not a glad-hander. He kept himself to himself and didn't mix socially.

I probably met Tony around the same time. I was in Newcastle for a Jobs and Industry rally. Tony was fluttering around. I remember him saying he was a lawyer but hoping to get into politics. He seemed able and likeable, a typical public schoolboy. But that's about all I can remember of that occasion.

When they were new MPs, in 1983, I did notice that neither went to Parliamentary Labour Party meetings. I got the impression that Tony didn't think the PLP was very important. He was a pleasant guy, said hello to everyone, but he wasn't an activist. Gordon was more into Labour Party politics and seemed to have more of a Labour Party background, but he wasn't into cliques. Neither seemed to support any of the main campaigning groups, so couldn't be described as a 'player'.

I knew they shared an office, and seemed to be good friends, and it was obvious that Tony looked up to Gordon. Oh, yes, Gordon was definitely the leader of the two. Tony hung on his every word.

But I didn't have much to do with either of them in their first few years. I had enough on my plate. I was being moved around quite a bit, from Transport to Employment to Energy, back to Transport, so I had a lot to think about. But in 1985, I did ask Kinnock for Gordon as one of my Employment spokesmen. Gordon turned it down, preferring to make his mark from the back benches and as a member of the Employment select committee.

When I started on Energy in 1987, the Party had no policy. 'What exactly are we doing about Energy?' people used to ask each other at PLP meetings. The answer was – forget it. Because I'd had so many different shadow ministerial positions, and in areas where we hadn't done much, I think I might have produced – along, of course with a group of Party comrades – more pamphlets than any other cabinet or shadow cabinet minister in modern times. But I'm proud to say that all did become Party policy and eventually got on the statute book.

The one on regional strategy and planning proposed elected regional assemblies and regional development agencies. The aim was to attempt a fairer distribution of power and finance among the regions. It wasn't adopted by the Party straight away, but later it was, and I suppose it's still a controversial issue.

Planning for Full Employment set out a new framework for full employment, and showed how regional development agencies could be used to create jobs. Then there was

Real Needs – Local Jobs, which was published in 1987, followed in 1989 by *Moving Britain into the 1990s*, which, for the first time, suggested a new way of financing future transport projects. In 1991 *Moving Britain into Europe* said there should be a private–public partnership for a Channel Tunnel high-speed link, and *Full Steam Ahead* in 1993 suggested expanding the British merchant shipping fleet from two million tons.

We were in opposition during all these years, so those documents and pamphlets were for discussion, hoping that, first, the Party would consider and adopt them as policy, or bits of them, and then, second, that if and when we ever got into power again, we might be able to do something concrete about them. So it was a busy time, from the mid-1980s to the mid-1990s. All this work was very important to the Party, if we were to be taken seriously again. Plus there were two other important documents in 1994, on finance and on social justice.

Anyway, with all that, I wasn't taking too much day-to-day notice of those two bright young MPs who had arrived, but I was aware that a new sort of person was appearing in the Party.

I first met Peter Mandelson around the time I met Gordon and Tony – some time in the early 1980s. Albert Booth, who had been a cabinet minister in both the Wilson and Callaghan governments, was still doing Transport and I was his second. We were planning an away day – a whole-day conference, a brain-storming session – to discuss the future of railways. We were looking for a bright guy to write it all up afterwards, getting down exactly what we had talked about and agreed upon and I negotiated with the transport union to fund a researcher.

Albert hired Peter, who'd been writing some anti-left-wing stuff, though at the time he, like Gordon, was still working in TV. I think that's how we'd heard of him, from his writings – then someone suggested he might write up our away-day notes. When you're in opposition, you don't have the resources or the civil servants to help you with reports and research.

I interviewed him and told him he would work with me because I did all the preparatory work for Albert. He said that was fine.

Some time after the conference – I thought we'd had a good session – Peter came to me. He said he was having trouble trying to produce our transport paper – it was all so complicated.

I said, 'Listen, son, go and dig out an Orange Paper Crosland did on Transport in the 1960s. The analysis is excellent but the conclusions were rubbish.' I remembered that one of his conclusions was that his Grimsby dockers wanted cars, they didn't want to go on railways, so we shouldn't subsidise rail travel. Which was wrong. Of course railways had to be helped. We all knew that. The problem, as always, was how to do it.

Anyway, I said to Peter, 'Dig out Crosland's report, follow how he did it, but bring the facts and figures up to date. Then add on our conclusions.' The most important one, the one I favoured, was that we should have an integrated system, using public and private money. Peter pulled the paper together as I'd suggested. It was seen as right-wing at the time, but eventually it became Party policy.

A couple of years later, in 1985, Peter asked me for a reference. He was leaving TV and had applied to be our spin-doctor – though I don't think that term was used at the time. The job was officially director of campaigns and communications. I agreed he could use my name as a referee, after pressure from Rosie Winterton, but I remember warning him, 'Stick to press and Party matters, not to internal Labour politics.'

Foot had gone, after the 1983 trouncing at the general election. I voted for Neil Kinnock as leader, and he got in. We differed on some clear policy issues – he was CND, I never was, he believed in central control, I believed in devolution – but we got on well at first. We came from a similar background – strong Labour families, working-class mining communities, both passionate and outspoken. Perhaps in the end we were too similar. That might be why we started falling out.

It was Neil Kinnock who asked me to stand for the Labour Party National Executive Committee – aiming to keep Ken Livingstone out, replacing him with me. My concern was getting on the NEC. Which worked. I was on it for the next twenty-five years.

As shadow Employment minister I was given the task of working out how Labour would reduce unemployment by one million within two years of getting into government. It had been in our manifesto, but was unrealistic, at least to achieve it in two years, but Kinnock had committed the Party to it. So working on *Real Needs – Local Jobs* was part of the process of deciding how to solve it.

I said we'd never manage a million. As a first step six

hundred thousand was more realistic. I managed to spell out in the pamphlet how this would be done and financed. That most of the jobs would be in the public sector. When I presented this to the shadow cabinet, Kinnock rubbished it.

'So, they're all going to be street sweepers, are they?' he said.

I said yes, in essence, meaning the jobs would come from all parts of the public sector, Civil Service, hospitals and suchlike, improving the quality of our public services. 'Anyone with any economic sense,' I told him, 'knows that creating one million jobs in two years can't come from capital investment. Capital can't work that quickly. They have to come from revenue-created jobs, i.e. the public sector. Obviously we want capital investment as well, but in two years, it can't be done. Yet you were the stupid bugger who said it could be . . .' After that, I never trusted Kinnock's political judgement. Today, the two million new jobs created in the last ten years have been mainly in the public service, as I advocated.

His judgement was right on Blair and Brown, though it surprised me at the time when he first started going on about them. He said they were the future, the bright young men who would lead our Party. And he started giving them junior shadow roles. Kinnock recognised their worth very early on, I will say that for him.

Brown was still the obvious leader of the two, everyone could see that, and so did Tony, who accepted this state of affairs.

But to me, they were still just OK guys. Not offensive. To us old hands, from trade-union backgrounds, they were a new sort of Labour politician. They didn't move in the same political or social circles as I did. I called them, Mandelson and the other advisers, the 'Beautiful People'. They were modernisers, as I was, but I was firmly old Labour and they were a new breed.

It took me a while to work out what they thought they there doing, what they were aiming for. It eventually struck me that their plan was to save Labour from itself and create a new kind of Labour Party. I didn't see that or them as a threat, not to me anyway. We'd had lots of little groups like this coming and going in the past, like Dick Taverne who in 1973 had resigned his Labour seat and stood against the Party in the subsequent by-election. He had quite a following, but then his lot went off and joined the SDP. I saw the SDP as traitors.

Blair especially seemed like an SDP type – bright young middle-class lawyer, living in Islington. He seemed committed to the future of the Labour Party, even if he was going about it in a different way from me. He didn't worry about groups or coteries, which I suppose was the Labour and trade-union world I had been brought up in. That was how things had always got done. Neither did Gordon. Their eyes were on higher things.

But when they first arrived they were not the only bright hopes for the Party. Apart from Blair, we already had several smart lawyers who were rising in the Labour Party. Blair was just one of them. No better or cleverer than the rest, or so it seemed to me.

The cleverest of them all was John Smith, our shadow chancellor. He was the sort of lawyer I did like. He enjoyed his whisky and a good laugh. I didn't drink whisky, or like the smoking room, but I liked him very much.

His background was Scottish Presbyterian, a Christian Socialist, if you like. He was from the centre right of the Party, among the so-called Solidarity group, the modernisers of their day. I was more the left-wing, trade-union militant – at least, I was in Harold Wilson's eyes. But we were both in our way modernisers – practical, non-ideological politicians, rolling up our sleeves to find realistic solutions and agreements.

More than me, I suppose, John was able to connect with all parts of the Party. Definitely more than Blair and Brown. They appeared to be cut off from the rest of us in the mainstream traditional Party.

After the 1987 general-election defeat, I stood in the Party election for the deputy leadership – against Roy Hattersley, who had been deputy since 1983. I was really standing on a matter of principle on what the role of the deputy leader should be. I disagreed with its historical role as a bonus for a defeated leadership candidate. I maintained the deputy should be concerned with politics and organisation. They were both equally important, yet organisation seemed to have been forgotten. Labour was in a period of decline. The militants had done us huge harm and Party membership was still falling, so organisation seemed vital to me.

I told Alastair Campbell, a political reporter at the time, that I was going to stand. Andy Smith, Party press officer, was also there. Alastair said to me, 'Won't Kinnock be upset?' He was, of course, a close pal of his. 'I don't bloody care,' I said.

I then got a message from Kinnock, wanting to see me

urgently. He had in his hand a brief of my meeting with the lobby. I hadn't realised that a report had been given to Mandelson, the Party's communication officer at the time, who, I suspect, must have sexed it up. Kinnock held it up in the air. 'Is this fucking true?' he screamed at me. He was red in the face, shouting.

'Listen, lad,' I replied. 'I can shout just as loud and just as long as you. If you go up the wall, I'll go up the wall. So just climb down and stay fucking calm.'

He eventually gave me the notes and I read them. Some remarks against Kinnock, which I certainly did make, had been included, but basically the account was distorted. Someone at some stage had put stuff in.

'You know this is a fucking lie,' I said, and stormed out. I think, actually, we both enjoyed a good fight and a screaming match.

Kinnock was furious. He said I was causing divisions, not healing them. That I was just being egotistical. I said, 'No. What concerns me is the function of the deputy. If it was redefined by the Party, on the lines I suggested, and the Party has the opportunity to vote on it, I won't stand.'

Kinnock's real worry was that Tony Benn would stand for leader. That would really have divided the Party. So me coming along and wanting a deputy leadership contest was making things worse, according to him. I said Benn would stand, whether I stood for deputy or not.

I needed union support if I was to have a chance. I went to Sam McCluskie of the NUS, Rodney Bickerstaffe of the National Union of Public Employees (NUPE) and Ron Todd of the TGWU – Kinnock's own union. And so, of course, did Kinnock, trying to get them to put me off standing. I told them my proposals for the function of the deputy – and agreed to step down if they managed to get a resolution at the Labour Party Conference on the new role. I got their agreement. We took it to Kinnock. He agreed, with some amendments, and signed it. So, because of that, I agreed to back out and not stand, unless Benn stood and caused an election.

That was all fine, until the details of my decision were made public. The press release from Kinnock's office put a very different spin from what I had been expecting on the circumstances. The statement said I had been forced to stand down. My deal with the three union leaders was rubbished and made to look as if I'd been working on a really pointless and stupid idea.

The general secretaries were appalled – because they knew what had actually happened. But I had to take a hit. I and my trade-union guarantors had been outmanoeuvred.

Then Benn decided to stand so I decided to run. I could have made it all public, but chose not to damage the leader of the Party. I relaunched my campaign to be deputy – but I got beaten by Hattersley. He got 67 per cent while I got 24 per cent. Kinnock got in again as leader, easily beating Benn. The election had not torn the Party apart after all, which was what Kinnock had been going on about. He was later to claim the election had been good for the Party – no doubt because he beat Benn.

It was later that year that Kinnock moved me. I'd been shadow minister for Employment for three years but I was now transferred to Energy. Still a big job, but in the papers it was described as a demotion. And you can guess who supplied that information.

I used to goad Neil Kinnock and he used to goad me. I remember him once introducing me to some foreign politicians in the House of Commons. He said, 'This is John Prescott, the salt in Labour's stew.' I'm sure he thought he was being amusing and affectionate, as I did at the time, but it struck me after later events that what he really meant was that too much salt in your food can kill you.

He used to tell me he thought the Tories, and the Tory press, hated both of us because we were working-class lads who had got on. Their way of mocking him was to say he was long-winded while with me it was, inevitably, my grammar.

While Kinnock was our leader, a painting was commissioned of the House of Commons while we were sitting. Photographs were taken to help the artist, and I saw them. I was sitting on the front bench, in my normal position. But when the painting was completed, I'd been removed from the front bench. I was now on the second bench, known in the House as 'the loyalty bench'. I went to see the artist, who said she had presented a rough of the painting to the whips' and leader's offices for them to designate who would be sitting where. And that was where she'd been told to put me. So, I went to our whips' office, and then to Kinnock's, and they all denied having had anything to do with it.

I was furious. There were people on our front bench who weren't even in the shadow cabinet. It was too late to do anything about it. Kinnock's office must have known what was going on, to instruct the artist, but I never got to the bottom of it.

I still have a copy of that painting, and a copy of the original photo, proof that I really was on the front bench. Such practices were not limited to Stalin's Russia.

One of the things that happened with the arrival of the Beautiful People was the increase in polls and focus groups. Kinnock was very keen on them, God knows why. I thought they were a waste of bloody time and replaced good political instinct.

In a shadow cabinet meeting one day, he was going on about the latest polls produced by Philip Gould, one of his advisers, which gave a rating to each shadow minister. Most were pretty low, though mine was quite high, as I remember it – but, then, I would. He finished by saying we all had to do better.

'What about the leader?' I asked. 'What about his rating? Aren't you going to tell us that?'

He was furious. He muttered something about it not being to hand, or not being done yet. Which was a lie. His rating was very poor. Philip Gould was there, but kept his head down, remaining silent.

In 1988, Kinnock moved me yet again – this time back to Transport. The person he put in my job at Energy was Tony Blair. Meanwhile Gordon Brown had become shadow chancellor, doing a brilliant job, taking over from John Smith who had become ill with heart problems in October 1988. Lucky for Gordon in a way, but we all thought it was deserved. The Beautiful People were certainly on their way.

Kinnock's biggest misjudgement was the 1992 Party Conference rally at Sheffield, the one before the general election. At the time, though, I have to admit there was a brilliant atmosphere. We were all caught up in it. But it was all yahoo, a rock 'n' roll, candy-floss conference. I'm sure, with hindsight, it helped bring about our defeat in that general election – and the end of Kinnock.

The 1992 loss was our fourth defeat in a row. The polls and focus groups had suggested we were going to win but you can't trust polls of any sort. In the 1970 election, when I first got in, we were ahead at one time by thirteen points, but we lost by seven.

So why did it keep happening? In a word, I'd say it was the economy – and the fear that Labour would not be able to run it properly. The joke, the irony, was that Harold Wilson had been a clever, academic, proper economist, while Alec Douglas-Home, the Tory PM, was useless at economics and worked it all out with matchsticks.

Wilson was supposed to come in with a white-hot technological revolution, but it didn't work. Inflation got out of control, we got into balance-of-payments deficits because things like buying jumbo jets and diamonds got put on the trade figures. Later governments made sure that things like planes were not counted. We had to make lots of public spending cuts, and then, of course, we had the strikes and industrial unrest. I think any party in power in the 1970s would have had a tough time, but Labour became seen as bad at managing the economy while the Tories were seen as the party of business, so they must be able to do better. The people knew we had a heart, but not a head. So that did for us for many years, plus our association in people's minds with trade unions and militants.

When Mrs Thatcher first appeared and then got elected

Tory leader in 1975, we were overjoyed. We thought, 'That's it, we'll win again, surely the British public won't stand for someone like her, the milk snatcher, so right wing, we'll hammer her.' But there did seem to be a lurch to the Right, with people like Keith Joseph, who was an advocate of free-market economics and went on to serve as a cabinet minister in Thatcher's government. They appealed to the mood of the times and won the 1979 election by ten points.

They left things to the market, cut back on state control and intervention, and were strong enough to take on the unions, which the public approved of. Mrs Thatcher was very combative, which we thought would lead to divisions, as she was never a consensus politician, but she dominated her party and was extremely competent. People forget that she wasn't personally liked. The Falklands War made her popular.

By 1992, we believed the public thought it was time for a change, with Mrs Thatcher gone and John Major looking pretty weak by comparison. It was a big shock to us to get beaten. I don't entirely blame that Sheffield rally. The public knew we were not united. Most of all, they weren't sure enough of us to want us to run the country. By the time the public got into the polling booths, they had left us. I also think they were not convinced by the personality of Kinnock.

It was obvious that if we were ever to win again, we had to be seen to be united and capable of running the economy.

After that 1992 defeat I stood for deputy leader for a second time. I argued once again that the role of deputy should be to overhaul the Party's organisation and also to ensure the leader well understood what the Party wanted. I'd pointed out that we were in a period of anti-Tory, anti-Thatcher feeling and yet we weren't growing our membership as we should. Far from it. We had to look into new technology, such as computers, to increase the involvement of members and improve access for women especially. I stressed that after four consecutive general-election defeats, we must not lose again: organisation was as important as policy.

Anyway, I lost. So that was my second failure to be elected deputy leader.

I did win one prize around that time. One day at the end of 1989 I got a call from someone saying they were from the *Spectator*. I said, 'You're a Tory rag, I don't speak to Tory rags.'

He said, 'No, no, this isn't for an interview or a quote. We sent you an invite for our awards ceremony, did you get it?'

I said, 'Yes – and I threw it in the bin.'

'What if you thought you might get an award?' said the voice. 'Would you come?'

I still thought it was someone taking the micky. He said, 'No, this is the *Spectator* and, er, don't tell anyone, but you have indeed won something.'

He didn't tell me what, or any details, but I decided I would go along – and discovered that John Smith had won Parliamentarian of the Year, Nigel Lawson had made the Speech of the Year and I was Debater of the Year. Apparently in my various times as shadow Transport minister, I had seen off four Tory Transport ministers. I'd never actually counted.

The awards ceremony was sponsored by a whisky firm, Famous Grouse, I think, so they were shoving glasses of whisky in everyone's hand from the moment they arrived. I don't drink whisky, as I've said, and rarely any alcohol at all, really. No one ever believes this. Sure, in the merchant navy, I did have a few bevvies when we arrived on shore after a long voyage of six months or so, going out to celebrate with the lads, but that was it. I never touch beer and I don't have wine with meals, though Pauline does. She's quite a connoisseur of white wines. The most I'll ever have, if I'm at a social occasion and I feel I have to have something, is half a pint of shandy, then spin it out all evening.

So I don't know what came over me that day. I was sat next to this young woman from the *Spectator*, Petrofino, Peregrino, something like that. I never did get her name right at the time but I gather now it was Petronella, Woodrow Wyatt's daughter. She was the one encouraging me to have another.

I managed to make an acceptance speech, saying I was not your usual Oxford rapier, I was more of an axe man. But of course I was very honoured. I did get the words out, in roughly the right order, but by then the whisky was taking effect and I was beginning to stagger.

It so happened I had to go to a meeting of the shadow cabinet, being chaired by Kinnock, at which we were going to be addressed by the cabinet permanent secretary. The thinking was we should know the inner workings of the cabinet, in case we ever got elected.

Despite being groggy, I was determined to attend. When I arrived at the House, they could all see my condition and immediately sat me down. Joan Hammell and Sue Nye, in Kinnock's office, poured coffee down my throat by the gallon, trying to sober me up. They were also trying to persuade me not to go into the meeting. But I was determined.

Eventually I stumbled in after it had been going on for an hour.

'I know I'm pissed,' I said, 'but I just want to ask one question . . . Why do I want some permanent cabinet secretary telling me things? I'll find out soon enough when we're in government.'

Then I was escorted out. Too much salt in the stew.

CHAPTER THIRTEEN

1992–94

One Member, One Vote

It was John Smith, now recovered, who became our leader in the election of 1992 – and Margaret Beckett who beat me to the deputy leadership. Clare Short told me before-hand that my grammar would hold me back, bloody cheeky, but I suspected she wasn't going to vote for me anyway, as she was part of the 'Sisters', which is what I called the hardened feminists. A lot of people, not just the women, had decided they'd like a woman in the post. Some of the unions saw Smith and Beckett as the dream ticket. And Margaret did very well. She got 57 per cent of the votes while I got 28 per cent.

I can't say I ever found Margaret a warm person but she's very able, far more so than the general public ever seemed to accept. But I don't think she ever forgave me for standing against her.

It was about this time I got to know Tony and Gordon a bit better. Following the 1992 election, they asked to see me and came to my office for a chat. It was clearly an attempt to improve relations, perhaps at the suggestion of John Smith. They chatted nervously for half an hour, then Gordon looked at his watch and said he needed to be on his way. I grinned at Tony. 'You'll probably be on your way too, then.'

That was still the basis of their relationship – Gordon as the teacher, Tony as his loyal, very able but nonetheless subservient pupil.

John Smith was so warm and humorous, and so clever and talented. I always got on with him, despite our political differences. I was anti the European Union, like most of the Party, while he was for it and voted against our policy, but it didn't spoil our relationship. He once complained to me that Kinnock didn't understand economics, which was a source of disagreement between them.

I had studied economics at Hull, so liked to think I'd grasped the basics. It helped me when I'd returned to Transport in 1988, which I looked after till 1993, trying to work out ways of introducing a better system of finance and investment.

During that period I went to talk to British Rail and could see they were starved of money. The engines were old, the infrastructure useless. A classic example of dis-investment in our public sector created by our public-sector finance rules and short-term decision-making. I went to see Jimmy Knapp, the Rail, Maritime and Transport Union (RMT) leader. 'How do you run the railways, Jimmy?' I asked him.

'Slowly,' he replied.

They did have trains capable of 120 m.p.h. but were running them at 60 m.p.h. for safety reasons. They didn't have the money to upgrade or improve the tracks.

I knew if Labour came in we'd need millions for schools and hospitals, so I couldn't see how the railways were going to get any money, not for a very long time.

It was while I was talking with Peter Parker, the chairman of British Rail, that I began to see there was an argument for private–public financing and leasing of assets in the public sector. I'd always been against it, on old socialist principles. I investigated how it could be done, how some capital could be brought in along with public money. I explained the thinking to the union leaders: that it was probably the only way to get funding. I produced a document on the subject, *Financing Infrastructure Investment*. John Smith, when he was shadow chancellor, came round to this view, and eventually so did many union people. Gordon Brown and Robin Cook also came to accept it, in a joint statement.

Later on, there was a strike at a railway works in York, which brought the problem home to us all. The factory was going to close through lack of orders for rolling stock. I felt it was absurd that the French railways could raise new investment in the City of London and yet it was denied to

171

our own nationalised British railways. I convinced John Smith, the shadow chancellor, to allow a leasing scheme to provide the investment needed in York with little cost to the public sector borrowing requirement. The Tories were against it as it looked like a subsidy for strikers. They couldn't really support it as it would have been bad publicity for them. We put the proposal in our 1992 manifesto. We won in York – but lost the general election. The Tory government implemented the idea, but just for the York investment, and the factory eventually closed.

I tried to work out how the York example might work in other situations – how British Rail could in essence borrow from the private sector against their assets and income flow. OK, it was getting involved with private finance and a private–public partnership, rather than total nationalisation, which had been one of my aims when I'd first become active in politics. In that 1966 pamphlet, *Not Wanted on Voyage*, I had called for nationalisation of all shipping and again in my maiden speech. In the twenty years or so since, I had modified my views in the light of brutal experience, but I didn't think I was compromising our basic principles. We would still *own* the railways.

I remember Heseltine mocking me: 'How can you as a socialist borrow from the private sector?' My reply was to ask where he thought all governments had always got money from. 'They borrow it privately and run up huge national debts,' I told him. 'That's where they get it from.'

I got the principle of some private–public financing into our 1992 manifesto, but in the event, it was the Tories who were first to introduce the notion – though they shaped it into a public financing initiative, which was largely designed for the purpose of privatisation. I remember saying to Norman Lamont, when he was chancellor, 'You buggers have pinched our public–private financing plans!'

He replied, 'Well, it's your own fault, for having a good idea . . .'

At the 1993 Labour Party Conference in Brighton, the big subject was 'One Member, One Vote'. Or OMOV, as it soon became known. The topic had been tearing the Party apart for decades.

The situation up to then was that trade unions had a block vote, which gave their general secretaries enormous power over selection processes and policy. Get two or three of the big unions on your side, and you could get anything through. OMOV would change all that, for the areas in which it applied. There would be no more block votes. Those for the status quo argued that it helped keep the militants in their place, as it made it hard for them to get control of vital issues. It also helped keep the unions in a position of power and influence. Those against the block vote system saw it as unfair and undemocratic, leaving power in the hands of the few.

It was a complex issue. In my days as a seaman, I had been generally pro the one member, one vote principle, seeing how union bosses and the owners could manipulate the situation that existed at the time, which allowed for one vote for every five years of service. This was, in effect, a block vote for older workers. That said, I could also see the other side of the coin. If thousands of your members were at sea at any one time, how could you organise a quick vote? You have to leave it to the leaders and trust them. So it cut both ways

I like to think I'm a pragmatist. I'm as much concerned with what I think will work as with what I would ideally like.

I actually voted against OMOV in 1984, specifically for the re-selection of MPs, which I felt was designed to get rid of certain MPs. Kinnock had proposed it then, but now I was in favour of it in certain situations, with certain provisos, which was what John Smith was trying to get agreement on in Conference.

The old Left were still mainly against OMOV, while the new Beautiful People, like Tony Blair and Gordon Brown, were for it. John Smith knew the Party was almost equally split. As the time got nearer for the big Conference debate on the subject, and then the final vote, it became clear that he was likely to lose the vote.

To my amazement, just a few hours before the big debate, he called me to his conference suite and asked if I would wind up the debate. 'Is this OK with Margaret?' I asked. 'She's your deputy.' He didn't really answer that, but I knew what he was thinking. Margaret had been equivocal, at best, as she was busy trying to reflect the views of the Transport and General Workers' Union.

I said, 'OK, then, but on one condition. You advise Margaret. But be aware, it could make me a hero in the Party.'

He said, 'I'll live with that.'

Although it seemed clear that defeat would mean John would have to resign as Party leader, he did have a possible fall-back position: he could go to the Party executive and ask them to back him, then return to the Conference and ask them to give him a vote of confidence. I told him he couldn't ask the Party to stand on its head. And if he did try it, I personally wouldn't back him. If he lost, he lost. That would be it. So, John had to win to survive. And he knew that.

'We'll just have to see what happens,' he said.

I was still writing my speech while the debate was in progress. There were shots on TV that showed me on the platform, scribbling furiously.

Usually, I have struggled hard with my major speeches, agonised over them, rewritten endlessly, up all night, just as I used to do at Ruskin with my essays. I know, no one ever has to tell me, that I don't have a natural command of English.

Dennis Skinner used to say I worked too hard on my speeches, moaning and groaning over them when he was trying to sleep. He said I set too high a standard and confused myself. He used to tell me the vital thing was to get the trunk of the speech right, then fill in the branches. But what I did, when writing my stuff, was get bogged down in the branches and lose sight of the trunk. I always wanted to bring in too much detail, too many facts to bolster my basic conclusion. Lack of confidence in my fluency, I suppose.

In the event, because it was a rush job, a lot of what I said that day was pretty spontaneous. That was probably why it went down so well. I allowed myself to be emotional – and to appeal to their emotions.

In essence, I was asking most of them to break their own mandate. To achieve this, I was trying to whip up an

175

atmosphere so that in the heat of the moment they found they had to change their minds, so much so that they would then be able to go back to their constituency parties and say, 'After John spoke, I had to do it.'

I don't like watching myself on TV making a speech and I usually avoid it. I don't like reading about it in the papers afterwards. That's why I rarely see Hansard. I know I will have said things that don't quite make sense on the page, but when I was saying them, I'd known what I meant. And that people listening had known what I meant.

Apparently, my words did come out in a bit of torrent, although I was trying to be calm, explaining what was a pretty complicated situation, allowing a block vote in certain situations but not in others. I knew it had to be theatre and convincing – which it was. I said we did have representative voting with levy-paying members, and representatives voting in electoral colleges. The situation could not be reduced to simply accepting that one member, one vote was a superior principle.

But, of course, our enemies, the Tories and the Tory press, were waiting for us to appear to be giving into the unions so they could turn it into a big story. We had to beware and not fall for it. 'God knows,' I said, 'I don't like the press setting the agenda. And you know I do not court publicity from the press.'

But I believed that the new proposal actually strengthened the trade unions. I finished with a rallying cry to support John Smith.

'There's no doubt this man, our leader, put his head on the block by saying, basically, "I fervently believe" – because that is what he believes – "in the relationship and a strong one between the trade unions and the Labour Party."

'He has put his head on the block. Now is the time to vote. Give us a bit of trust and let us vote to support him . . .'

The vote was carried and tremendous cheering broke out. Pauline was in the audience. She said later she thought it was the best speech she'd ever heard me make. She had always been on at me for taking too long working on speeches, telling me to keep them simpler.

She happened to speak to Alastair Campbell, who was sitting beside her, covering it as a journalist. She said to him how good she thought the speech had been. 'I'm quite sure he'll be doing many more good speeches,' he replied.

Lots and lots of people came up to me afterwards, shook my hand, said well done, congratulating me. Except my dad.

Bert used to come to all the Party Conferences, had done most of his adult life, long before I'd become an MP. Once I'd risen up the Party, and become a member of the shadow cabinet, a big attraction for him was the free drinks. He didn't get an invite to most of the parties, but of course I did, being on the NEC and all that, loads of invites from lobby groups, action groups, newspapers, unions and all the rest.

His habit each year was to get from me the list of receptions I'd been invited to. He'd then go to each of them ahead of me. At the door, he'd say, 'Has my son arrived?' They'd ask who his son was and he'd tell them, making the most of his artificial leg, wearing his old Royal Artillery tie,

177

doing his poor-old-gent act. And, of course, they'd welcome him. And he would go straight for the brandy.

If I arrived, he would leave at once, moving on smartish to the next. He did this trick at all Conferences. Talked his way into loads of receptions, and still came out walking upright.

Anyway, at that Party Conference, with the last-minute panic for me, having to give the closing speech, I hadn't been able to see him beforehand as usual. So when he rushed up to me afterwards, with everyone still patting my back, I was expecting him to say, 'Well done, lad.' What he said was, 'Where's the bloody receptions list?'

I gather later he did say to others how well I'd done, but he never said it to me, not to my face. I knew he always wanted to be an MP, and probably always thought he could have made a better job of it than I had so far. He was a character, though, and thinking of him makes me smile now, but at the time I admit I was hurt.

The thing about speeches is that you can get carried away thinking that what matters most is courage, courage to say what you really feel, or what you feel *has* to be said. You're convinced in your guts that what you think is right, so you get swept away by your own rightness and virtue. Kinnock could be like that, thinking he was fighting World War Three when he was attacking the militants.

But judgement is as important as courage, knowing what to say, when to say it, and what not to say.

I've always liked to think that even when I wasn't making grammatical sense, I was making emotional sense. People still understood me.

I suppose the worst ridicule I had to put up with was

from Matthew Parris in *The Times* in his report of that 1993 Conference speech:

> John Prescott went twelve rounds with the English language and left it slumped and bleeding over the ropes. Among the collateral damage were thousands of Mr Smith's critics, many trade union dinosaurs, several big composite motions and Margaret Beckett's political career . . . The very thought of a Prescott transcript is laughable. . . . Any transcript would be gibberish nouns, adjectives, and unattached parts of speech lying among the verbal wreckage like a rose garden after a bulldozer. Yet, somehow, everybody guesses what he meant.

In fact, I didn't get too upset at the time over this piece. I would have liked him not to take the piss, of course, but the way I read it, it seemed to me he was trying to help. And he got it spot on – that people did know what I meant. Otherwise we would never have won the vote. But the damage was done by people not as witty and clever as Matthew Parris, who started to climb on the bandwagon. Over the years, I've seen scores of examples of daft things I'm supposed to have said in a speech – which I never did. For example, I'm supposed to have said, 'As I stand here on terracotta' as opposed to '*terra firma*'. That's funny, I suppose, but I never said it. 'The green belt is a Labour policy and we are going to build on it.' That's another that always gets quoted, and I did say that one. I became a sort of urban myth. Stupid things said and supposed to have been said by John Prescott.

I think my main problem is that my brain works faster than my mouth. I'm always thinking about what I'm going to say next while I'm still saying the last bit, so I butt into myself, go off at a tangent, which is when my sentences start to look confused. I sometimes forget what my mouth has been saying, which is a strange experience. I can hear my brain saying to me, 'Don't forget Point B,' when my mouth is still explaining Point A.

One reason I go so fast is that I was brought up making speeches to striking seamen, usually in the open air. You had to get used to being heckled and interrupted. It paid to speak quickly, and keep going, otherwise some other bugger would get in. So I learned to keep talking with no gaps.

With difficult or long words, or difficult names, I still tend to do what I've always done when I'm trying to write them. I scribble the end of the word, to disguise the fact I don't know how to spell it, just as I gabble the end of a name to hide that I don't know how to say it.

On the last night of that 1993 Conference, we did a Red Revue, as we always did, taking the piss out of ourselves, with music and sketches. I did a sketch with Rodney Bickerstaffe, based on John Smith asking me to make my speech. I've always enjoyed appearing on stage, ever since I was in those school shows. I suppose politics is theatre, after all.

But my best fun was always being out and about in the constituencies. One of my jobs, in the shadow cabinet, was to improve our membership figures. To do that I had a sort of travelling roadshow, which I called the Red Rose Show, sponsored by the *Daily Mirror*. I had my own bus, which later became known as the battle bus. I had it before they became popular with other politicians. For the election of 1992, and later in 1997, I went to almost every constituency in the country with my roadshow. Especially the marginal ones. I had music, sketches, a jazz band and speeches. I'd arrive with the bus, tour the town, then we'd have a rally in a local hall, putting on music and entertainment as well as speeches. The local Labour MP, or our candidate, would be on the platform, along with any other Labour MPs we could raise.

The theme of each event was 'We're on the road to victory', which, of course, had looked pretty unlikely for many years, after our endless defeats. I'd finish the show with a passionate speech, aimed at our supporters, to thank them for their work and rally them to the cause. The show was free, aimed at Party workers and Labour voters, but everyone was encouraged to bring a friend, which made it easy for Tories or hecklers to get in. Not that I minded. I loved all that, arguing with the hecklers. I remember at one hall we got invaded by some pro-fox-hunting demonstrators, who always hated me. They got on the stage and wouldn't leave until the police arrived and chased them away. Our jazz band burst into 'Run, Rabbit, Run' and the whole audience started laughing. Mind you, our anti-hunting activities weren't always so successful. At another roadshow one of our team was dressed up in a fox outfit – and managed to set fire to his bushy tail. We had to pay for a new costume.

I was always very keen on those grassroots occasions, getting out into the heartland and mixing with our supporters, while the Beautiful People were busy in locked

181

rooms at some country house listening to reports from focus groups. There's room for both, of course, though I didn't always think that at the time. The roadshow events took me back to my old days when being a member of your local Labour Party meant sports days, parties, tons of amusements and games. Much of that sort of fun went out of politics when the flowcharts flooded in. But I knew pumping up the membership was vital. And, slowly, we began to do it. We managed to increase Party members from around two hundred and sixty thousand in 1992 to over four hundred thousand five years later.

We all knew, old and young, traditional and modern, that we needed a good base to build on, if we were ever to get into power again.

CHAPTER FOURTEEN

1994

Deputy Leader

On the evening of 11 May 1994, John Smith was the life and soul of the party at a fund-raising banquet in Park Lane. Afterwards I had a chat with him about France. He was sending me there to speak to some leading politicians. I was probably one of the last people from the Party to talk to him. He died the next morning after a heart-attack. He'd seemed to have got over his earlier heart trouble, and had looked so fit, well and cheerful that night. It was a tragedy for his family, his friends, the Party and the country.

I was shattered and cried when I heard the news. I had admired and liked him so much, as a man and a politician. We were from the same generation, born in the same year, but from very different backgrounds. He was a brilliant debater and a naturally fluent speaker. We had arrived in the House by completely different routes but we had both been new MPs in 1970. His death made me think about my own mortality.

Margaret Beckett took over as acting leader, and did an excellent job, calm and organised, far better than some had expected, until we were ready to think about holding elections.

Very quickly the front runners were saying, 'Of course it's far too early to be going round, it wouldn't be seemly or respectful,' by which they meant, 'It's too early for anyone to be going round – except me.'

I offered Margaret Beckett a deal. She was obviously going to stand for leader, having been doing the job, so I said I would only stand for deputy if she didn't stand for deputy *and* leader. A woman and a man at the top seemed a good idea. But Margaret declined. She decided to stand for both positions, deputy as some form of insurance I'm sure. She may well have faced pressure from some of the feminists, the Sisters. Maybe they wouldn't let her stand down. So, I decided to stand for both positions. At such a time, with the elections sprung on us out of the blue, when we had never expected to have to make such decisions, anything could happen.

The heir apparent, until John Smith died, was Gordon Brown, not Margaret, John's deputy. Everyone agreed on that. As I did. He'd been shadow chancellor under John and seemed the most talented of the new younger generation.

I should think Margaret was probably a bit resentful that Gordon and Tony had arrived from nowhere, promoted by Kinnock and Smith as our shining hopes for the future. I don't think Tony trusted her politically because of her disagreement with John over one member, one vote, and her lack of total support for him at that vital time.

But then strange things began to happen: assumptions were questioned, allegiances changed, new possibilities arose. To me, as I said, Tony Blair had always seemed a nice chap, inoffensive, but I still had the feeling he was an SDP type. But at least he had never left the Party, so I'd always rated him.

With Gordon, I'd had a few run-ins. In shadow cabinet meetings, when we were discussing finance and I was shadow Employment minister, I challenged him on lots of things – for example, in trying to get a million into work within two years: Kinnock's mad idea, which I thought was impossible and Gordon had supported. I actually thought then that Robin Cook would have made a better shadow chancellor – and so, of course, did Robin. But, then, Cooky always believed he could do everyone's job better than they could.

I remember once going into a shadow cabinet meeting and bellowing, 'Hello, Gordon.' He just sat there at the table, head down, reading figures, ignoring me. I don't think he ever liked being challenged on his figures, by me or anyone, and he certainly didn't like my battleaxe approach.

I think at that moment, when John Smith died, Tony

Blair himself accepted that Gordon would be the leader, as he was the best person for the job. Tony was still obviously in awe of him. The teacher–student relationship had hardly changed. Gordon, as shadow chancellor, was the more senior shadow cabinet minister although Tony had done well and was shadow home secretary.

Theories and suggestions began to circulate, get into the air, just gossip and rumour at first. Then some influential people began to take them seriously. Perhaps Tony might have a better chance of winning a general election than Gordon. In that case, wouldn't he make the better leader?

Some so-called experts now think that Tony had already emerged as the next leader by the time John Smith died, and point to all the friends and contacts he'd been building up since 1992, and various newspapers tipping him. But you can always find examples of that. As far as I'm concerned, at the moment John died, Gordon was still our most likely next leader.

Mandelson had been for Gordon, but now he changed sides, spinning away, determined to get Tony in.

Alastair Campbell, still working as a tabloid journalist, was publicly writing stories to the effect that Tony would be the best leader.

Philip Gould, who had come in during Kinnock's reign as the Party witch-doctor, reading the tea leaves and other such nonsense, produced research to show Blair would be the most acceptable leader.

I used to argue with Gould in meetings, saying, 'I've had decades at the heart of the Labour Party, I've developed political instincts, I don't need stupid focus groups to tell me what I should believe.' I was hostile to his methods and dismissed most of his conclusions as little more than throwing bones in the sand. It was funny with his surveys – they always seemed to be leaked to the press when they were what the Beautiful People liked to believe. Those to the contrary, and there were some, never made it.

The press made a lot of Gordon being very Scottish, as if that might be a bad thing, and harped on about how he appeared grey and dour.

Tony was also Scottish, by birth and schooling, but it didn't appear to be held against him because, of course, he didn't look or sound Scottish. Unlike Gordon. And Tony didn't consider himself Scottish. He said his favourite football team was Newcastle United. And he had an attractive, clever wife and a young, attractive family.

The upshot was that in just weeks, accepted wisdom had swung round. Everyone at the top of the Party seemed to believe now that Tony was the better bet. He'd appeal to the middle classes, women, the southern voters, the Tories, far more than Gordon would.

I don't know what happened at that famous Granita restaurant meeting in Islington, when they met together to discuss the leadership election. But it seems to me, from how things were at the time and what happened after-wards, that Tony finally got Gordon's agreement not to stand as leader. In return, if Labour got in, he would make Gordon chancellor, with control over all spending, perhaps even over most domestic matters, but I'm not sure about that. Then, in due course, he would hand over the reins to Gordon. Whatever the details, Gordon accepted the inevitable, but in return got a deal.

Perhaps Tony really meant it as such, when it came out

of his mouth, that it was a proper deal, but then Tony has a habit of saying things people want to hear. They believe him, because they are charmed by his smiles and nods. That's his way. That's why I used to call him Bambi when he first appeared on the political scene.

I don't actually think Tony was Machiavellian or manoeuvring in all this – whatever Gordon might later have suspected. Tony isn't wicked. I don't believe he had always schemed to do Gordon down, keeping in with him all those years, waiting to knife him in the back at the vital moment. I'm sure he wasn't pretending when he appeared content to be in Gordon's shadow, looking up to him. He hadn't been secretly jealous or two-faced. He was genuine.

But now that this election was upon us, long before we ever thought it would be, Tony, like everyone else, had begun to accept that perhaps he was the better bet. He probably wobbled a bit, but all the polls were now indicating that he had a stronger chance of leading Labour to victory than Gordon. Tony understood that for the good of the Party, even though I'm sure he felt guilty about what was happening to Gordon, that he appeared to have been carved up.

God knows what Gordon thought when all this became apparent and then inevitable. Really pissed off, I should think. I'm sure he believed Tony had stolen it from him. But he had to accept, as Tony had done, what the polls were telling us, probably before that Granita meeting. The result was that he withdrew from the leadership race.

Some commentators have suggested he had to do it, because if he had run against Blair, it would have split their camps and could have let in either me or Margaret as leader. Which neither of them wanted to happen. And then, of course, any deal Gordon may have made with Tony would have been useless. Labour politics would have gone a different way. Anyway, when Gordon withdrew, his supporters moved to Tony and assured the likelihood of his election.

I learned from various go-betweens, such as Ian McCartney, that Tony felt his deputy should be me, not Margaret. But Gordon was against me as deputy leader. His thinking was that I would blow up, explode, make trouble. He also didn't like the idea of me challenging him, being aggressive towards him, as happened in the shadow cabinet. So Gordon voted for Margaret as deputy. But Tony stuck to his guns. He said he could get on with me, but, then, he believes he can get on with everyone. Which is true, more or less.

I also decided to stand as leader as well as deputy leader, even though I knew I had no chance. But it gave me a chance to put forward my policies. Who did I vote for, as leader and as deputy? Myself. You were allowed to do that.

Tony, of course, won the leadership election easily – getting 57 per cent of the vote. I got 24 per cent and Margaret 19 per cent. For deputy leader, I polled 56.5 per cent, and Margaret 43.5 per cent. Hattersley voted for me as deputy, having changed his mind, deciding that I wasn't a trouble-maker, after all.

It was all very amicable, as we knew roughly what the outcome was going to be. There was a nice quote afterwards from Denis Healey – who had never been a fan of mine. When he was asked how he felt about me being elected deputy, he was very positive:

> Well, it would be stupid of me to give advice. I would simply say that Prescott must be intimately involved in Tony's working out policy with policy bodies because I think he can speak directly to ordinary people in a way nobody else in politics can at the moment in any party. He also is extremely intelligent. He has got a lot of Ernie Bevin's qualities and as I say the two of them together are an extra-ordinarily powerful team. I thought the wonderful thing about the leadership contest was not only that it was short but it was also very well mannered. When I consider the appalling contest we had between Benn and me for deputy leader, and many of the ones after we lost power, the leadership contests in the eighties were so appalling.

Many years later Anthony Seldon, in his biography of Blair, said that Tony's decision to back me as his deputy leader 'was to be one of the shrewdest personal judgements of his political life'. But, of course, we didn't know that then.

Almost immediately, Tony embarked on what I thought was a mad idea – getting rid of Clause Four, sacred to all true Labour supporters: it tied the Party to fight for common ownership of the means of production and distribution. In other words, total nationalisation.

We had done a lot of nationalisation under the Attlee

government, and there was more we could do, or might do, but with the years most of us, even those on the traditional wing of the Party, like me, realised it was a fond dream rather than a true reality. It became a symbolic aim rather than an active campaign. Nobody thought we'd ever do it, but we liked to see it there, in our manifesto each election and on our membership cards. To get rid of it, I thought, was a mistake – and would spark up unnecessary ideological controversy. It would give out the wrong signals to our grassroots supporters.

So, when Tony first mentioned it, because he was planning to include it in his first Conference speech, I said, 'It's a step too far.' I was dead against it and believed the Party would not accept it. But I didn't immediately blow up. I said, 'But give me time to think about it.'

I went away. And thought hard. I could understand that Tony, as the new leader, had to be seen to be doing things, challenging conventional Party views, forward-looking. I could also see that if we were going to win the next election, get over the magical 45 per cent of the votes, which we hadn't been near for a very long time, we had to do things that encouraged past Labour supporters and Tories to switch their votes.

I've always been convinced by the art of the possible, to believe in what will work. I could see Tony was desperate for my support. He told me he wouldn't be able to carry it with the Party, if I said, 'No, I'm all against it.'

I went back to see him and said, 'OK, then, but I have three conditions. I want you to take it round the Party, explain your thinking to them, make it look as if you're having a proper debate, and let the Party decide. You must

191

persuade them it's the right thing to do, not just announce it with no discussion.

'Second, when you make your big speech at our October Party Conference, leave the mention of dropping Clause Four to the last page.' The normal thing is that a big speech is released the day before, so the press have advance warning and can read it, as it's being spoken. 'If you give it away in advance, they'll make trouble, stir things up. Don't tell anyone about it till they hear you speaking it. If you don't keep it to the last page, and announce it too early in your speech, people like Scargill will lead a walk-out, and that will be a fatal start to the debate.

'Third,' I said, 'if the clause is being changed, then the words "Democratic Socialist" should still appear there somewhere.' And I had the right to approve it.

Rosie Winterton, my chief of staff at the time, went round to Tony's Islington house with me and worked on the words. It began, 'We are a democratic socialist party . . .' I was proud of those words.

At Conference in 1994, I supported him – and said the Party should. I got a huge personal reception, which surprised Cherie, Tony's wife. She said as much to Pauline, who was sitting beside her. Then, for a month or so, Tony went round the country, holding Party rallies to explain the changes in Clause Four. And it was all accepted.

Some time in 1995, I can't remember the exact date now, we had a secret meeting with seven or eight of the most important trade-union general secretaries. Tony had been on *The Jimmy Young Show* and said in passing that, as Labour leader, he would be showing no special favours to the unions. Naturally, many of them were worried by this, and wanted to talk to him personally and privately.

A meal was arranged at an Indian restaurant. I wasn't included at first, but when I heard it was being organised, I said I should be there, if just as an observer. So I went along to the meal. Bill Morris, leader of the TGWU, was there, Jimmy Knapp, Rodney Bickerstaffe, Garfield Davis and other union leaders.

Over the meal, Tony made it absolutely clear that the old days were gone and he wouldn't be following any union diktat, and they should not expect any deals.

What amazed me was their timidity. It was obvious to me that he was challenging them, expecting them to complain or argue, but the response was muted. Only Rodney, with the support of Jimmy, spoke out. I felt that evening that Tony had got the measure of the trade-union movement, which I regretted.

Soon after I became deputy leader, I got a call from John Major, the prime minister. I was surprised by this, as Tories generally didn't ring me. He said, 'Congratulations.'

'Oh, aye?'

'You're going to be made a member of the Privy Council.'

'Oh, yeah?' I said.

He explained it meant I would become a Right Honourable.

I said, 'Oh, no, I don't want all that stuff.' I'd been reading Barbara Castle's autobiography and there was a bit about how you had to go on your knees, then lightly brush the Queen's hand with your lips. It all sounded daft to me, part of the royal flunkery.

I had met the Queen before, back in 1970 when she was on an official visit to Hull and I'd just become an MP. I didn't want to attend, though the Labour Party was quite insistent. So I'd agreed, but I said I wasn't going to bow to her. All three of the Hull MPs were going to be presented to her when the *Britannia* docked in the harbour. So we lined up, with Pauline, a convinced monarchist, doing her curtsey.

I was surprised at how small the Queen was and when it came to my turn, she mumbled something. I couldn't hear what it was, so naturally I bent down. She just smiled. She knew she'd got me. As far as everyone watching was concerned, and the local photographers, it looked as if I was bowing. But I wasn't. She'd deliberately lowered her voice and caught me out.

Anyway, John Major said I'd have to go through with the ceremony, in order to become a member of the Privy Council. Otherwise vital information of state could be withheld from me. He said it would be just a small ceremony on this occasion, just me and Tony together, the two of us, as Labour's new leader and deputy. So I agreed to go.

We shared a car. On the way to Buckingham Palace, I was grumbling that I didn't want to do it. Tony said it was the only honour worth having for a politician, so I had to go through with it.

It was the first time I'd ever been to Buckingham Palace. When we got there, it turned out there was a garden party being held at the same time and we could hear the band playing outside in the gardens.

Tony swore on the Bible, of course, while I affirmed. I

managed not to turn my back on the Queen, as I'd been warned. I knelt on a chair to kiss her hand. But I was still moaning all the way home in the car.

I gathered later on that it became one of Tony's party pieces: Tony used to imitate me at Buckingham Palace, so he says, going, 'By heck, bloody hell, I'm not having all this fucking nonsense . . .'

CHAPTER FIFTEEN

1994–97

Rows and Exclusions

My first big row with Tony occurred in the autumn of 1994, before Conference. I had agreed to support him on Clause Four, then he made a further request that Labour should be described as 'New Labour'. At first I rejected it, saying that Labour was capable of change without calling it 'New'. Again, he said he would only propose it if I agreed. I decided I'd think about it and said I'd let him know before his big Conference speech. I could see the need for changes to be made, and to be seen to be made, so I agreed. We couldn't go on as we had been. Those voters who had left for the Tories or Liberals would not come back, I was sure, unless they could see we had changed.

Mind you, I was still determined not to use the phrase 'New Labour' myself – and I never did. I just couldn't bear those words to come out of my mouth. I much preferred to say that the Party now stood for 'traditional values in a modern setting', a phrase I'd been given by Rodney Bickerstaffe that was eventually used by the Party in election leaflets.

However, I was worried about the use of all this slick presentation, the pet pollsters and analysts who were becoming so important. Kinnock had first brought them in, thought they were wonderful, but they had done him no good in the end. Now they were gaining even more influence in the Party under Tony.

I discovered one day, through my adviser Rosie Winterton, that there had been a secret meeting in a house on the south coast. It had apparently discussed election strategy, among other things, which was supposed to be my field, as deputy leader. Heaven knows what else they talked about but Gordon Brown, Peter Mandelson, Alastair Campbell, David Miliband, Jonathan Powell and Tom Sawyer were at the meeting with Tony. Whatever Party matters they were discussing, I should have been there, as deputy leader and Old Labour. I was bloody furious. I had trusted Tony to be open with me, as he'd promised on our election.

I rang Alastair and said, 'Is it true, you've all had a secret meeting?' He said I'd better talk to Tony. I rang Joy Johnson, who'd just been made the Party's communications director, thanks to support from myself, Tony and others. I presumed she must have been there as well. I rang her at home and was told she was in the shower. 'Get her out of the bloody shower,' I shouted.

I asked her if she had been at the meeting. It was clear she had, but was giving nothing away. 'Just shows you where your loyalty lies, love,' I said, and put down the phone.

I made a few other calls, and got it confirmed who had been there and roughly what had taken place. There was part of me that saw it as a personal slight, the college-boys coterie, the Beautiful People deliberately excluding the old bruiser, stirring up my chip-on-the-shoulder sense of inferiority. They had all been nice to me so far, to my face, and I'd had a lot of sleeve patting and sob stuff, saying how important I was to the cause, but I'd begun to suspect I was being used.

But more important than my pride was the fact that as deputy leader I should have been at all meetings where future policy and strategy were discussed. The elected deputy represents the mass body of the Party, keeps an eye on what the executive is doing.

It so happened that I had arranged to meet Tony the following Saturday: I was coming down from Hull and he was catching the same train at Grantham. When he got on with his entourage and came into my coach, he plonked himself down, all smiles and charm, and I started on him. 'Listen you little shit, I've got a question to ask you and you'd better be clear and truthful about the answer. Did you take all that lot down to this secret country meeting and discuss policy?'

He tried to say there were other things being discussed. Then he said he hadn't realised till he got there that I hadn't been invited. It was an oversight. He then admitted it had happened. So he said he was very sorry.

'I don't believe you,' I said. 'It's all a load of crap.'

He asked me to come to his house and we could discuss it privately. I was getting heated and other passengers could hear. But I said no. So for the rest of the journey to London I sat there, keeping him squirming.

I did think of resigning. I'd never contemplated it in my political life before. I'd never used it as a threat, the way some people do. It just seemed to me I'd been betrayed. They obviously didn't want anyone from Old Labour in the inner circle. So they'd excluded me deliberately.

Yet only a few months earlier they'd been so grateful to me for supporting their New Labour project, which I had done, if not with those words. But it was clear they saw me more as a performing seal, trotted out to entertain and amuse the faithful, then pushed back into my cave and told to shut up. Perhaps they were hoping I'd resign. But the important thing was to stay and fight.

Anyway, on arrival at King's Cross I'd cooled down. I did go with Tony to his home. He tried to suggest it was all Brown and Mandelson's doing. They hadn't wanted me at that meeting because I might have challenged them. Which I would. I saw it as part of my job not to let them get away with any nonsense.

He maintained that they were just raising topics at the meeting, trying out ideas, and my challenges could have been obstructive. But I knew that Gordon was trying to take over responsibility for Party strategy, and keep me out.

I admitted he was good at it, but that wasn't the point. I should still have been there.

Anyway, Tony gave me a lot of soft soap and nice words and I felt reassured, happier. I believed that he himself did not want to exclude me.

Of course, I didn't know at that time that the Beautiful People, and even New Labour's Big Four – Blair, Brown, Mandelson and Campbell – were continually getting pissed off with each other, jealous and furious when in turn they felt carved up, excluded or briefed against, working themselves into sulks and rages.

Alastair Campbell's *Diaries* describes petty, stupid tensions between them. He even says there was a fight between him and Mandelson. I thought that was rubbish. Mandelson fighting? No chance. You could blow him away. More like a hissy fit.

At the end of my private meeting with Tony at his house, he promised me that in the event of us winning the next election, I would be made deputy prime minister. I hadn't to tell anyone. Was it a con? I didn't think so. I decided he'd believed it when he said it. Which in politics goes a long way.

Not long afterwards Harriet Harman infuriated me and the Party when she revealed that she was sending one of her sons to a grammar school. Having a child at the Oratory, where Tony Blair sent Euan, was bad enough, but they could vaguely defend that on religious grounds and by saying it was still a comprehensive. But using a grammar school, selective and grant maintained? That, to me, was a direct rejection of a central plank of our policies.

I did have words in private with Tony about Euan, when he'd sent him to the Oratory. He explained it was a personal decision. I said, 'Once you're in politics, not all personal decisions can be divided from the political.'

Both my sons, Johnathan and David, went to local comprehensives in Hull. I would never for one second have contemplated sending them anywhere else. David, when he started his comp, got attacked by a boy with a knife, but he fought back and it didn't happen again. He also played the bass guitar in a group, which helped make him popular.

Johnathan couldn't get into his first-choice comprehensive, or his second. He was one of five per cent who didn't get either their first or second choice. So he ended up in the least popular school. I don't know why. At the time, they were trying to balance the proportion of A and B grade kids entering each school, to distribute the available talent. I thought that was fair enough. It was probably part of the explanation, but no one ever said. He was just told he was going to a comp eight miles away – which wasn't even in my constituency.

Pauline asked why I didn't go down to the education department and protest, as other parents had done. We would have had a good case, with him having to travel so far, but I said I couldn't. The Tory tabloids would turn it against me: 'Prescott Intervenes to Help His Son.' I've never, ever done that sort of thing, pulled any strings to help my kids – probably to their disadvantage. If I hadn't been a politician, and a target for all Tories, I would probably have helped them more than I did. As it was, the press made me a target and contacted their schools for their grades.

I've always believed in the comprehensive principle. I have never forgotten how I suffered from being classed as an 11-plus failure, along with millions of others. So I was pleased when the exam was stopped and the grammar schools closed, but I'm not saying the comps got it right. We never fully thought out our policy on streaming. It seems to me you have to allow streaming if certain kids move ahead faster than others in some subjects.

The other problem with the comps was, of course, that the middle classes, as ever, found out how to play the system. They always know which is the best comp in the area and work fiddles to get their kids in – such as moving house or giving the granny's address, pretending their kids live there, not at their own home.

Every time I made an official visit to a comp, anywhere in the country, I always cross-examined the teachers on what was happening, what they thought was going right or wrong. I was amazed when I started discovering that teacher administrators were paid more than classroom teachers, the ones supposedly looking after other teachers, sitting in little offices but doing hardly any teaching themselves. They were the ones getting the big money whenever teachers got increases. Seemed wrong to me. We need as many teachers in the classrooms as possible, correcting things like spelling mistakes and enthusing the kids. I know how the lack of that held me back.

Anyway, I felt what Harriet did was unacceptable. She was in the shadow cabinet, shadow minister for Health, at the time. She was going totally against Party policy.

I know that other Labour figures had rejected the state system in the past – Harold Wilson and James Callaghan

203

had both sent their kids to private schools – but now we were pledged to support the comprehensive system. I thought Harriet Harman should have resigned.

I didn't know about her decision till I read it in the paper, though other shadow ministers did. They'd been told beforehand, but it had been kept from me, in the knowledge that I'd make trouble. Harriet later wrote and apologised that I hadn't been informed before the papers got the story.

There was enormous discontent in the shadow cabinet as the story rumbled on, with moves to get her to resign. But Tony stuck by her. He didn't think it was a big enough crime for him to sacrifice her, giving Tories a scalp.

The subject came up in Prime Minister's Questions and John Major enjoyed baiting Tony with what had happened. In fact, Major cruelly taunted him. It was one of Tony's worst displays ever at PMQ. He just couldn't defend her.

I was sitting near Harriet on our front bench and was still furious with her. Later, on TV, they had cut-aways of my expression – and it was pretty clear what I thought. Mandelson said I'd done it deliberately. I said, 'No, I didn't. I can't help my face, can I?'

Tony called me into his office. He was furious that I hadn't supported him in his defence of Harman. He said I should have done, as his deputy. 'You should be like Ernie Bevin, supporting Attlee.'

'Rubbish,' I said. 'First of all, you know nothing about Ernie Bevin. He was never deputy leader, elected by the Party. Secondly, I'm not going to support that woman on her selfish decision to send her child to a grammar school. But thirdly, when it does come to the crunch on something that *does* matter to us, the Labour Party and the Government, I'll go to the stake for you. I know that one day, I don't know when or what for, I'll take a knife in the back to support and protect you and the Party, but this is not the day, not for her . . .'

It was the most serious personal row we ever had, with us both sticking to our guns. Even when much more important dramas later turned up for me, for Tony and for the Party, I can't think of one disagreement that was as heated.

That was an occasion when my face had let me down, but around the same time, towards the end of 1995, I woke up one day to find I'd become a sex symbol.

The Times had published on its front page a poem by a poet I'd never heard of, Fleur Adcock. She'd had a fantasy of sleeping with me, or something daft like that, all about 'we were leaning avidly forward, lips out-thrust, certain protuberances under our clothing brushing each other's fronts . . .' I didn't know what she was on about. I had to look up 'protuberances' in the dictionary.

All the papers followed it up. Melanie McDonagh, in the *Evening Standard*, said she'd had lunch with me and Tony Blair, 'but as far as fanciability goes, Mr Prescott is well ahead of the leader'.

The *Daily Express* carried a feature called 'The Strange Allure of Thumper Prescott' and the *Mail* examined 'the reasons why Prescott is attractive to women'. *The Times* even sent a reporter, Valerie Grove, with me all the way to Brussels, where I was going to a Socialist International meeting, just to ask me about it.

Then bloody Heseltine read out the whole poem in the House of Commons. It got more coverage than my speech in the Budget debate, which I'd been slaving over.

I suppose it was funny, and probably meant affectionately, but at the time I was so busy with serious things that I suspected they were all just taking the piss.

We won an important by-election in April 1996 at Staffordshire South East, turning a Tory majority of seven thousand into a Labour majority of thirteen thousand. We were on our way – which most of the commentators were beginning to realise.

I went on the *Today* programme as I had been mainly responsible for masterminding that particular campaign. John Humphrys tried to have a go at us by suggesting that Labour was now the party of the middle class. I said the middle class had always been an important part of the Labour Party. I also admitted I was now middle class. Well, that started a right discussion, which went on for days in the papers. All I was saying was that I was brought up working class, my roots would always be working class, but as an MP, I was now living a middle-class lifestyle. No argument about it. My salary, my house, my car all meant I was middle class. So what?

My old dad got in on the act. He was then eighty-five, living in a sheltered flat in Chester. He came on the *Today* programme to say I had to stop all this middle class nonsense. I was working class and should be proud of it. I think he quite enjoyed the sudden exposure he was getting.

I've admired Humphrys over the years as a broadcaster.

He usually gives you a chance to reply, and he's done his homework – but I think he was always at his best when he was doing the half-hour interviews on Sunday TV, on the programme *On the Record*. Then you can have a proper discussion. Now he's caught up in the usual fixation broadcasters get of falling in love with their own questions. All those BBC types think their questions are more important than any possible answers.

As the 1997 general election approached, we were all aware of the need to be united, despite various differences and the feuds that had been going on, such as those between Blairites and Brownites.

Clare Short got herself demoted again, for not sticking to the Party line. She loved the media and playing to the gallery. Peter Mandelson was too full of his own importance, convinced he had the most influence over Tony.

But Mandelson was vital to the establishment of New Labour. He was good at assessing how other people would react and was helpful to me – but he turned out to be a bad judge when it came to himself. He didn't seem aware of the effects of his own actions or lifestyle, which ultimately resulted in him being forced to leave the Government twice. As for Alastair Campbell, I always saw him as more than just a press officer. I felt he was a very strong Labour person, very committed and very able.

Over the years, he gave me quite a bit of good advice when I got into certain scrapes. He also passed on to me some good jokes, which Tony, as a possible prime minister, considered a bit rude. I think some of them had been written for us by Roy Hudd. I remember when Heseltine was deputy prime minister and had acquired for himself several different jobs. I stood up at a Party Conference and said, 'Heseltine has now got more positions than in the *Kama Sutra*.' I did worry some of the women in the audience might not be amused, but they all laughed. I suppose I could get away with a joke like that, with my image, but Tony had to be more careful.

I was worried about Gordon and we had a few set-tos as he tried to take over all financial and economic matters. We argued, for example, over the details of our policy for the privatisation of Railtrack, the part of British Rail that owned the track and stations. Then Gordon was upset that Tony had said I would be looking after the regions. He didn't think I should be – he wanted to do it.

In a bid to improve the relationship between me and Gordon, Geoffrey Robinson, the wealthy Labour MP for Coventry, who was one of our front-bench spokesmen and an ally of Gordon's, invited us in June 1996 to his luxury apartment in Mayfair to watch the England v. Scotland game. I had a bet on with Gordon of ten pounds that England would win.

When you're not at all used to it, a drop of brandy can quickly go to your head. If you're not careful. Which I wasn't. Geoffrey's hospitality flowed and flowed and I got pretty sloshed. Charlie Whelan, Gordon's press secretary, had to help me into my car. I remember thinking, through the haze, Oh, God, this will get in the papers, someone will leak it, and I'll be able to guess who did it. But, surprisingly, there wasn't a word.

I saw that as a good sign. It showed that, despite

everything, we were all working together, not stabbing each other in the back or leaking nasty stories. And I got my ten pounds from Gordon. That was a triumph in itself.

With election day in sight I was spending more and more of my time on my battle bus, the Prescott Express. I covered ten thousand miles during that 1997 campaign. Yes, while I was on the road, I did suspect they might be up to their old tricks, making decisions behind my back, or at least listening to focus groups and coming to dopey conclusions based on a load of nonsense figures and opinion polls. So I insisted on a personal phone link whenever any important meetings were taking place. They stuck to it, in the main.

I was tempted sometimes to stay in London, stick in Whitehall or Millbank, but I've always preferred to be out there meeting people, encouraging our Party workers, being shouted at by Tories, rather than sitting in a room looking at flipcharts.

And I knew that if we were to win a general election at long last, we had to rally the troops, the grassroots supporters, rather than worrying too much about any focus groups.

CHAPTER SIXTEEN

Victory at Last

I went up to Sedgefield, to Tony's constituency, on the afternoon of election day, 1 May 1997. We knew we would win, had done for some time, but we didn't expect a landslide. A helicopter was sent for me, I don't know who organised it, it just appeared and I flew up with Joan Hammell to talk to Tony at his house.

There was a huge amount of bustle and rushing around, lots of people there. Someone gave me some tea and a sandwich, and Tony and I discussed what was going to happen. He had already agreed I would be deputy prime minister, though it had never been made public. I suppose part of me suspected it might not happen, but he immediately confirmed it.

We then talked about exactly what job I'd be doing. I had really wanted to be at the heart of government as advocated in my earlier pamphlets, in the Cabinet Office, in a strengthened No. 10. He'd already told me he wanted me to take a department, a big new one. For some time he'd been thinking of combining several ministries to create 'super-ministries'. I wasn't sure about that. I would still have preferred to be based at No. 10, with him, but he said I should have some experience of running a big department. It would stand me in good stead for future work. At the next election, he'd consider placing me in the Cabinet Office with him. So I agreed to do it, for the first term anyway.

We discussed briefly what the big new department would contain, then I flew back to Hull and watched the results coming in. In my constituency I had a huge majority, once again – almost twenty-nine thousand votes while the Tories got just over five and a half thousand – but our overall majority of 179 MPs surprised us all. It was Labour's largest ever landslide, greater even than Attlee's in 1945.

About midnight, I caught a plane, specially chartered by Tony's office, to take me from Humberside to London. I got on it with Pauline, my family and some of the staff. They were all singing 'Come Fly With Me', drinking champagne and eating smoked salmon.

I didn't realise at first there was also a security man on board. This bloke just seemed to have appeared, and was sitting there, saying that as I was going to be deputy prime

212

minister, I needed security from now on. Pauline didn't really believe he was security, and thought he might be a tabloid journalist. When he seemed to close his eyes and looked as if he was nodding off, Pauline grabbed me and said, 'I'm going to attack you, John Prescott.'

The security man opened one eye and said, 'Just you try.' We had arrived in another world.

In London, I met up with my battle bus and we drove round Smith Square, past the Tory Party HQ. We went round and round the square with all of us singing 'OUT OUT OUT, AT LAST YOU'RE OUT OUT OUT'. You could see their hangdog faces at the windows.

Next morning I went round to Downing Street, to see Tony and get the official appointment. I'd been told not to take the battle bus, but I just ignored that and got it to take me down Whitehall, letting me off at the entrance to Downing Street.

The new enlarged department I was to take over covered Environment, Local Government, Transport and the Regional Agencies. Yes, a pretty big responsibility. And a bit of a mouthful. I inherited two permanent secretaries, who had been at Transport and at Environment, but I only needed one, to be placed in overall charge of this big new department.

I'd met one of them some time previously, a chap called Patrick Brown, at Transport, back in 1992 when Neil Kinnock had asked me to meet him, prior to the election. I was shadow minister for Transport and I wanted him to come and see me in my office. I asked him to pop round the following day but he said he couldn't, as his number two would be in Southampton. 'Fine,' I said, 'then send your number two round today as he is clearly running the

213

department.' That did it. They were both round soon afterwards. Mine wasn't a big office, so we had difficulty finding enough chairs. We laid out for them an armchair and pouffe, wondering who would choose which. The permanent secretary took the pouffe while his number two sat in the chair. That gave me an insight into his character. The top men should always act like the top men. I thought then, if I ever make it to a minister, I wouldn't want him as my permanent secretary. We lost that election, but he was still there in 1997 when I arrived as secretary of state.

During the election, I arranged to see the other permanent secretary, Andrew Turnbull, from the Department of Environment. We met privately at Rosie Winterton's house at Doncaster. I got on with him, and told him if I took over all the departments, he would be my permanent secretary.

When I got to the D of E building on the first afternoon, the staff were hanging out of all five floors in the atrium, cheering and clapping. For me, that was probably the biggest, most thrilling moment of the whole election. It was amazing, realising that all those civil servants were genuinely pleased to see a Labour government taking over and pleased that the deputy prime minister was to be their secretary of state.

There was then a tussle between Environment and Transport about which building I would make my headquarters. I chose Environment. It seemed a nicer, friendlier building.

I immediately sat at my desk, got my head down and started work. Unlike some others. Robin Cook seemed more interested in rushing to the press to tell them about the changes he was going to make at the Foreign Office, how it was going to be ethical foreign policy from now on. He was probably the most brilliant parliamentarian of our times – but he was well aware of it. All politicians are self-centred, but he was the worst I ever met. Tony and Gordon didn't like it when he would suggest behind their backs that he could do a better job than they were doing.

The suggestions and gossip about me were that I would blow up, once I was in office, that I'd get into some row and lose my head, or I would be like Eric Heffer, the left-wing Labour MP always threatening to resign. But I had waited too long to be in government to fall into that trap. I just concentrated on working as hard as possible and avoiding any rows or eruptions, though the major changes I planned would be controversial.

On my first day, I called a dozen of the top civil servants from the departments I was looking after, the real mandarins, who had seen it all. I invited them for a cup of tea in my office. I went round them, asking who wanted tea, who wanted coffee. A woman called Mavis McDonald said she'd prefer a gin and tonic. It was late afternoon and I said nothing. I knew she was a very important, high-powered woman. (Later she became my very good permanent secretary in the deputy prime minister's office.)

I stepped out into the corridor, went into a few offices and eventually found some gin and a bottle of tonic. I also found a tea towel. I held it over my arm, the way I did as a waiter, and walked back into my office with her gin and tonic on a tray. 'Here you are, madam,' I said, 'one gin and tonic.' Everyone laughed.

Tony then appointed Gavin Strang as minister for Transport, under me but with a seat in the cabinet. I could understand his thinking. It was only fair that people who had served in the shadow cabinet should get a chance in the real cabinet, at least for a while. Tony asked me first if I would take him. He wasn't forced upon me, as such, as I agreed to the rationale, but it made it a bit difficult for him. The Department of Transport then tried to use him to undermine me in order to secure control of the department themselves. So in the end he didn't last long.

I'd only been in the post a few weeks when the Treasury asked me to make changes to some figures my department had produced. They wanted the possible cost of something to read X million not Y million in some projection. I called in the permanent secretary and asked him to change it. 'I think we can't do that,' he replied. I asked him why. He said the new figure would not be correct. 'You can, of course, direct me to do it,' he said, 'and I will, but that will then go down on the record.'

I made him change the figure, but he was right to point out the danger. If questioned about it in the House, I would have to defend the figure. And he was right. In the end, his costing proved correct.

I had great respect for all the civil servants I ever worked with and it made me a great admirer of the Civil Service.

I did have problems with one of them, though. It was decided that as deputy prime minister I was required to live in London and would have a grace-and-favour residence in Whitehall, at Admiralty House. It's a massive building with a big courtyard in front and huge columns at the front door. When Pauline first saw it, she said, 'Where do we put our milk bottles, John?'

Anyway, we went up to inspect our apartment – and

found it was fully furnished. It had previously been occupied by Michael Portillo, the Tory defence minister, and Winston Churchill at one time. Pauline fell for it. The next day we visited the flat again – and all the furniture had gone. Apparently, so I was told, the permanent secretary at the Ministry of Defence, Sir Richard Mottram, had ordered all the furniture to be removed, once Portillo moved out. I don't know whether he knew we were about to move in, but I was furious. I got my own back, though.

A few years later, Sir Richard became a permanent secretary in my department. On his arrival I had great pleasure in taking him to his room. I opened the door and said, 'This is your new office, Sir Richard.' It was totally empty, except for a packing case in the middle of the floor with a telephone on it. He took it with good grace and a Civil Service enigmatic smile on his face.

All senior ministers get a government car and a driver and we were told we would all be having a Rover, apart from the prime minister who would get a Jaguar. I complained to my civil servants because Michael Heseltine, as the Tory deputy prime minister, had had a Jaguar, so why couldn't I? I was told he'd paid for it himself. I suppose when you have a stately home and private wealth, you can do that sort of thing. Heseltine also had black despatch boxes, not red, as he didn't like the colour. That didn't bother me. I don't care about colours. But the Jag I did.

Since 1970, I'd only ever been an MP, with no other source of income or any private money, so obviously I couldn't afford an office Jaguar. But I was determined to get one. I like Jaguars. They are traditional English cars. We should support them. Why couldn't I have one?

It took three months of messing around, but then they suddenly decided they could, after all, provide me with a Jaguar – as my official car. So that's how the Two Jags image came about. If I'd stuck to the government Rover, it would never have made a story. Obviously I never *owned* two Jags, that just became the story. All I had was an old one for my private life, plus the use of one on government business. Less well known is that my own Jag was paid for by the *Daily Telegraph*. I bought it after I won damages against them for a wrongful story.

I got a lot of stick at one Labour Party Conference in Bournemouth when I got a car to drive me and Pauline 250 yards from our hotel to the conference centre. As the person responsible for Transport, I had been trying to get more people out of their cars and on to public transport. So they got me for that.

I made the mistake of saying it was because of Pauline – she didn't want her hair messed up in the wind. It was a mistake because I was ungallant and it dragged her into the papers when all her life she has been trying to keep out of them, always refusing to give any interviews. There were security reasons for taking the car, but the main reason was that I was in a hurry, running late. I'd spent hours sweating on my speech, so every minute counted.

Not long after we took power, Tony told me he was thinking of bringing Paddy Ashdown, leader of the Liberal Democrats, into government – Tony's so-called Big Tent. Now, on previous controversial topics, like Clause Four, I might have been initially against it, but I was still willing to go away and consider it, work out what was best for the Party.

This time it took me one second. 'If Ashdown walks in the back door and gets a cabinet job, I'm straight out the front door. It's not a negotiable issue for me.'

And I meant it. I would have resigned if Ashdown had got any sort of cabinet job. But I could see what Tony was trying to do. He was trying to create a party of the centre, involving the Liberal Democrats, which would destroy the Tories and keep us in power for ever. That was the theory, and there was a lot in it, but I was totally against it.

He sent Ashdown to see me and ask me why. I told Ashdown, '(a) You're a Lib, so I'd never join forces with you and (b) We don't need you. We've got a massive majority and I don't like Big Tents.'

Callaghan had flirted with the Liberals, but that was a different situation as he had had effectively no majority. This time it was unnecessary. Even if it had been, I would still have been against the idea. We're Labour. They're Liberal. That's it. Tony felt it was a tribal response.

'Yes, that's me,' I said. 'Old Labour.'

I'd had enough problems getting to grips with so-called New Labour to have to worry about absorbing Liberal Democrats. We had done well enough on our own, changing and developing as society changed, and had enough to be getting on with.

Anyway, Ashdown was never given a job. I'm not sure if it was my reaction and threat of resigning that brought it to a halt, or because others had said much the same thing. Anyway, it was a bloody stupid idea.

My department was enormous, but it included many areas I'd always deeply cared about. Now was the chance to bring about some of the changes I'd longed for during the years in opposition and had spelt out in my policy documents. I gave them to the department to implement, which they did.

For instance, those flags of convenience. They had been one of the many maritime issues I'd campaigned against, but got nowhere. Now, with Gordon and Tony's backing, we were able in 1998 to start changing the system. New legislation allowed owners to pay tax on the tonnage of their ships rather than their profits so there became no need for them to register their ships in dodgy foreign countries and obscure islands to avoid tax.

It had a dramatic effect on the Red Ensign which started to fly again, all over the globe, including later on the new *Queen Mary 2*. More than sixty companies and at least seven hundred ships began sailing under the British flag. The total registered tonnage went up from 2.8 million tonnes in 1997, before we made the change, to 12 million by 2003. It also meant, of course, that millions more were being raised in tax to help Britain. The transfer of my old Cunard company to the UK with its new *Queens* brought pride back to the British fleet, along with my announcement of an Annual Day for the merchant navy, to be held on 3 September each year, with the Red Ensign flying over No. 10. Great.

There were lots of road-building schemes and plans left over from the Tories, many of which I scrapped, but I did give the go-ahead to one or two. I brought in the legislation to establish congestion charges in cities and priority routes for buses. Both were very controversial. Drivers loathed the bus lanes, which slowed them down, but proved to be successful.

My designation of part of the M4 between Heathrow

220

and Hammersmith flyover for buses and taxis proved to be particularly unpopular. Some motorists hated it. Terry Wogan certainly made his views known on his morning radio programme. However, the journey time did become quicker on that stretch of road and there were fewer accidents.

I was trying all the time for an integrated transport system, on the lines of the pamphlets I'd worked on in opposition, aiming to balance the needs of all forms of transport. I hoped eventually to reduce our dependency on cars and increase public-transport use.

I did one big favour for Gordon in negotiating the sale of the National Air Traffic Services – the air-traffic-control people, who guide the planes in and out of our airports. It had not been in our manifesto, so it was a dodgy subject for us. It was among the Tories' public expenditure plans, which we said we'd adopt. A lot of people were against it, but Gordon needed the money. He was determined to stick to the Tory spending plans and revenue-raising proposals, like the sale of the NATS.

It was tricky as various rebels on our back benches opposed it. The Treasury naturally wanted to raise as much as possible, but I negotiated a compromise, selling 42 per cent to a consortium of airlines for £800 million. I gave five per cent to the air-traffic-control staff. BAA, the new operator, got four per cent and we, the Government, kept the largest share, 49 per cent. I didn't see it as an ideological sell-out. I saw it as the best financial deal for the taxpayer, which raised money to meet the investment needed to modernise air-traffic control. Again, it's been very successful.

*

I suppose the most important thing in our first term that I played a part in was negotiating the Kyoto agreement.

In our 1997 manifesto we had promised to create a 'green office' in every Whitehall department, but there wasn't a lot of interest in it at the time, or much understanding. I knew a bit more than most because of my years shadowing the Environment minister.

The UK was taking a leading role because it was our turn in a few weeks to have the presidency of the EU. Tony sent me, as DPM, to lead the UK delegation which, in practice as the talks progressed, meant fronting for Europe. Tony told Al Gore, the US vice president, that he was sending me as a skilled trade-union negotiator. 'So if anyone can do it, John can.' That's what Al himself told me later on, in one of our many meetings.

The object of the Kyoto conference, held in Japan in December 1997, was to try to get a promise from the leading industrial countries that they would stabilise their carbon emissions and set a framework for future reductions.

President Clinton, despite his friendship with Tony, had made it clear that the USA would not cut their emissions, but would not increase them. On the way to Japan, I dropped off in Washington and had a private meeting with Al Gore. I found him very receptive. He made it clear to me that the US position was negotiable.

There had been months of discussions and meetings between the different countries before we eventually arrived in Kyoto. Angela Merkel, now Chancellor of Germany, was with the German delegation as their Environment minister. On the whole the rich countries didn't want any reduction, or only a minimal one. The newly developing countries weren't keen either, as they felt it would hold back their industrial and economic progress.

I remember going on *Today* and John Humphrys saying I had no chance. The countries that mattered wanted nought per cent cuts, so how could we get any agreements? Which wasn't far off the truth.

In my meetings and arguments, I tried to use the fact of the USA's opposition to our advantage. By saying beforehand they would not sign up and not reduce, the USA had in effect, they thought, vetoed the whole process. If the US wasn't taking part, what was the point? That was what many countries thought.

I argued with the European, African and Asian countries that we must not let the USA dictate to us what *they* wanted to do. We shouldn't give in to their veto. We should go ahead with our talks, regardless of the Americans. When that began to have an effect, and the US saw we were going ahead anyway, they joined in the talks.

There were some brilliant civil servants – especially the British team led by Peter Unwin – and experts helping us, from all over the world, but with 176 countries to consider, all wanting different levels, it became incredibly complicated.

The main countries were each offering to accept different rates of reductions, but at the same time they were worried about what other countries would accept, saying they wouldn't do it if the others weren't doing the same, or if they were offering to accept less. It was like an enormous jigsaw puzzle, trying to fit all the different-shaped pieces together.

The European starting position was that we should cut

by 15 per cent, higher than anyone else. As the European presidency representative, I was arguing the European case as a whole. The other rich countries were offering contributions which ranged from expansion not cuts, zero expansion, to 15 per cent cuts.

It was very like the trade-union negotiations I had grown up with, only on a global scale, going from one group to another, doing bargains, trade-offs, threatening, pleading and banging a few heads together.

The Japanese Environment minister was nearly in tears, saying he couldn't possibly go above five per cent, which was the minimum figure we had agreed possible to make the conference work. He said he would have to resign, if Japan went over five per cent. It would be such a loss of face.

I got Tony to ring the Japanese prime minister, and he persuaded him to change their offer, pointing out that the conference was in his country, the first one in the world which would for ever be known as the Kyoto agreement, so surely he didn't want it to end in no agreement.

Behind the scenes, I persuaded Tony to ring up fifteen different prime ministers to lobby them to lean on their delegates.

We had a problem with one East European country's delegate who became obsessed with one word in the agreement. His prime minister rang Tony to ask him to lean on me to agree to it. I didn't know what the hell he was worried about, as the particular word he was bothered about didn't seem all that important. I went to see Michael Meacher, one of my team, who was doing a great job, and said, 'Look, whatever it is he's worried about, agree to it.'

'But the word he wants put in is not grammatical,' said Michael.

'Bugger the grammar,' I said. 'Just do it.'

At midnight on the final day, after countless meetings, some lasting most of the night, I thought we'd got an agreement. I packed up and went to have a shower – only to be called out because the talks had broken down once again.

I quickly dragged the Japanese and US negotiators back and all three of us sat down. I rang Al Gore, who agreed to instruct his representative to sign the agreement. The rest of the delegates were scattered around the building, shattered. The three of us could hardly keep our eyes open.

What it boiled down to in the end was that I got Japan to settle for a figure, as long as it was less than the USA's. The USA would agree a figure, as long as it was less than Europe's. We, the Europeans, were willing to accept a higher figure than either, as we were taking the high moral ground.

We then started this final round of hard bargaining. I knew we had to vacate the hall by nine the next morning, then that would be it, the conference would be over, for ever.

I think it was at about five o'clock that I finally got an agreement. The global average reduction in greenhouse gas emissions by the year 2012 would work out at five per cent.

I think I managed to swing it by staying more awake than anyone else. I just kept going, hour after hour, pummelling away, till they had to admit defeat. I went forty-eight hours without sleep. But it was well worth it.

Having got the agreement, we went into the chamber and the president of the conference, who was Argentinian, when he heard the three of us had reached an agreement, said, 'That's it,' and announced our decision. He didn't take a vote.

Later President Bush repudiated the USA's Kyoto agreement, arguing that it would harm America's economy, but today at last the Americans are coming to their senses. I think the US government does realise that global warming is a threat to us all. And, of course, Al Gore is still at the forefront of the battle to change American opinions and policies.

Just imagine the difference in world politics if Gore had become president. The irony is that some American environmental NGOs told him, and me, that they would support Gore in his fight for the White House. They were delighted with his achievement at Kyoto yet they ran away from backing him when the time came for his presidential bid. The narrow defeat in 2000 could fairly be laid at the door of those environmental NGOs who failed to give the support they had indicated.

You could say that five per cent was a small aim, which many countries never reached, and not enough has been done since, but the point was that it was the first world-wide attempt to do anything. Since then, it's been on the global political agenda. Without Kyoto, I am sure that global emissions would have gone up by 30 per cent, not down.

So, I consider Kyoto a big success. Looking back, you could call it diplomacy by exhaustion.

CHAPTER SEVENTEEN

1990s

Getting Stuffed

I'm not sure when it was that I first realised I was suffering from bulimia. I've never confessed it before. Out of shame, I suppose, or embarrassment or just because it's such a strange thing for someone like me to confess to. People normally associate it with young women – anorexic girls, models trying to keep their weight down, or women in stressful situations, like Princess Diana.

Then, of course, with my weight, people wouldn't suspect it. I never looked as if I was bulimic, unless you know some of the telltale signs. You could say I wasn't a very successful bulimic, in that my weight didn't really drop. But, of course, that wasn't the main reason it started.

It was at its worst during the years when we first came to power and I was running that very big department, but it had really begun some years earlier.

In my case, it was partly associated with stress. I was working too hard, putting in enormously long days, sixteen and eighteen hours of solid work. I've always done that, of course, since I first entered politics, as if trying to prove that I was up to the job. That time I broke down and cried, after the dinner with Crosland, was, I suppose, an early example of overdoing it, overdosing on work.

Once I got into the shadow cabinet, trying to produce all those pamphlets and documents, stuck in an office, hour after hour, the only break I ever took was to eat. That's all I did. Work, and then quickly eat something. It became my main pleasure, having access to my comfort food. So what I did was stuff my face with anything around, any old rubbish, burgers, chocolate, crisps, fish and chips, loads of it, till I felt sick – but at least I'd had the pleasure of stuffing my face and feeling really full. Then there would be a weird kind of pleasure in vomiting and feeling relieved.

I suppose other people might have taken to the bottle, but I didn't. Well, now and again, once or twice a year, when I was absolutely knackered, I did get out a bottle of vodka and place it on my desk. The office hated it when they saw that happening. They knew I'd go at it full pelt, as I always do with everything in life, and empty the bottle. But that was very rare. As I say, once or twice a year.

I think getting out that vodka bottle was a cry for help, a cry for sympathy, to let people see how I exhausted I was. It seemed to ease the stress, loosen the inhibitions, but I never liked doing it, or the after-effects. And, really, I didn't enjoy it. I don't like the taste of alcohol.

But food, I've always loved the taste of food. So, instead of the odd vodka, I'd just turn to some digestive biscuits, which meant a packet of them, scoffing the lot, then perhaps another packet. I could sup a whole tin of Carnation condensed milk, just for the taste, stupid things like that. Marks & Spencer trifles, I still love them, one of my favourites. I can eat them for ever. Whenever I go to Mr Chu's in Hull, my favourite Chinese restaurant in the whole world, great atmosphere, great people, I could eat my way through the entire menu.

But I was ashamed of this gorging, this greed, and pretended I wasn't doing it. At home, I would say, 'No thanks,' to Pauline when she offered seconds, but behind her back, I'd raid the kitchen or the fridge. Same at the office. I became a secret eater, hiding food and snacks, then trying to eat them when no one could see me.

When I was younger, at sea, my weight had been just over eleven stone, which was pretty normal for my height. I always say it's five ten but I think it's nearer five nine. I blame that accident in the car on the Humber Bridge when I broke my back and lost an inch. In my wedding photos, I look quite slim, still around eleven or perhaps twelve stone. I think thirteen stone is probably what I should be, for my build. I'm large-boned, and I was always quite muscular, especially in my boxing days.

My weight gradually crept up over the years, with more sitting around, less exercise, more binge-eating. The most I've been is sixteen and a half stone. I certainly didn't want to be any more than that.

I don't know how I learned about what bulimics do. I can't remember reading about it or being told by anyone. I just worked it out for myself. As I was getting all this pleasure stuffing food in, perhaps if I could get it out, I could carry on eating, do the same the next day. So I started deliberately sicking it up. I'd go to the toilet after guzzling, put a finger down my throat, and make it all come up. It was surprisingly easy.

I thought, of course, I was being clever, and no one would ever know, but Pauline realised in the end. The signs in the toilet gave it away, and all the missing food.

Pauline knew about bulimia, having read about it in women's magazines and followed Princess Diana's story. Apparently, when her marriage was under stress, she became a bulimic. Pauline warned me of the consequences, which I hadn't been aware of – how it can damage your kidneys. Also, the bile rises and affects your glands so you look all swollen-faced and swollen-necked. It's to do with the acids, causing inflammation, I think. I hadn't been aware of the effects, but I can look back now at old photos and work out what was causing me to have such a swollen face at certain times.

They soon found out in my office, just as Pauline had. You think you're keeping it a secret, but you're not.

Pauline persuaded me to seek medical help. I went to see the House of Commons doctor, who sent me to a consultant. My appointment was on 19 February 1991. I turned up and found his waiting room full of young women. I was the only man there. I felt a right twerp. Luckily none of them shopped me to the press. Perhaps they thought I was on a fact-finding mission, never for one moment thinking that a man of my age and build could be suffering from bulimia nervosa, but that's what the consultant said I had.

He asked me lots of questions, most of which I thought were daft – about my childhood, early sexual experiences, that sort of stuff, which I don't think had anything to do with it. I was just under pressure and seeking relief in eating too much, then sicking it up – that was all there was to it, as far as I was aware.

He explained all the side-effects and advised certain diets, which I did try to stick to, but not always with much success.

Around the same time, I found I had diabetes, which was another reason why I was feeling so tired. The medication was a great help and I felt better after that was sorted.

I was also driving Pauline mad by my snoring. I was found to suffer from sleep apnoea – a symptom of which is heavy snoring. That was connected with the overeating and bulimia.

I also had lots of tests for allergies. I discovered that when I was eating a lot of digestive biscuits I was more bad tempered than normal. They gave me tests in case I had any flour allergies. It looked as if I might, but the tests proved nothing. But cutting down on digestives seemed to help.

I haven't suffered from bulimia for more than a year now. I try to exercise in the gym for forty-five minutes every day. My weight, though, is still over fifteen stone – as I do love my food – but I try not to snack between meals and to eat at sensible times.

I'm sure it was to do with stress. I wasn't doing it all the time, and there would be gaps of weeks and months, but during those years when we first got into power, I let things get on top of me and took refuge in stuffing my face.

After I developed diabetes in 1990, I made it public, getting involved in a government initiative to make people more aware of the illness. Then in the 2001 election, I launched a mobile diabetic unit to tour rural areas to examine people's eyes and identify the early stage of diabetes cases. I have continued to keep in contact with the unit and launched a diabetic awareness NHS campaign with Alan Milburn, the then Health secretary. I heard that it led to capital investment in a nationwide NHS scheme to increase awareness of the illness.

Now I've come out about my bulimia, I hope I might do something to help the many young women – and others – who suffer from it. I'm aware of an NHS campaign on food disorders which will help to play a part in the public debate on anorexia and bulimia. I hope that it will encourage people to come out and discuss these matters and not suffer in silence.

CHAPTER EIGHTEEN

1997–2001

Acting as Prime Minister

As deputy prime minister, I naturally had to deputise for Tony when he was on holiday or otherwise unavailable. The first time I did Prime Minister's Questions I was terrified. But, then, even the most experienced and fluent PM has butterflies, as their memoirs usually reveal. It's so easy to be caught out and fall flat on your face because you really don't know what's coming.

The trick, of course, is to guess the questions that might come up and have suitable stock answers ready. It was hard for me to get briefed properly. Since taking office, I had been immersed every day and every minute in my own large department. I knew about its problems, but I wasn't quite up to scratch on what was happening in all the others. Tony tended to know, or was kept informed on, the main running problems in every department. Also, I hadn't been involved in all the meetings or policy decisions when they were outside my own field. New policies were continually being worked on that I didn't know anything about.

I had a tremendous team helping me from No. 10, led by Claire Sumner and Kath Rimmer, plus my own team led by Joan Hammell and Mick Halloran. Dennis Skinner, Rosie Winterton and Lord Bruce Grocott also helped. Their job was not just to guess the questions but think of answers.

All the same, I got floored completely by a question on a 'withholding tax'. I didn't know what it was, but I'd actually misheard the question. All I'd heard was the word 'tax', not the first bit, so I just guessed the rest. I damaged my ear diving many years ago, when I was working on that North Sea campaign, and my hearing had suddenly begun to get a bit weak. The Tories twigged this and would deliberately ask me questions in a low voice, short and quick. I'd have to ask them to speak up, or guess what had been said. That day, though, I decided it must be a question on council tax, so I replied about that. And got some stick when it was soon revealed I hadn't understood the question.

Perhaps the worst mockery I got was in April 1999: standing in for Tony at PMQ, I mispronounced 'Milosevic'.

I did my usual thing when I see a difficult word – pronounce the first bit and gabble the rest, hoping I'll get it right, or people won't notice. I got hammered for that, my single most humiliating experience in Parliament. From then on, I asked the office to write out phonetically any hard words. Like 'phonetically', that's another . . .

Prime Minister's Questions are like a circus for either party. If you appear to land a hit, your own back-benchers shout and cheer, as if you've scored a goal. The Tories always give the loudest support to their front benches, regardless of how well they're doing, but our side, if you're doing badly, just sits there, letting you slide deeper into the shit. They don't always get behind you. That made it harder going.

I also had to preside at cabinet meetings when Tony was not available. By chance, the very first one I had to take concerned the Dome, dreamed up by Michael Heseltine in the Major government, as a national celebration of the Millennium, situated at Greenwich; it was also seen as a way of regenerating a run-down area of the Thames. We either had to give it the final go-ahead or cancel it quickly and save millions, although scores of millions had already been spent on decontaminating the site.

I was for it, as I remembered how much I had enjoyed visiting the Festival of Britain in the early fifties on a trip with the Sea Scouts. It had had an uplifting effect on the whole of the country. Mandelson was for it because it had been his grandfather, Herbert Morrison, who had sponsored the Festival of Britain. Tony was for it as well, but he'd buggered off and left me to find out what the cabinet thought. He'd suddenly had to go to a House of

Commons church service. I asked him to pray for me as well, being left with the Dome as I was.

There was a lot of arguing as soon as Tony left the room. A few were dead against the Dome. I had to calm everyone down, then give each a chance to speak. Gordon as usual had three conditions, such as it mustn't cost much more public money than it had already. Clare Short was against it. Robin Cook was dismissive and superior.

I knew and they knew that Tony was for it, even though most were critical. I asked if anyone disagreed with the formula set out by Gordon. I said I would report their views when Tony returned. Don't forget, this was one of the first meetings of the cabinet since we'd taken over, so no one was wanting at this early stage to come out against the PM. And it worked. When Tony came back, he said, 'What happened?'

I said, 'Don't worry. It's settled.'

'Let's go,' he said. Me and Tony got on our hard hats and wellies, then went down to look at the site and announce our support.

It did cause a lot of controversy, especially when the editors of the national newspapers got stranded in their special train on the way to the opening ceremony. That pissed them off. And, of course, it cost a lot more than we ever expected and the function and format had to be changed. In the end, though, it's turned out a great success: the O_2 is an amazing arena. It's the biggest indoor venue in the world. It's making money and has revitalised the most polluted land in London and played a part in securing Britain's Olympic bid.

Also at the Greenwich site we developed a new concept

for the twenty-first century – the Millennium Village. It was built to the highest standards of construction and greater efficiency with energy saving and the necessary infrastructure and support to create a sustainable environment. Nine of these have been built in the United Kingdom with the same goals.

I also like to think that my £60,000-house idea has turned out well. That was one of the other ideas we had as a sort of Millennium concept, setting up something that would be vital in the future: eco-houses, done as cheaply as possible for first-time buyers but environmentally friendly.

I said to the building industry, 'Can you build us a house for sixty grand? A house that can be manufactured off site and then assembled?' None of them seemed interested. I realised then that they are in a oligopoly situation, all part of the same group, but I also understood, which is what they told me, that they'd been through so many booms and busts that they were suspicious of any government projects. Even when I told them I could get £300 million in government funds to help the off-site manufacturing, they were still not interested.

I found an Irish builder who said he could build a £60,000 house. We displayed it in Manchester at our Sustainability Conference in 2002 and Tony Blair went along and approved it. The building industry huffed and puffed, and finally agreed that it could be done – but not at that price if you included the cost of the land.

So I went to see Gordon. The Treasury was planning a subsidy of something like £100,000 per key worker house to help them get on the property ladder. I suggested we look at the idea in a different way. 'Why not keep any land we were thinking of selling off to create these key worker houses? We'll continue to own the land but let developers build on it, putting up sixty-K houses? If the final value is, say, a hundred and twenty thousand – sixty for the land and sixty for the house – the Government will end up with 50 per cent of the equity. But we've created some affordable housing. When the houses themselves are sold, we'll own half, but in due course, the owners can buy us out, once they have the money.' That, in simple terms, was how it would work.

The building trade was never totally sold on this idea, but they eventually did their bit. Today, some sixteen thousand of these houses have been built – and I hope more will in the future through English Partnerships. I was interested to see the other day that IKEA is now doing affordable houses, and giving priority to potential purchasers on low income. That's encouraging.

Whenever Tony was on holiday, in France, Tuscany, Barbados or wherever, enjoying a deserved rest, something awful seemed to happen. My watch seemed to be fated. The tsunami, the airports terror alert and the Tube bombing happened when Tony was away.

Perhaps the most tragic I got involved in was the Omagh bombing in August 1998. Tony had just arrived at his holiday home in France when the news came through that twenty-nine people had been killed by a bomb and two hundred injured.

I went off immediately to visit the scene of the devastation – and found I had a horrible political decision to take. The police and army suspected who the bombers were but they needed to do some phone-tapping – at once.

Many years earlier during the seamen's strike, I had known that phone-tapping was going on – and being done to us. It was common knowledge that all so-called trade-union militants were having their phones tapped by the secret services. I went to see Merlyn Rees, the home secretary, to protest.

'John, John,' he said, trying to calm me down, 'it only happens ten or twelve times a year and only when it's really vital, so don't worry about it.'

I suspected it was more like hundreds, but I couldn't prove it. I came away from that meeting telling myself that, if I was ever in such a position of power, I would never sanction phone-tapping.

But here it was, happening to me. And I had to decide in minutes. Tony was still away or not available and so was Mo Mowlam, secretary of state for Northern Ireland. The official document was stuck in front of me to allow the phones of suspects to be tapped. I was told it was the only way to catch the terrorists – and we had to act now. I read through every word, very slowly – and signed. It showed me that principles and practicalities are not always the same thing.

I went to the hospital to visit some of the injured survivors. In one of the wards, I came to this bed where a young lad who'd been caught in the explosion was lying. He was still unconscious. His mum and dad were there and they were telling me that their son's biggest passion in life was for Liverpool FC. At the mention of 'Liverpool' the lad opened his eyes and said, 'What's the score?'

He somehow managed to stay awake for a few minutes,

just long enough for me to promise that if and when he got out of this, I'd take him to a Liverpool game.

Months later when he came out of hospital, I wrote to Liverpool and told them the story. They said, 'No problem, we'll fix up some tickets for you.'

I went with the lad to the game and we met the whole team. That was when I discovered that Phil Thompson, the former Liverpool captain, was the son of one of my best friends when I was at sea, Owen Thompson. I'd never made the connection before, though I'd known that his son had been a keen player.

Robbie Fowler was the Omagh lad's favourite player and he met him as well – and Michael Owen and the others. All the players were brilliant with him and the lad was in tears of happiness.

When I think of Omagh today, I think of the horror, but I also remember a nice thing that came out of it.

As deputy prime minister, I was offered the use of Dorneywood as my country home. It was reported that Gordon didn't want it, which was true, but because of that the papers suggested I was getting above myself, taking the country home meant for the chancellor, as if I'd somehow worked a fiddle. But this wasn't the case. Over the years, lots and lots of different secretaries of state, of all departments, have used it. That's what it was meant for.

In London, I'd moved into Admiralty House, which meant that at long last I was out of the flat in Maritime House, owned by the NUS, which I'd shared with Dennis Skinner. Dennis himself had moved out a few years earlier. The NUS had had their assets sequestered when they were fined for a strike at Dover docks. That strike and the court cases went on for a long time but, meanwhile, Dennis had decided to move away from 'Thatcher's sequestor'.

I kept the flat on after I relocated to Admiralty House as DPM, because I would still need a London base if Labour were to lose power or if I were to stop being a minister. I continued to pay the controlled rent for Maritime House, which applied to all tenants in the block of forty flats, the amount being decided by the rent regulator.

There was plenty of precedent for this in law – keeping on such accommodation for an MP who has left ministerial office but who still needs to have a place in London. This was all done in full agreement with Jimmy Knapp and the NUS.

The situation changed a bit when the NUS and the National Union of Railwaymen joined in 1990 to form the RMT union, but Jimmy Knapp agreed I could stay on. At one time I tried to buy the place, as a sitting tenant. Jimmy Knapp had said yes and we had worked out a price, but then Bob Crow became general secretary in 2002 and stopped it. So I never owned the flat, despite what some papers alleged. I was always living there as a tenant, until 1997 when we got into government and I was offered the Admiralty House apartment.

Stories about me living it up at the taxpayer's expense became a tabloid myth, like owning two Jags, or being a lager lout. Once such stories get into the files or public consciousness, they follow you for years. I eventually gave up the flat in 2003 – there was such a lot of hassle and nonsense flying around about me renting it that it just became too much.

I did get into one spot of bother, which the tabloids loved. It turned out I hadn't been paying council tax on Admiralty House. Margaret Beckett and Geoff Hoon had had demands on their government apartments, but I'd never got one. I was fully aware I had to pay charges on Admiralty House – for gas and electricity etc. – and tax. I knew the apartment was a perk of the job and therefore I had to pay the appropriate tax as a 'benefit in kind'. A bit like the notional value that is attributed to a company car for tax purposes. My department made the necessary arrangements and I thought I was paying the appropriate amounts, deducted straight from my wages. The confusion within the department, in terms of the council tax, seems to have stemmed from a misunderstanding as to what would be regarded as my 'first' home. It was thought that Hull was my main residence, but as I was a minister it turned out that Admiralty House was deemed to be my primary home, as I had to stay in London to do my job.

In Hull, I'd always paid council tax, and on the union flat, but I honestly hadn't realised I hadn't been paying it on Admiralty House. So when I got the demand for unpaid council tax, the papers loved it. But it was all a mistake.

I used Dorneywood for department away-days, and the family loved it. Pauline especially enjoyed the gardens, the trees and flowers. My biggest pleasure was at Christmas when I invited my old mates from my seafaring days, from ships like the *Britannic*, to come for a party, or to stay. It was probably my happiest time in government, when I was most relaxed, in the company of people I felt completely at ease with.

CHAPTER NINETEEN

2001–05

Punch-ups

For the general-election campaign of May 2001, I was out as usual in my battle bus, canvassing up and down the country with my great team of Joan Hammell, my press secretary Beverley Priest and Sue Phillips. On 16 May I was due to speak at Rhyl in North Wales, just a few miles away from where I was born in Prestatyn.

The election campaign was going well and we were ahead in the polls – but, of course, you can never be too sure. Some unexpected incident can be blown up out of all proportion and knock everything off course.

A dramatic example was the fuel crisis of the previous year when what seemed to be a minor incident became a national crisis. Some lorry drivers, protesting about the tax on petrol and diesel, along with some farmers, began a blockade against certain oil refineries. The country panicked, thinking there was going to be no petrol, and massive queues built up all round the country. Tony's popularity took a right hammering.

It also ruined my party to celebrate thirty years of being an MP. I had arranged a celebration at Mr Chu's restaurant, in Hull, and Tony had agreed to be there as guest of honour. People were still queuing up for petrol, because of the crisis, and feelings were running high. The police heard that some protesters were going to organise a demonstration and would disrupt my party, aided by some idiots from the pro-fox-hunting barmy army. Tony's security people cancelled his visit. I was furious about that. Tony went back to Sedgefield, eating a bag of fish and chips, bought in Hull. I had to apologise to all the guests for his absence. The party went ahead, despite lorries blocking the route and protesters outside.

So I knew the Countryside Alliance hated my guts, and were looking out for another chance to disrupt things. During my battle-bus tour we had been keeping an eye on things, alerting the local police well ahead about where we were going and what we were planning to do.

What I didn't know, as I approached Rhyl, was that there had already been two incidents elsewhere that day, minor events that can turn nasty and attract the sort of headlines you don't want when you're trying to win an election. We had launched our manifesto in Birmingham and were spreading out to get our message across and connect with the electorate.

Tony was visiting a hospital in Birmingham when he was cornered by a woman protester, Sharron Storer. Her partner had cancer but he'd been unable to get a bed in a bone-marrow unit. She had a right go at Tony and he had to put up with her tirade, but he didn't know anything about the case. He just had to stand there, and take it, live on TV, while the nation watched. Perfect fodder for the Tories and the right-wing press who could then throw back at Tony his promises to 'rescue the NHS'.

Meanwhile Jack Straw, the home secretary, was up in Blackpool at the Police Federation annual conference. In his speech, he was coming on strong about law and order – and suddenly found himself being slow clapped by hundreds of police, again live on TV.

Poor old Tony. It was proving a bad day for him. Not that I knew any of this, as I prepared to arrive in Rhyl. I remember thinking, Hmm, there's a lot of press here, for what's just a routine visit. It was going to be the same sort of thing I'd been doing for weeks, rolling up in the battle bus, parking near the local hall or theatre, or whatever it was we'd hired, then going in and doing the show. I kept spotting a lot of stepladders, the sort photographers use when they know there's going to be a crush and perhaps a good photo opportunity.

The local police had warned us that some Welsh farmers would be waiting, plus some petrol strikers and hunting people. I'd recently described the hunting people as having 'contorted faces', which didn't make me very popular with them. I could see all the crowds as we got off the bus and I said to the police, 'This isn't safe.' For some reason, they decided to lead me into the crowds, through the middle of them, instead of keeping them all behind a railing and letting me walk down a cleared stretch. My own stewards protested, saying it was dangerous. But I set off, with two coppers in front of me, pushing their way through the crowds.

Suddenly, I felt a blow on my neck. Then it seemed that blood was flowing down the side of my face. I didn't know at that moment it was just an egg. It certainly didn't feel like one but, then, I would never have believed an egg crashing into you can feel so powerful. I was expecting jeers and boos from some of the crowd, and I was used to that, but not any sort of physical assault. It was the sudden shock of the attack that got me.

The 'blow' appeared to have been struck from some-where behind me. I instantly turned, trying to see where it had come from. I saw this big feller jeering at me – so I lashed out at him. I gave him a good punch with my left fist – which I suppose was one way of connect-ing with the electorate. Beverley and Joan were knocked over. I was going to give the big bloke a second punch when the stewards grabbed me and him and kept us apart.

In the hall, I realised it was an egg that had hit me. I found my suit, collar and tie were ruined, but luckily I had a spare set of clothes on the bus. I felt a bit shaken, and still furious, but I changed in the hall, determined to carry on as planned. I did our show, but then the police in their wisdom decided to lock us in the hall for two hours, supposedly for our own protection. After that I didn't have a very high opinion of the local North Wales police.

Or of some of the broadcast media. They were mostly all there, of course, filming it. I had noticed some satellite vans when I arrived, yet no one had access to the meeting. That was a surprise. With hindsight, I'm sure some of them must have suspected what was going to happen – or, more likely, had been tipped off. I know what protesters are like. I did it myself in my Ruskin days in anti-apartheid campaigns. You organise a protest and tip off the local media to be there, telling them they might see something interesting. I remember once, as a student, being asked to jump on the bonnet of the South African ambassador's car by a TV crew.

The egg-throwing might even have been a set-up. Some TV people colluding with the protesters, encouraging them to do something to get themselves on TV. I don't know. But I have my strong suspicions.

The main damage was done by Sky, obsessed by 'breaking news': in the first transmissions they put out they only showed me delivering the punch, not the bloke throwing the egg or attacking me. So it looked to the nation watching the event that I'd just lashed out, unprovoked, whereas in reality I had been reacting in self-defence. They showed this film over and over, for the rest of the day. Sky TV's Adam Boulton, egotistical as ever, was encouraging viewers to press some red button or ring in and say Prescott should resign. He obviously thought I should, the way he was going on about it. In a recent article, Boulton said he was convinced I should resign when he first saw the pictures.

Apparently people in offices and homes all over the country were talking about it, ringing their friends and saying, 'You must turn on the TV – Prescott's punched someone.'

Rosie Winterton was canvassing in Doncaster that day. A lady opened her door and said, 'Sorry, I can't stop and talk, I want to watch John Prescott smacking that bloke again.'

The BBC coverage came in later and they showed it in the right sequence. You can clearly see that this bloke had hit me with an egg, and it was only then that I lashed out, but by then most of the country had accepted I'd gone ape and thumped someone in the crowd.

I rang Alastair Campbell, and then Tony, to tell them what had happened, not knowing they were already aware of what was appearing on Sky.

Tony had come out of a TV show saying, 'Thank goodness today's over. Nothing more can happen.'

To which Alastair said: 'John's punched someone.'

'You mean someone's punched John,' replied Tony.

'No, it's John who's done the punching.'

'Did anyone see it?'

'Only the whole nation – it's going out on television.'

'That's all we need,' Tony groaned.

When I spoke to Tony I explained that it wasn't my fault, I hadn't started it, but he said I shouldn't have done it, even if I had been provoked. After all, I was the deputy prime minister.

'I might be,' I said, 'but I'm also an ordinary bloke, and an ordinary bloke would react as I did.'

'But if you're an ordinary bloke you cannot be deputy prime minister,' Tony said.

'Then take the job back if you want,' I replied.

'You'll be pressed to apologise, John,' said Tony.

'No way,' I replied. 'I'm not apologising. I've done nothing wrong.' And Tony didn't ask me to do it.

At this stage, No. 10 had only seen the first bit of film, which had gone out on Sky. Several of the No. 10 coterie were saying I should be sacked, or made to resign, not just apologise.

At Millbank, the election headquarters, they were all rushing around, going, 'Oh my God, Prescott's hit someone! He's really lost it this time – the *Daily Mail* will crucify him. He'll have to go.' All rubbish, of course. Joe Irvin, my chief of staff, was based at Millbank and insisted they wait till they had more information. But I admit I was a bit worried for a time, wondering where it would lead, what might happen to me and what damage it might do to the Party. Gordon Brown, though, was more sensible. He apparently said that they should wait for the full story to come out. The Sisters were demanding my resignation, but Charlie Falconer, then minister of state at the Cabinet Office with responsibility for the Dome, and Douglas Alexander, who was co-ordinating the election campaign, argued that it had been justifiable personal defence.

Eventually the story did emerge, of course – and then a surprising thing happened. Instead of all the papers calling for my resignation, they began to realise that the general public was supporting me. Instead of viewers ringing Sky and demanding I should resign, they were saying, 'Hurrah for Prescott, good on you, John, about time someone gave these violent protesters a taste of their own medicine.'

In the next few days I was getting messages and calls

from people in all walks of life, sending their support, ranging from Alex Ferguson in Manchester to Sean Connery in the Bahamas. I didn't speak to him personally, but he'd seen it on the Internet and got through to my office. I could hear the girls saying, 'It's James Bond, he's sending his support for John.' Helen Clark, the prime minister of New Zealand, who was also in an election campaign, asked me to come and 'give some punch' to her campaign.

One thing that did puzzle me at the time was why the egg running down my face felt warm, like blood. On reflection, I realised it must have been because the bloke had been holding the egg in his hand for a long time, waiting for me to show up.

It wasn't the first occasion in my political career that I had punched someone in a public place – but the previous time, for various reasons, had never made the papers.

In 1998, as DPM, I was invited to the Brit Awards being held at the Docklands Arena. I went with Pauline and some others, including Della Georgeson, then a civil servant, later my chief of staff. We had our own table. Cherie Blair was also there, but at another table. We were all enjoying it, listening to Fleetwood Mac, when suddenly this big guy in short trousers jumps on the table and shouts, 'Don't forget the dockers.' I didn't recognise him but apparently he was a pop star, in a group called Chumbawamba. He then emptied a big bucket of ice-cold water over us all. It was huge, more of a dustbin than an ordinary ice bucket. We were all drenched, including the women. They were screaming, bottles and glasses were flying across the table, and he's still shouting crap about the dockers. So I lashed out with my fist, into his ribs. I hit him so hard he fell off the table. I then stood up, about to press my foot on his throat, and give him a few choice words of advice for what he had done to the women, when I realised the photographers had arrived. So I just stood there, over him, not touching him, just glaring at him, then I sat down again. All the photographers got was my face, livid. They'd all missed me hitting the bloke, at the beginning of the incident, which was fortunate.

I don't think the bloke had pre-planned the stunt. He had just suddenly done it. If he'd planned it, he would probably have tipped off the press and they'd have got the beginning of it and my fist flying.

One of the Spice Girls, Geri I think it was, came over and apologised to us for his behaviour, saying how sorry she was.

Pauline wanted to leave, there and then, but I wanted to stick it out. Fleetwood Mac had continued playing, during all the commotion. When they finished, they must have been told, or have seen what had happened, for they took us into their dressing room and Pauline and I got our clothes dried.

The incident was in the papers the next day, with pictures of me looking furious, but they all said what the photos showed – that I'd managed to keep cool and not react. Little did they know.

I understand that by chance Tony was seeing the Queen and she must have read about the incident. 'I see Mr Prescott has been looking very angry today,' she said to Tony. What was pleasing was that the dockers rang up to say it was nothing to do with them and they did not agree with him.

I suppose in the end the egg incident did me more good than harm. The papers kept up the story for days, going over my time at sea when I'd been a boxer. They managed to dig up some bloke who said he'd taught me boxing in Rhyl, with a photo of me in his gym when I was a little lad, which was rubbish – it wasn't me: I'd left North Wales when I was four. But he probably got something for his photo. So he did well out of it too.

After throwing the punch, as I was walking to the hall, I remember wondering if it would make the papers at all, and if it did, I hoped the photo would show how big the bloke was and not portray me as a sixteen-stone bruiser. I hoped the headline would be something like 'Young Man Attacks Pensioner'.

Today it's probably the single incident most people associate with me – in all my ten years as deputy prime minister. Perhaps it might have helped us, in a small way, to win that 2001 election so decisively . . .

Even today, when I meet President Clinton, he always says to me, 'Who have you punched today, John?'

CHAPTER TWENTY

2001–05

Second Term
Negatives and Positives

After our general-election victory in June 2001, I flew again to Sedgefield to discuss Tony's reshuffle in which he was thinking of replacing Robin Cook as foreign secretary. I warned that it would not be easy or understood.

Tony kept his agreement with me, that I would establish a separate DPM office working with No. 10, moving to the main Admiralty House building in Whitehall – next to my apartment – when some construction work had been completed there. This would keep me more actively involved in cabinet meetings and able to help Tony both here and in Europe.

My large omnibus Department of the Environment, Transport and the Regions was going to be taken over by Jack Straw. That was the plan. At four o'clock, I would show him round. Then at the last moment Tony persuaded Robin Cook to give up being foreign secretary and become leader of the House. He was fed up with Cooky not supporting him enough, and wanted to be more involved in foreign affairs himself. So there were lots of last-minute changes to make.

Jack Straw was then given the Foreign Office, instead of my old department, which would be broken up. Margaret Beckett took over Environment and Rural Affairs. Stephen Byers was made minister for Transport, Local Government and the Regions.

At six o'clock, I learned of the break-up. I was appalled – there had been no discussion or agreement with me. I rang Tony to ask why. He said it was to do with the difficulties of the reshuffle and the fact that Michael Meacher had written a private report on how to break up my department, which I wasn't aware of. I think he was hoping he would get some of it. But he didn't get anything. So that taught him a lesson.

With my new department, the Office of the Deputy Prime Minister, I would be more involved in what was going on, chairing more cabinet meetings, acting as enforcer, if you like, when Tony wanted things done, leaving him to worry about the bigger picture, such as foreign affairs.

In the first term, for the initial twelve months or so, apart from cabinet meetings, we'd had regular meetings of what we called the Big Three – Tony, Gordon and me. But there were always tensions in the air between Gordon and Tony. Gordon would get in a sulk and say nothing, leaving all the talking to me so these meetings petered out.

In order to win the 1997 election, we all had to work together, forget any jealousies and rivalries, put aside the splits on policy between Left and Right, over CND, pro- and anti-Europe, and the other issues that had bedevilled us for so long and had made us unelectable.

We'd done that, won that first election, but now, in our second term, we were getting back to the old ways, with groups and coteries trying to see who could have most influence. I was often finding out from the press that there had been some new policy document, because no one had told me about it.

I believed it was vital that all important things should be discussed openly in cabinet, but it happened less and less. Tony did seem at times to treat the cabinet like a shadow cabinet, making his decisions with his chums on the sofa – which I admit sometimes included me. His theory was that if you told too many people there was more chance of leaks. I argued that you had to keep things transparent and inclusive, and take a chance on leaks.

I remember complaining to Robin Butler, the cabinet secretary, in the early days of our first government, saying, 'Didn't you tell Tony how a cabinet's run?' He said he had – but Tony had told him it wasn't his intention to run it that way.

So this 'sofa government' developed, with the cabinet becoming less and less involved. We all agreed that Gordon was our best strategist, and I handed over any responsibilities I'd had in that area to him, but now it was the Big Four who were tending to decide things among themselves – Blair, Brown, Campbell and Mandelson – in the back room, away from cabinet. I felt excluded now and again, and I did get upset when little groups were making policy decisions. I realised that I might have to say things publicly, speak out, leak things, in order to be heard, but it wasn't my style to rock the boat. That's why I wanted to be more on the inside, in the Cabinet Office, so that I'd know what was going on. Perhaps that's why some people opposed my role.

I railed against most of the No. 10 advisers, the Beautiful People who had arrived when we were in opposition. They used to ring up and say, 'Number Ten here,' and I would say, 'No, you're not, you're just Joe Bloggs. Tony's Number Ten.' Then I'd hang up. Some of them imagined they'd taken over the Government and were running everything.

When I started at Environment, Transport and the Regions, I gave orders that none of the No. 10 advisers were to be allowed in the building without my express permission. What they then tried to do was to creep in lower down, trying to influence junior civil servants. I wasn't having that either.

In June 2002, I got really annoyed when I read about some policy away-day held in a country house in Buckinghamshire organised by Mandelson, who was now back in government again after having resigned in 1998 over not declaring a loan he'd received to buy a house. Blair and Brown had attended but I hadn't. I was determined to have a real go at them this time, not just on my behalf but for generally ignoring the whole cabinet.

I waited for the full cabinet to assemble and then I laid into Tony. I'd mentioned it in a pre-cabinet meeting with him, but I wanted to raise it in a full cabinet as that's where such things should be discussed, not in little groups. I said I was reading stuff in the press about our policies before the cabinet knew about it.

'Don't believe everything you read in the press,' said Tony.

'I don't,' I said. 'But I do believe it if I read about things which are not then denied.'

I complained it was now typical of the way things were going. I reminded Tony that all strategy had to be discussed right here. We'd had six brilliant years in government, done so many good things, but here we were, splitting into groups again. We were lucky we didn't have all the problems previous Labour governments had had, and now here we were causing ourselves difficulties. We, not the Tories, would make ourselves fail.

I could see Tony was angry with me, but I was determined to keep going. Before anyone could interrupt or reply, I finished by saying, 'I've now got the Indonesian president coming to see me, so that's it.' And I walked out.

Later Alastair invited me and Pauline to his house for dinner, and listened to my grievances. Clearly Tony had asked him to keep me happy. He said he felt I'd declared war on Tony in the cabinet. I said that as deputy prime minister I needed to be properly involved in all decision-making and so did the cabinet.

On the whole, after that, things went well. I can't remember another occasion when I got upset because I hadn't been told in advance about something I considered important. I also started getting on much better with Gordon. I think he began to realise how much influence I had with Tony, so for the future good, he should co-operate more fully.

The firemen's strike, which was to test our resolve with the unions, began at the end of 2002. It shouldn't really have been my problem but Stephen Byers had resigned and I found myself back looking after Transport and Local Government within the DPM office. Traditionally, the firemen had come under the Home Office, with the police, but David Blunkett had cleverly separated them and Byers had accepted it.

First of all, the firefighters came out on strike for forty-eight hours, in November 2002, and then for eight days, the army stepping in with old-fashioned Green Goddess fire engines. There was a lot of public sympathy for them and it looked as if the strike might go on for weeks, if not months. Tony left it totally to me. Everyone in the cabinet was pleased it was me trying to sort it out, not them.

The firemen had not long had a new general secretary and they were determined to demand a 40 per cent pay increase – with no compromise. I said no chance, even though the TUC was backing them. We couldn't do it, because all the other unions would come out on strike and want the same. If local authorities wanted to pay them more money, that was up to them, but the Government wouldn't budge.

Their union leaders were coming out of the front door after our meetings, effing and blinding to the press and their supporters, denouncing me – but they were also coming in the back door where we got down quietly to working out a settlement without the public and press being aware.

From the beginning, while I made clear that 40 per cent was impossible, I promised I'd get a better deal for them.

I told them privately I wasn't going to worry about, or try to stop them having, second jobs. This had become a tradition among many firemen. Because of their shift work, many managed to fit in extra jobs on the side. I wasn't going to interfere with their hours and make it impossible, as some people wanted, but I did want them to reform some of their practices. The strikes went on a long time, firemen on the street with their burning braziers and a sympathetic public giving them money.

I got attacked personally by someone I considered one of my oldest friends, a *Britannic* steward I'd been at sea with. His son was a fireman, out on strike. His dad told me I was a 'fucking sell-out', letting down the workers when I was supposed to be a union man. I'd been all for the workers, he said, when I'd been at sea with him. I tried to explain the Government's position, that 40 per cent was unrealistic, but didn't get very far. It was sad. He hasn't spoken to me since.

Eventually it was settled. They got between 12 and 14 per cent over the next two or three years, and in return they promised to modernise.

That was the worst union problem we had, in the ten years of the Blair government. Remarkable when you remember all the strikes that damaged previous Labour governments.

*

One of the more long-term projects I got very involved with in our second term was China. Tony called me in one day and said he wanted me to work on our relations with the Chinese, as they were going to be a huge economic and political force in the future. We weren't thinking of trade at that time, as there still wasn't much coming out of China, but rather of establishing better cultural and educational understanding. I was made joint chairman of the China Task Force with Councillor Tang, representing Premier Wen Jiabao.

I visited China ten times in ten years and sent a dozen or so of our ministers, from various departments, and Chinese ministers were sent to Britain.

On one of my first trips, a cultural mission, I had to open a Henry Moore exhibition in the Imperial Palace in Beijing. I couldn't work out why the figures had no heads or arms, so I asked one of the art experts. He was shocked by my ignorance. But I tell you what, I never got a proper answer. Nobody has yet explained to me the point of all the holes.

Those early cultural exchanges were a big success, and began to grow. In fact we've recently seen one of the results – the Terracotta Army at the British Museum in 2007. That's due to the good cultural relations we've been building over several years.

We were also interested in exchanging information and expertise in health and science. We did a lot of joint work on Asian flu and in education, which led the University of Nottingham to set up their own campus in China.

As the years went on, and our contacts and friendship improved, I moved the main thrust of the Task Force into sustainable communities. With all the research work I'd done for Kyoto I knew that China, with its 1.3 billion population, was going to face enormous pollution problems. We had lots of meetings on carbon emissions, discussed what we could all do to reduce them, and came up with the idea of eco-cities. It was agreed we should each create special eco-areas, where all the new buildings would use minimal energy and cause minimal pollution. In Britain, we have had a history of urban innovations, with the garden cities in the nineteenth century, then the new towns in the twentieth.

In China, 15 million people a year emigrate from rural to urban areas and the authorities know they will need a thousand new cities to cope. China always gets hammered for the extent of its pollution, which, of course, in absolute terms is as big as the USA's, but you have to remember their population is five times greater. And they do care. They recognise the threat of climate change and are doing something about it.

In November 2005, Tony Blair and President Hu Jintao witnessed the signing of a major agreement between the UK and China to work together to create new sustainable cities. The British company involved was ARUP, working with the Shanghai Industrial Investment Corporation. They are to develop a new type of eco-city at Dongtan, a 650-hectare site, on Chongming island, the third largest island in China and not far from Shanghai. Eighty thousand people are expected to be living in Dongtan by 2020.

The China Task Force had been instructed to work out in more detail the concepts surrounding sustainable cities. We brought together the universities, industry and planning authorities and we produced a discussion paper called *Sustainable Cities*. This made the point that the Thames Gateway Development, incorporating the Millennium Village which has come out of the regeneration of the Dome site at Greenwich and was further advanced in terms of its aims of energy efficiency and being carbon-free, should be developed along with Dongtan. The intention being that the two areas would work together and be used as examples of how such eco-cities and towns can thrive.

I was absolutely delighted when this report was presented at the next summit held in China in January of 2008, between Gordon Brown and Premier Wen Jiabao. They endorsed the concept, and are taking it forward.

I got on well with all the Chinese people I met. Very easy to deal with. They stuck to their promises, after the handover of Hong Kong, and didn't let us down.

On one of my early visits I said I wanted to go and see the mother-in-law of my Chinese restaurant friends from Hull, Mr and Mrs Chu. They didn't want me to go there, as it was in a working-class area. They preferred us to look at palaces. But I managed to persuade them.

It was an interesting experience, driving through the tower-block estates, very like the ones we have in Britain, with graffiti and vandalism. We were in a motor cavalcade, with Chinese government flags flying. As we drove along, trying to find this woman's flat, curtains were twitching with people gaping out. She was pleasant, living in a nice little 'council' flat. Back in Hull, I was able to tell Jack and Jia-qi Chu, and the children, all about our visit.

I had a bit of a drama when I went to Beijing to meet the prime minister. All my baggage got lost. I had no suit, tie or shirt and had to meet him first thing in the morning. At two a.m., the officials got a shop to open and they fitted me with new clothes. I still wear my Beijing suit.

The Chinese do have a sense of humour, despite what some people think, and it's very like our own. It's just that they hold back because they are more formal, traditional people, who believe in respect.

When I met a delegation of them, just after my punch-up had been in the papers, I knew they would be aware of it. Their London embassy briefs them on everything going on in our country. But during the day of meetings, meals and drinks not a word was said about the incident. Then, very late in the evening, one of their officials, who was a friend of mine – he had been at Kyoto as Environment minister – asked me if it was true I'd hit the guy. They had been desperate to know, but nobody had been willing to mention it. They are just as nosy as we are. And they all had a good laugh when I filled them in about it.

In Britain, the papers were still having a go at me, the usual Two Jags thing, plus my so-called vast empire. I knew they were on the lookout for any minor incident they could build up and use to hammer me.

I have a theory that one of the reasons I used to be attacked so much, ridiculed and sneered at, was because they could.

I look back to that time early in Tony's leadership when he went off to Australia to address the Rupert Murdoch editors. From then on, they mainly kept in with him, and he did with them, having tea all the time in Downing Street with any editor, not just from the Murdoch press but even creeps like Piers Morgan.

They also tended to keep off Gordon, assuming he might be prime minister one day. Better keep in with him, they thought, or we might regret it.

But they always need a public figure they can give a good kicking to, someone they don't have to worry about keeping in with. In this case, they managed to find two. They always felt free to hammer me – and Cherie.

If you look at the coverage over the years you'll see that Cherie always got far worse stick than Tony ever did. I think me and Cherie were on a par, with every little thing we did or said, or supposedly did or said, being turned against us.

When Tony first became PM, Cherie was very nervous about the public engagements she had to attend. When he and I had to be somewhere with our wives, at parties or functions, she would hold Pauline's hand for moral support. She was very worried at the 1997 Party Conference about being in the limelight, suddenly self-conscious about her dress sense and her hair, which she'd never fussed about before.

All that changed when she started using Carole Caplin. I didn't know who this woman was when I first saw her during the Party Conference. Then she started fluttering around No. 10 as if she owned the place. I assumed she must be a new secretary or adviser. But she gave Cherie much more confidence in her appearance, made her less nervous in public. I think Tony appreciated Carole's help, and was aware of Cherie's increased confidence, which had been more than he'd been able to give her. I also think he felt a little guilty that Cherie's career had been curtailed for the sake of his.

During the Bristol flats controversy, when it had come out that Cherie had used Carole's dodgy boyfriend to help buy them, Cherie was forced to apologise for misleading the public. I was at No. 10 the day she was going to have to make her statement. I happened to meet her in the corridor, having come out of some meeting where she'd had her arm twisted to make her apology.

As we talked, circus clowns suddenly appeared, followed by some little children, arriving for some charity event.

Anyway, Cherie said to me, 'What are these people doing?'

'They look like clowns to me,' I said.

'We have enough of them in there already,' said Cherie, pointing to the door she'd just come out of.

One of the things about her growing confidence in her own style was that she did make the odd sarky remark, which often rebounded on her. As it can do to us all.

At the same time, unfortunately, I felt she began to be very unkind to Sarah Brown. I was at the 2005 election victory celebration for Party workers, with Pauline. Gordon and Sarah were there as well, waiting for Tony and Cherie to arrive. It was a public event, in that the press and photographers were around. We were standing and chatting idly, the four of us, as we waited for Tony and Cherie to appear.

When they eventually got there, Cherie did the kissy-kissy bit, which I still don't like, after all these years. So, it was kissy-kissy to Pauline, to me and then to Gordon – but she totally ignored Sarah. I thought it was appalling behaviour, putting poor Sarah down in front of her husband, in front of us and all the other people who happened to be about.

I don't know what was going on that day, but I suppose it was all part of the Blair–Brown saga, and things were beginning to change. Their relationship had been slowly worsening as the end of our second term approached.

CHAPTER TWENTY-ONE

2001

Pauline's Baby Reappears

Pauline never forgot her first baby, the one born when she was just sixteen, before I had met her. She still felt guilty about what had happened, even forty-plus years after she'd been forced to let Paul be adopted. She still referred to him as Paul, the name she'd given him, though she didn't know, of course, if that was still his name or, indeed, anything else.

We didn't tell people about him, not even our own sons, Johnathan and David. They grew up knowing nothing about Paul's existence. Only a few people who were our friends at that time remembered what had happened back in 1955.

Then one day in 2000 I got a call from the leader of the Cheshire County Council in Chester. This was where we used to live, where Pauline was born and where we'd first met. He said some reporters had been sniffing around the birth-certificates department and might be trying to find out details about me and my wife. Apparently they'd been using various tricks to try and get hold of certificates – tricks such as using false names and the like. Did I have any idea what the man might be after? I knew at once.

I told Peter Mandelson about it. He was brilliant, and immediately very helpful, even though I'd recently called him a crab. I'd been running against him for the National Executive and someone happened to have a crab in a jar. I said, 'Oh, look, it's Peter.' Just a joke. He hadn't held it against me.

He gave me some good advice, which was to go to the Press Complaints Commission. They managed to put a stop to further investigations as invasion of privacy. At this stage, I think the press thought I'd fathered a baby before I met Pauline, or perhaps afterwards. Anyway, one of us had had a baby out of wedlock, which had been adopted. Someone in Chester must have been gossiping and some reporters had picked up the rumour and were checking birth certificates.

Around this time there appeared a series of adverts in the *Liverpool Echo* – the sort of thing I've seen a lot of over the years, before and since, with papers trying to dredge for any dirt about me. They said things like, 'Have you got any seafaring stories about John Prescott? If so ring this number.' It was pretty clear what sort of seafaring stories they were really after. It once happened during a Labour Party Conference, so in my speech I told everyone to ring the number in the paper – saying that if they all did it at once, they could block the lines.

Over the years, photographs of me have been doctored, to make out I'm a lager lout and a big boozer. One paper even airbrushed out a bottle of beer at a black-tie function and substituted champagne to make out I was a champagne socialist. I got an apology for that. Another paper went on for ages that I wore a wig, and offered money to anyone who could prove it. And you wonder why I hate the press.

Anyway, the PCC ban seemed to silence them and we heard nothing else about the search for Pauline's baby. I had begun to think they'd given up. Then one day, in September 2001, we were visiting Brenda Dean, who had been general secretary of SOGAT (Society of Graphical and Allied Trades) and is now a life peer, and her husband at their holiday home in Falmouth.

The phone rang, and it was for me. It was Joan Hammell, my chief of staff. As I picked up the receiver, Pauline was taking my photo. She dropped her camera when I told her what Joan was saying.

'They've found Paul,' I said. 'The holiday's over.'

We went back to Hull and discussed what we had to do. We decided that, before anything else happened, we must tell the boys.

They were, of course, grown-up. I think they'd heard

rumours of newspapers sniffing around, in search of some baby. So when I began to tell them, they assumed it was to do with me. 'No, it's your mum,' I said. I then told them the whole story, about what had happened long before they were born.

They were brilliant about it. Pauline had worried they might think badly of her, as you always have an idealised image of your mother. But they cuddled and reassured her and were wonderful.

Bit by bit Joan managed to find out what had happened. Someone from the *News of the World* had tracked Paul down and doorstepped him. It turned out he was still called Paul and had become an army officer. He was now based at Edinburgh Castle, in Scotland. I don't know how the reporter got past all the security, but they'd got to him.

Paul opens his door and the reporter says, 'Do you know who your mum is?' He is, of course, completely taken aback.

'The wife of the deputy prime minister!'

Paul shuts the door and has several glasses of brandy to steady himself. It took him some time to take in what had been said. It was a terrible, terrible thing to do to him. He had obviously had no idea who his birth mother was, yet here was a total stranger who seemed to know all about her.

I spoke to Geoff Hoon, who was then the Defence secretary and asked him for any details about Paul. He came back and said, 'He's really bright and clever.' He'd gone to Sandhurst and was now a lieutenant colonel who had won medals and awards. He had an OBE and an MBE. He could have been appointed one of the security people who'd been looking after me and Pauline since I'd become deputy prime minister.

I thought, Bloody hell, a colonel. I bet he's a Tory as well. Which turned out true. And a fox-hunting one – though not one of those people who have always hated me.

We learned that Rebekah Wade, who was then at the *News of the World*, was desperate for a photo of Paul with Pauline. They'd printed nothing yet as they wanted to stage the great reunion, and have a proper interview – otherwise they would publish what they managed to dig up on their own. After a lot of discussion, negotiated by my son David, we decided to agree. And so did Paul. In turn they agreed to wait till Pauline and Paul had met and got to know each other, before doing anything else.

There were phone calls and letters between Paul and Pauline and eventually a meeting was arranged. We decided not to have it in Edinburgh, where Paul was still stationed, as some of the press would probably find out. So it was arranged he would come to Hull.

I met him at Hull railway station, with Johnathan. We had coffee and a chat, just to break the ice, get to know each other a bit, then I took him home.

I led him into the room where Pauline was waiting – and left them together. Pauline had had a sherry or two to steady her nerves. She'd seen a photo of him, which he'd sent to her in the post, but this, of course, was their first meeting in the flesh since he was three. She was thrilled by how handsome he was, and so wonderful and nice.

They chatted for a while, got on really well, but she was waiting for the two questions she knew would come. She'd been dreading having to answer them.

271

The first: who was my father? She told him what she knew, which was very little. The second was harder. He knew he had been adopted at the age of three. But why had she done it then? Over the years, this had always puzzled and worried him, raising so many other questions in his mind. Was it because there was something wrong with him? Was he perhaps not good enough in some way? Apparently, this had always been at the back of his mind. I suppose it could explain why he had done so well in life, with his brilliant military career, determined to prove himself.

Me and Johnathan were walking round the garden all this time, while Pauline and Paul talked. Eventually, at a sign, we trooped in. I found he was a great bloke, lovely feller, no side, straightforward, not at all the posh high-up officer. I got on with him and liked him very much.

Over the next few months we got to know him, and his then girlfriend. He fitted into the family so well, which was a relief.

I worried that perhaps Johnathan and David might have been a bit nervous of this total stranger coming into our family life. They had always been Number One Son and Number Two Son, and had assumed these roles in the unspoken pecking order. Now it could look as if they were being demoted to Number Two and Number Three, with Paul at Number One, possibly becoming the apple of his mother's eye.

Pauline did and does love him dearly, but there was never any tension or rivalry. None of that happened. They all got on so well. As Pauline said to Paul, 'I don't know you as well as my other two boys, but I love you as much.'

Perhaps if they'd been younger, adolescents, when all this happened, it might have been more fraught.

After eighteen months or so, we told Rebekah Wade that she could have her story and photograph, as agreed. She had been ringing us regularly, to check progress. But it turned out she'd now gone to the *Sun*. That, apparently, led to some internal problems, nothing to do with us and I don't know the details. But I gather the *News of the World* maintained it was their story, as the investigation had been done while she was on their paper. In the end the *News of the World* ran it.

Anyway, it went well. The news was out. Paul did his bit, co-operated, and so did Pauline, and afterwards we were left alone.

It was a sad story, originally, but it had ended happily. Just as well, though, it had not come out earlier. Not just because the boys would have been younger, but society's attitudes to such things have totally changed since the 1950s. Then it was a terrible disgrace to have a child without being married. Now it's totally normal. We got some very moving letters from mothers who had gone through a similar experience.

As for who leaked the story in the first place, gossiped that Pauline had had a baby, I have my suspicions. It might have been my own mother, Phyllis. She's dead now. She was one of those who never approved of what had happened to Pauline. I have a feeling she might have blurted it out when meeting reporters over the years. Ironically, it's only recently I worked out that I'd been born just seven months after my parents had got married . . .

*

Paul's parents, the ones who had brought him up and whom he loved dearly, were still alive in 2001, at the time of the reunion. He had been thinking that one day he would try to find out about his birth mother, but he'd never got round to it. He'd told himself he wouldn't even think of it until his mother, Mary, had died.

Once the papers got on to the story, he didn't need to do his own investigation – at least, not into who his birth mother was.

Very recently, there has been a new development.

When Paul first met Pauline, he had asked her about his father. Pauline knew very little, but she had told him his name. She had never told anyone else, not even me. But that was all she knew, just his name, because there had been no communication from him during all those decades. He might be living anywhere, or he might be dead.

Paul got to work on the Internet, and Pauline managed to recall a few other details. She had wondered about him, of course, from time to time, and had tried to imagine what he might be doing, if he was still alive.

Paul, amazingly, managed to track him down. At least, he came up with the name and address of a man who seemed to fit all the details. It turned out he lived in America, not far from where we have some friends. Paul decided to go and visit them and have a holiday. One day he hired a car and drove to the address he'd found. In the garden a man was doing his lawn. I wonder if that's my dad, thought Paul.

He let down one of his tyres, then drove round the block again and stopped his car outside the bungalow where the man was still mowing his lawn. Paul got out of his car, looked at his flat tyre, then struggled to get out the spare wheel. The man looked over his hedge and said, 'Can I help you?' Out he came and together they got the spare wheel fixed.

Naturally, by this time, they were chatting away to each other.

'Are you English?' he said to Paul, which, of course, is pretty obvious, Paul being an officer and a gentleman. 'What a coincidence,' said the man. 'I used to be stationed near Chester when I was in the forces. And I knew this lovely girl called Pauline.'

I know, it sounds like a corny soap, but he did say it. So they chatted about Chester and then moved on to music, which Paul likes very much, both classical and popular.

Paul asked, before he left, if he could take a photo of the man – just as a keepsake, for his holiday album, a memento of someone who had helped him. The man agreed and stood dutifully against a wall. Finally, they shook hands and Paul drove away.

But back at our friends' house, Paul discovered he'd had no film in his camera. He was going back to England the next day, his holiday over. He wanted to study it for family resemblances, and show it to Pauline. Not that she would have recognised him.

Paul returned to the man's house and apologised for his stupidity. He persuaded the man to pose again, though by now the man was beginning to think it was a bit strange, this complete stranger being so keen to take his photograph.

On his return to England, Paul showed the photo to Pauline and they could see a likeness. They discussed what to do next. Should Paul come clean and tell the man the truth or not? It would be unfair if it resulted in the media getting on to the story and upsetting his life.

Anyway, after several months, Paul decided to write to him – revealing that he was his son. The man phoned up. He had kinda guessed something strange was going on that day, but he'd never suspected who Paul was. But once he'd got the letter, the strange conversation had made sense.

After lots of calls and letters, Paul decided to go and meet his father properly. The entire family turned out at the airport to meet him, and they gave him a great welcome. He could see the family resemblance right away. No need for a DNA test.

One of the things Paul wanted to know was his father's medical history. All through his life he'd been asked about any diseases in his family and, of course, he never knew. So now he was able to check it all out.

He's still friendly with his American family – and, of course, with us. He visited us at Dorneywood a few times, and Admiralty House, comes to our family gatherings and social occasions. He was at David's wedding in the House of Commons. He likes music and dancing, as Pauline does.

Pauline was amazed that one of his favourite tunes is 'Unchained Melody' – the original version, the one that was top of the pops around the time he was born. He couldn't, of course, have been aware of it, but Pauline was singing it all the time that year.

CHAPTER TWENTY-TWO

2001–05

Transport and Iraq

When Stephen Byers left Transport in May 2002, I found myself responsible for it again, while still DPM, working from the Cabinet Office. Over the years, I seem to have spent a lot of time with Transport, with several spells as shadow Transport minister, and had been responsible for lots of Transport papers.

I did get one thing wrong – or, at least, I got a bit carried away and made a rash prediction. When I first took over Transport in our first term in government, I made a speech in which I said that in five years' time we would have failed if there were not more people using public transport and making far fewer car journeys. I even added, 'I urge you to hold me to it.'

I like to think today that public transport is being better used, so the first part came true, but I didn't envisage the economy doing so well that families would want and be able to afford second and even third cars. We now have something like an additional seven million cars since 1997. Because of that, the number of car journeys has probably doubled, rather than fallen. I know from my own experience the effects of all this. My journey to Hull on the motorway now takes longer than it did ten years ago because of the volume of traffic. But most of my journeys are by rail, which is better and quicker.

I wasn't anti-car, as such, but my object during my years at Transport was to improve and encourage people to use public transport. I think now, looking back, that the changes I helped bring about, which were controversial at the time, are now seen as successes. The congestion charge, for example: I managed to push through the legislation that allowed local authorities to impose it and, of course, Ken Livingstone went ahead with it in London.

I even got written into the Act the theory of 'hypo-thecation' – a long word that, yes, I can pronounce, as I used it often enough – which clearly outlined the purpose for which the tax should be used. 'Hypothecation' means any income from a particular source must be earmarked for a specific purpose, not just put in the general tax pool. The congestion charge had to go into improving public transport. It also led to a 30 per cent drop in congestion in

Addressing my first union executive, in 1963

Right: 1970. Brand-new MP. Brand-new suit. On the Commons Terrace

Below: The new MP for Hull East meets the Queen. I was determined not to bow. But Her Majesty was too clever for me

Above: Riveted by the Common Market referendum discussion. I was PPS to Peter Shore

Left: With Mum in Luxembourg, at the European Parliament

Right: In London just after the announcement of the result for leader and deputy leader of the Party. I wonder if Pauline has just noticed Tony's suit and tie

Far right: Deputy leader and leader, planning for victory in Sedgefield, 1995. The beginning of 'sofa government'?

In opposition

Above: Talking to myself, apparently

Left: Brighton Conference, 1987. With Dennis Skinner

Below left: With Jim Callaghan in the '80s

Below: The shadow cabinet, 1991

How I see myself ...

Above left: Fit enough for a ten-mile charity swim (with an incentive to get to the end)

Above: Dedicated enough to swim in the Thames to demonstrate against the dumping of nuclear waste into the sea

Left: Sporty enough to play football against German MPs (we won 2–0). The roar of the crowd was deafening

And smart enough to get a snap of myself on Lady Thatcher's plinth in the Commons

How others see me ...

Making headlines

I know in the last year I let you down.. I want to say..

SORRY

Prezza quits .. and bids an emotional farewell

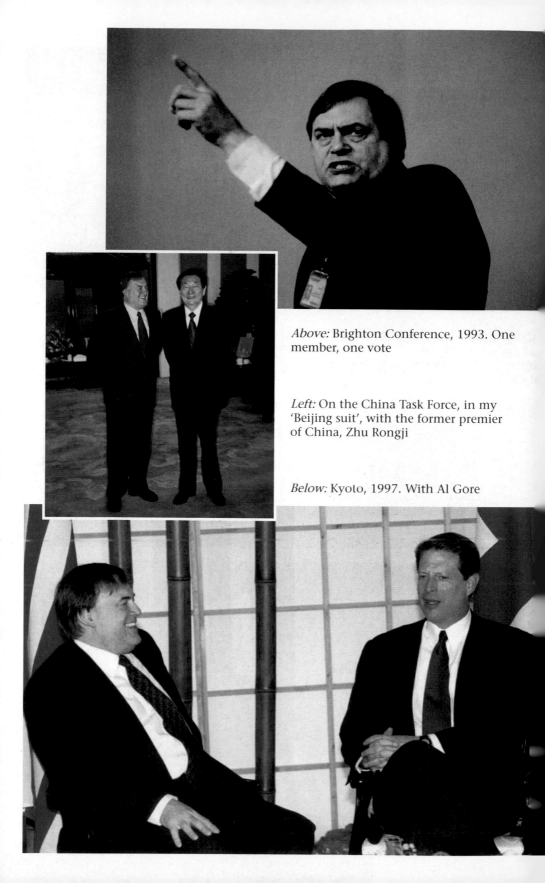

Above: Brighton Conference, 1993. One member, one vote

Left: On the China Task Force, in my 'Beijing suit', with the former premier of China, Zhu Rongji

Below: Kyoto, 1997. With Al Gore

Above: The joys of government

Right: Gordon and Tony enjoying a video of my greatest hits

Above: Cherie and Pauline, State Opening of Parliament, November 1998

Right: The last days of sofa government in Tony's Cabinet Office den

Above: Now where's Pauline gone? I told her not to wear that camouflage blouse in the garden

Right: At home in Hull

Above: Pauline and her three boys, Johnathan, David and Paul

Right: David, Pauline and Johnathan in Admiralty House on their way to the first State Opening of Parliament with me as deputy prime minister

London – for a while anyway – and five per cent more people on the buses.

The Treasury never likes hypothecation. They prefer to collect taxes and spend the money on the things they want. I had to secure Gordon's agreement for this, and got it. But Tony was worried. I got a message from him, ten minutes before I was to make a statement in the House, telling me not to promise hypothecation. I ignored the message. I pretended I hadn't got it, and went ahead. I think this was probably the first tax ever to have hypothecation built into it. I did it with speed cameras too: when they were introduced, I made it a principle that the money raised had to go back into police expenditure.

With the congestion-charge legislation, I was also trying to include in it that supermarket and company car parks would pay the levy, regardless of where they were. Supermarkets have massive car parks, many able to take up to two thousand cars, usually for free, unless they happen to be part of a council car park. This naturally encourages people to use their car, not buses, for shopping. Company car parks encourage more people to drive to work. But I failed on that. Tony got nobbled by the supermarket lobby. Their pressure meant I eventually had to drop it to secure the Bill.

When I took over the first time as minister, I asked for a list of all the current road-improvement plans, all the new motorway projects in the pipeline, and tried to trim them down, wanting the money to go into public transport, not private cars. But I did allow the M6 toll road, Britain's first motorway toll. The project was in trouble as the contract had been passed from bank to bank with none of them wanting to put up the necessary finance. It seemed to me a good way of speeding up traffic round Birmingham and easing congestion elsewhere. In my mind, I was also thinking this could be a trial run, to see if the public would support the idea of paying a toll on a road. Today, I believe most people consider it a success. In the future, we might have tolls on almost all our main roads in order to balance the unfair financial costs between public and private transport.

I was a bit disappointed when it came to buses. I wanted all public buses to be regulated by one local authority in each area. But it didn't happen. I should have pushed harder, but I settled for a compromise. We now have all these different companies, some gobbling up the others, who are making most of their money from public subsidies. I was persuaded that competition was best. I think now I should have persevered with my original aim. I should have accepted the advice of Rosie Winterton to be tougher.

The Channel Tunnel Rail Link project was in terrible trouble when I arrived. This was Michael Heseltine's big project but it was about to collapse financially. He had given the company twelve months to raise the money, but they had been unable to manage it. The City wasn't interested. The company came to see me and said they needed £1.5 billion from the Government (which we didn't have) in the next two months, or they would go bust.

'Fine,' I said to them. 'Just leave me the keys when you go.' But I knew it was vital for the country as a whole. It would regenerate a lot of run-down areas, such as Stratford East. The press were attacking us, saying it was stupid to spend £5 billion in total, just to save twenty minutes on the train from the Channel to London. I argued it was less about saving minutes than saving whole areas. It was a strategic decision for our transport infrastructure and links to Europe, encouraging greater use of the train than the plane.

I realised the only way to move forward was to take the Rail Link back somehow into public ownership, and therefore be in control. It was too late to put it out to tender and find a new company who might complete it – that could have taken as much as three years. So I kept the existing company but got new people to run it and new engineers. The company already had debts of £2 billion, which we realised we would have to take on. The Treasury said, 'Oh, no, we won't. We don't want any more public debts.' Gordon, as chancellor, had promised not to increase public debt at all.

The Treasury agreed on a system of bond financing, as recommended in my document *Moving Britain into Europe*, to get the project up and running again, but that still left the problem of the debts we were taking on. I said to the Treasury that they had to find a way round this – and they did. They discovered a Eurostat (Statistics Office of the EU) principle I'd never heard of – I'm sure they'd kept it pretty quiet: it said that if a debt had less than a 15 per cent chance of not being repaid – i.e. there was an 85 per cent chance that the money would come back – it didn't have to count as public-sector borrowing. I think I've got the figures right. But the point was, they eventually came up with a solution, after me badgering them. We were therefore able as a government to take on the debts. Today it can't be done in the same way. The Treasury has changed its own rules after EU intervention.

It meant the company was able to go ahead and they did, as everyone now knows. They finished the Channel Tunnel link at the end of 2007 – bang on time and on budget. It's now looked upon as a huge success and a triumph of engineering.

When I said that at the back of my mind I'd always been thinking of regeneration advantages, I didn't know, and nobody else did, that we were going to be awarded the 2012 Olympics. What a disaster it would have been if we'd never gone ahead and completed the improvement of that vital rail link to Europe.

There's a book being done about the whole project – probably out by the time you read this. The author, Nicholas Faith, has recently been to see me about it. I was very amused when he told me that two heroes emerged from the whole long saga – Heseltine and me. I'm not sure Heseltine will be quite so amused or pleased. He thinks it was all his doing, which it was till it collapsed and I inherited it.

In my view the Americans were determined to invade Iraq long before it happened. I'd had talks with friends in the Senate and Congress in 2002 and it was clear they were going to go in and get rid of Saddam Hussein, whatever happened. Both Republican and Democratic senators, including my old friend for twenty-five years, Senator Chris Dodd, saw it as unfinished business.

They were still, of course, in shock from 9/11. Shortly after that awful tragedy took place, after flights were back up and running, I was in the White House on a video-link, talking to Dick Cheney, the vice president. I asked him where he was and he said he was in a secure location. From what he said it sounded as if he was in some sort of cave or at least an underground bunker. Which I think, actually, he was.

'You must know now what it's like being Bin Laden,' I said to him. I don't think he found that very funny.

Even when it became clear that the US were determined to somehow get rid of Saddam, we were still going through the UN resolutions. The cabinet spent a long time discussing how we should proceed. At this stage, Clare Short was the only one who said she would resign if we went in with the Americans.

Personally I didn't like the way she was acting. She was always convinced that she was the moral soul of the Party, always in the right. But she was doing a good job at International Development and she was loved overseas. Her department was the one most graduates wanted to work in, according to a poll I saw, which was interesting. It showed how well the public liked her. But she was still a pain.

At that stage, Robin Cook didn't really come out fully against. He just tried to be superior. He was always careful, unemotional in his objections or criticisms. He made a big issue of not going into Iraq unless we had the UN mandate. And yet, the US used UK bases on what some members of the public saw as legally questionable grounds. I asked him why several times. But I never got a proper reply.

Eventually he did threaten to resign and Tony asked me to try to persuade him not to. I argued that Tony thought going into Iraq would help us and the Americans with a road map for Palestine.

In the end, he did resign, which was a great loss, just before it came to the final vote, on 18 March 2003. Clare was still threatening to resign. The massive anti-war protest march in London had been very worrying, but I felt we were all in this, so the cabinet should stick together. Apart from Clare and Robin, everyone understood and accepted what was happening. Although we all had worries, we tended to go along with the feeling that we were stuck with Bush. Tony couldn't walk away. We were blaming the French, for backing out of supporting an invasion, but we knew the Americans would go in, whatever happened, so the French didn't really matter.

Our relationship with the US has always been fund-amental. All British prime ministers have to decide whether we're with the US or not, and Tony had decided we were. Most of us agreed with that, deep down. During the run-up to the invasion, we all had our own reser-vations, and we were genuinely trying to delay an actual invasion, and go the UN route, if not stop it altogether, for as long as possible. But once it was inevitable we felt that was it.

My attitude was that Tony, having made up his mind, should be supported. I took one of the cabinet meetings on Iraq and got quite carried away, saying it was vital to stick together. We should do the brave thing, not be cowards.

After that massive march in London, and all the protests from so many people all over the country, Bush realised that Tony had put himself in danger of being kicked out for supporting him and gave him the opportunity to leave it to the Americans, saying he wouldn't hold it against him. He said it was more important to him personally to have Tony in office. But Tony declined the offer. Tony is not a fair-weather friend. He had decided to support Bush and would go through with it. Tony has always been like that. He doesn't let friends down, unless he really, really has to. That's why twice he gave Peter Mandelson his chance.

There were more than a hundred Labour rebels who voted against the Government on the vital vote but, with the Tories, we scraped through.

During Tony's big speech, he had been seen to whisper something to me. The *News of the World* hired a voice expert to try and work it out and it was assumed he had said to me something like, 'Don't you say anything . . . just shut up.' In fact all he'd said was one word: 'Smile.' I tend to glare and look grim when I know cameras are on me.

I read in Alastair's *Diaries* that Tony was expecting to resign if he'd lost that vote. Apparently the cabinet secretary, Sir Andrew Turnbull, was making plans, taking soundings, on what would happen in the event of Tony being forced to resign. It would mean me taking over as prime minister, so they had to prepare for that. But no one ever discussed it with me. And it never came into my mind. All I thought about was supporting Tony and our joint cabinet decisions.

Clare finally resigned in May. Once she and Robin had gone, the cabinet was totally united. In fact the vital decisions were taken while Clare and Robin were still with us – and carried unanimously. Some might have been unhappy at what we were getting ourselves into, but we felt it was the right thing and had to be done.

Once the invasion got going, the cabinet stayed united, even when things began to go wrong and at times it became very frightening.

I once took part in a video-link to the White House, talking to Bush himself. I was amazed by Bush's language. It was like cowboys and Indians, the goodies going in to fight the baddies, kicking ass, teaching them a lesson. It was pretty raw, rough, emotional, simplistic stuff, not the sort of language he ever used when addressing the American public.

When the government scientist Dr David Kelly – who was involved in the leak about the published dossier on Saddam's weapons of mass destruction, the so-called 'dodgy dossier' – committed suicide in July 2003, I was on summer watch, so I could have guessed something awful was going to happen. Tony was on his hols, though on the day in question I happened to be in Cyprus. I told Alastair Campbell, who was also on his holiday, I could be back at once. Geoff Hoon was also away, so I agreed I would go to Dr Kelly's funeral, to represent the Government.

There was a report in one of the papers, the *Independent*, that No. 10 was putting it around that Dr Kelly had been a Walter Mitty character. I was shocked they were doing this to a dead man and started an investigation. I rang one of Alastair's assistants. 'Who said that about Dr Kelly?'

She said she didn't know. I said, 'In that case find out. If nobody at Number Ten or in the Government said it, put out a statement emphatically denying it. And if we are denying it, I'll say the reporter got it wrong.'

Nothing happened. I listened to the news, and it wasn't mentioned, or on the next news. I rang the woman again – in fact I shouted at her. She was clearly becoming upset. I had to find out the truth. I suspected that such a remark could not have got into the papers without the knowledge of Alastair or Tony. I rang Tony on holiday, told him I was going to flush out the truth, and he said I was right to do so. However, Alastair's book makes it clear that Blair knew more than he told me about the incident.

I rang the No. 10 office again and gave them a deadline of eight the next morning to get to the bottom of it. That was when it was at last admitted that Tom Kelly, no relation, a man I liked and respected, who was one of the No. 10 spokesmen, had indeed been the source of the remark. He apologised publicly, as I demanded.

I'd been determined to get to the bottom of it because I felt I couldn't go to the funeral while it was still hanging in the air.

Alastair was most upset and wanted to write a personal letter to Mrs Kelly. He asked my advice. I said we didn't know how she was feeling and how she would react. It might make matters worse. I offered to take it with me and give it to her at the funeral – if I judged it was suitable. Which I did.

She turned out to be a wonderful woman. She kissed me at the funeral, said she was grateful to me for coming. Dr Kelly's death was tragic, but I don't think anyone was specifically to blame.

Looking back on the Iraq invasion, which has had tragic effects all round, I would still do the same again. I read all the documents and thought we had a reason for our actions, even though it would be a gamble. I believed the evidence we were given, about weapons of mass destruction, and so did Tony. The dossier was just a way of making it easier for the public to appreciate.

I believed, too, that the invasion might help the situation in the Middle East. If Blair backed Bush over Iraq, Bush might then lean on Israel to get a settlement in Palestine. So I felt we had to support the US and stay united. When things started to go wrong, we had no alternative but to stick by America.

So I went along with our decisions then and I'm not willing to change my view now. Some have done so, saying they were always against it. So why didn't more of them resign?

Tony was proved right in intervening in Sierra Leone and in Bosnia, and also on all the work he did in Northern Ireland, against all the odds. That's not necessarily so on Iraq, but I won't disassociate myself from what we did, even with the benefit of hindsight.

And when I left the cabinet, I vowed never to whine and moan or comment on what those in power are doing now. They have to get on with the situation, as they find it, as best as they can. All I can say is good luck to them.

CHAPTER TWENTY-THREE

2006

The Tracey
Aftermath

I had an affair with Tracey Temple, my diary secretary. I accept full responsibility. I've admitted it, apologised, and I won't go into any further personal details. I know the tabloids are still waiting to jump on me, so if I say anything else about what did or did not happen, it will start up all over again and cause more hurt for the people concerned, especially those I have hurt more than enough already, for which I'm deeply sorry.

I first heard that the *Daily Mirror* was on to it at the end of April 2006. I got a call at the airport when I was leaving for Barcelona with my press secretary, Alan Schofield. It was from political journalist Kevin Maguire, who said they were going to run a story about my affair: had I any comment? I said I had no comment to make. Which I know is the same thing as admitting it, as far as the press is concerned, but I couldn't believe they had any proof. Then he said they had Tracey's diary, and began reading out bits to me. I didn't recognise some of it, and I couldn't believe the *Mirror* would have it. I guessed they were just fishing for confirmation. I still said, 'No comment,' hung up and got on the plane.

On the plane, I told Alan. It so happened that he knew Tracey very well. She had rented a room in his flat at one time. Not as a couple, just as friends. She had a boyfriend she was always falling out with and for a time she left him and shared with Alan in central London.

Alan rang Tracey from the plane. He asked her if it was true, that the *Mirror* had a story and her diary. She admitted they had something, but it was nothing to do with her. She thought her old boyfriend must have given the diary to the paper.

She said stuff in the diary had been enhanced, just to make her boyfriend jealous, knowing he would probably look for it and find it one day. But, of course, she'd never thought it would become public.

When we landed in Barcelona, I collected my bags, then caught the next plane back to London. I went straight up to Hull. On the way, I confirmed to the *Mirror* that the story was true.

I arrived late in the evening. Pauline had just washed

her hair and was about to go to bed, not expecting me home till the next day. She heard me on the intercom, saw my car arriving and, of course, was very surprised, wondering what on earth had brought me back so early.

I came in, looking ashen, she says, and told her to go upstairs. She giggled for a moment, not knowing what was going on. We got up to the bedroom and I sat her down and said straight away, 'I've had an affair. It's in the papers in the morning.'

It was the most terrible thing I've had to tell her in my life, but I felt I had to do it quickly, and prepare her. She asked how long it had been going on. I said about eighteen months to two years. It took her a while to ask who it was. When I said it was Tracey, she was totally devastated.

Pauline and Tracey had gone to engagements together, had sat together at public events, like memorial services, when I had to be present. Pauline had looked upon her as a personal friend. She had regarded my driver Alan in much the same way. She'd got to know Tracey well – and liked her so much.

I said, 'We'll have to leave. This place is going to be bedlam in the morning with the press pack.' Pauline said she wasn't leaving. She'd done nothing wrong, so why should she? Anyway, we had painters coming in the morning, so she'd have to be here to let them in and look after them.

I said I'd probably have to resign. I'd brought shame on myself, on her and the family, the Government, the Party and everyone. A huge load of crap was now going to fall on my head, so it would be better all round if I resigned now.

The press had me in a corner. They'd got rid of David

Blunkett over allegations surrounding his relationship with Kimberly Quinn, and now were determined to get rid of me. Pauline said, 'No. It's the coward's way out. It's going to happen to you whether you resign now or not.' But I reckoned I'd cut the pain short by getting out immediately.

We discussed it for some time. Yes, there were heated words. She could hardly take it in and was stunned by what I had confessed, and so disappointed in me.

But still she would not leave. I said again that we should both go to Dorneywood, now, where there would be proper privacy and security. It would discourage the press from surrounding our own home. In the end, she told me to go. So off I went, alone.

Next morning it was hellish for Pauline. Hundreds of press and TV people were camped outside our house and the painters were on the scaffolding, wondering where all these people had come from, and what was going on.

She wouldn't speak to me for a while. Johnathan was in America but David came straight up from London to be with his mother. He acted as intermediary for a few days.

But I began to gather that Pauline and the boys thought I should carry on with my job, continue being deputy prime minister. It was important and it mattered so much to me. We were a united family. We'd all been in it together, helping my career, so why give it up for this? Anyway, I didn't resign.

Tony Blair was very supportive. He never for a moment suggested I should go – no one did – and encouraged me to stick it out. His main concern was for Pauline and the boys, what I had put them through. Gordon was equally supportive, worrying about Pauline, what I had done to her through my my own stupidity.

Some of the papers tried to suggest I'd been a security risk as it had happened with one of my own staff, and wanted the police or the security service to investigate, but this was pure mischief, trying to spin the story out. The authorities dismissed it and no investigation took place.

The boys, of course, were bitterly disappointed in me too. They'd had to take a bit of flak when it came out about their mother's child, but this was far, far worse. What I'd done to my name affected theirs as well. Everywhere they went, people were talking about it.

The shit did pour down and was far worse than I expected. The papers had a feeding frenzy, desperate for any women from anywhere to come forward and reveal something about me. They were offering fortunes, tens of thousands of pounds, for any woman with a story about me. And, of course, some came forward with unbelievable rubbish. Appalling allegations were trotted out in many cases from people I'd never even met.

One paper had a story that at Blackpool, during a Labour Party Conference, I'd taken this woman to a restaurant frequented by MPs and journalists and disappeared upstairs with her. I'd come down later with a smile on my face and the sheets on the bed had been ruffled. I rang the paper and said this was utter nonsense, where had they got it from? They said from a man who had been the manager. I said, 'What's his name and where is he?' They said he was now in Spain and they couldn't contact him. I said, 'OK, then, when was this supposed to have happened?'

They eventually gave a date and I was able to prove that on that day and at that time I was in the conference. I said, 'There must be a guesthouse register. See if you can find if I booked a room.' But, of course, they didn't even try. They were just so desperate to keep the story going that they were willing to accept any old rubbish almost anyone was telling them.

Lies and gossip kept pouring out, most of it absolutely trivial. If they couldn't find things I'd supposedly done, they went for things I'd supposedly said. I'm alleged to have said to an air stewardess, while accepting a pear from the trolley, 'That's a nice pair.' They worked that up into a big story. I had been on that flight, with Richard Branson, but I never spoke to any air stewardess like that.

Then I was supposed to have groped another woman in my department. The story then got changed and it was said it happened to her sister. It was all gossip, based on nothing. But the papers fell for it, carrying any allegations.

People said, 'Sue the papers who have reported these things as facts,' and I said, 'I'd have to mortgage my house to do that. I haven't got that sort of money.' So I complained to the Press Complaints Commission, who had helped me when the papers were trying to find out about Pauline's son Paul, but otherwise with whom I'd been having a running battle for years. The tabloids had always been after me, getting away with mistakes, but refusing to print proper apologies.

I think when a paper has been found to have got it wrong they should admit it and give as much space to the truth as they did to the original story. But, of course, they'll never do that. You're lucky to get one line, ages after it's all happened. They hire expensive lawyers to keep you at bay and can put it off for years.

I note in a recent book by journalist Nick Davies that he conducted a survey of the PCC's handling of complaints over ten years. It received 28,277 complaints from the public, but only 197 complaints were upheld for adjudication. That just shows you how futile it is complaining.

Anyway, after about a week, I went back home to Pauline, covered in guilt and shame, hoping to try to get on with our life and rebuild our relationship. But the story rumbled on.

The croquet incident, not long afterwards, was the one I couldn't understand. They made such a huge meal of it. All they had was a blurry photograph of me playing croquet with some people from my office on the lawn at Dorneywood – as if this was somehow a crime. Yet every paper picked it up, all the columnists and comedians, and it went on and on. The croquet set had been donated by a previous occupant – Kenneth Clarke.

I knew what point they were trying to make – the same one they've always been trying to make about me for thirty-odd years. They want to expose a working-class man for enjoying the good things in life. Living it up while others are doing the hard graft. That's their angle, their sneer. Pathetic. Afterwards, so I was told, sales of croquet sets went up 30 per cent. I also noticed in the papers that the British croquet champion was working class.

It was part of their campaign to prove that I'm living it up, running my two Jags, having lots of houses. They suggested, without quite saying it, that I was always milking the taxpayer.

Then they got more serious and political, so they imagined, and alleged that Tracey had stayed overnight at Dorneywood – in other words, that I'd been abusing my position. But it simply wasn't true. She was only there during the day, for an away-day, with about ten other people from my office, plus Pauline, the sort of away-day all government people have. No one stayed the night, except me and Pauline.

I knew it was all untrue, but what can you do about it? You deny it till you're blue in the face, but no one reports the denials. So the lies and allegations go on.

I was recently in touch with Bernard Donoughue – Lord Donoughue, who used to be an adviser to Harold Wilson and James Callaghan. It so happened that he's a trustee of Dorneywood, and knows what happens there, so when he was reading the stories in the papers about me playing croquet, he knew what the true position was.

He contacted the *Daily Mail* and other papers to tell them three things. First, that not a penny from the Government or the taxpayer is ever spent on Dorneywood – it's all financed and run by the Dorneywood private trust. Second, under the deeds, the house is for a minister of the Government for 'rest and relaxation'. That's its purpose, so there's nothing wrong with playing croquet, or cricket, or tennis or bagatelle. Third, he had gone through the security records for the period in question, and Dorneywood has a sophisticated security system. He looked at the lists of people who had visited, and those who had stayed – and there was no record of Tracey staying. And there would have been, if she had. Did the newspapers print any of these corrections? Did they hell.

Not even low down, in small print on page 27.

Then, of course, the final event in the saga was the TV drama documentary, about a year later, which started it all over again – this time adding a lot more fiction.

I never watched it. I refused. But afterwards people told me about it, so I heard about the things that were completely made up. I never set Tracey up in a flat. I never made her cook a meal for Tony and Gordon. She was once in Admiralty House, on official business, when Gordon did visit me for a private meeting – but not with Tony. She went out into Whitehall and bought us two pizzas. That's what junior civil servants often have to do, get food if ministers are working late. Nothing unusual in that. But, of course, they worked it up into a big scene, with her cooking this huge meal and serving it to the prime minister. The viewers wouldn't know it was pure fiction.

I told Pauline not to watch it – but she did. It was quite funny, I suppose. Two of her close Hull friends, a couple we have known for years, Frank and Janet Brown, came round to watch it with her, and she cooked up a meal for them. But it was still a humiliating experience for her. She was grateful to all her close friends, including another couple, Sally and Ernie Bamforth.

The papers tried to suggest I later got demoted, because of the Tracey affair. But that wasn't true either. It had been agreed a long time before that I'd give up my departmental positions and move into the Cabinet Office. When that happened, they saw it as a sign that I was being pushed out, which wasn't the case.

Life has now moved on. Pauline has forgiven me. Our relationship has got back to normal. She says the only way things have changed is when we're looking in shop windows. When she sees a handbag she fancies, she goes, 'Oh, no, not at that price.' I say, 'Go on, love, you buy it.' According to her, I would never have said that before. And it's probably true. Only now she goes through the whole shop, doesn't just buy one bag. That bit's a joke.

Throughout the whole thing, Pauline showed much more maturity than I did. I underestimated her good sense and wisdom. I owe my whole career to her, for supporting me through thick and thin, going out to work when I was a student, taking in lodgers, always believing in me when others didn't. I can't apologise to her enough for what I did. It did teach me a terrible lesson.

And it was all caused by my own stupidity. I let down Pauline, and the boys, put them through so much.

But I'm not going to say anything about Tracey. She was an adult. I was an adult. Yes, I know she later sold her story, thanks to Max Clifford. But I'm sure she had her share of grief as well.

I never blamed it on the life of an MP, being cut off from my wife and family all week, stuck in London on my own, getting into temptations. I know some MPs have used that excuse when they've been caught. I never did. It had nothing to do with it. I was just stupid. I let myself down.

I didn't deny it, once the story broke. I apologised to Pauline, and the boys, and gave a public statement admitting it, then asked the media to respect our privacy as we tried to rebuild our marriage.

I later made an apology at the next Labour Party Conference. Tony had spoken and then Gordon, making a few remarks about me, all nice ones. I was going to bring it in at the end of my speech, but Alastair Campbell said, 'No, do it right away, at the beginning, don't leave it to the end.' So I apologised to the Party, and the Government, for my personal behaviour. I said I'd let them all down.

I'll always feel guilty and ashamed. I made a terrible mistake, but let's leave it at that. I know I can never make it up to Pauline. She has been a rock and put up with a lot because of me. But she has always stood by me.

She says she can always take knocks from outside the family, people having a go at me. What she can never bear are knocks inside the family. For example, if I have arguments with the boys. That's what upsets her, not the outside world. She can take what the outside world says, and what they throw. Always has done.

She is sensible, mature and grown-up, more than I was shown to be.

CHAPTER TWENTY-FOUR

1997–2005

Blair and Brown

I'm pretty sure that the unvarnished truth will never be known about the exact relationship between Tony Blair and Gordon Brown. They'll no doubt give their own accounts and memories and I bet their versions will not match up. They will be based on their own interpretations of what happened, or what they think happened.

Writing a history of events, even those that took place as recently as 1994, is never easy. Thousands of words have already been written about the Granita restaurant agreement between Tony and Gordon, and there are many different interpretations. Whatever the truth and the detail, one thing should not be forgotten. That meeting was the foundation of one of the most successful partnerships in British politics. But it also sowed the seeds of much of the dissent that occurred after 2003.

Understandably, Tony and Gordon remembered those bits of Granita that suited them best. For Tony, the basis was Gordon's loyalty to him as leader. To Gordon, it was control of economic and much domestic policy and, crucially, that Tony would go at some point to allow him to take over. Tony's close friends say that a date was never talked about. That is probably true but Gordon clearly believed that Tony would resign during the second term. That was the cause of much of the friction.

But we shouldn't overplay it. A prime minister rowing with his chancellor is as newsworthy as 'dog bites man'. Attlee and Cripps; Wilson and Callaghan; Callaghan and Healey; Thatcher and Lawson; Major and Lamont – they all rowed. Some walked, some were sacked. The surprise isn't that Tony and Gordon had rows, but that they stayed together for so long. I was often cast in the role of conciliator.

In many ways, I was ideally suited to it. I am instinctively the trade unionist looking for agreement. But, as deputy leader, I was also the only person who owed his position to the Party and not to the prime minister. As deputy prime minister, I was obviously privy to the details of policy disagreements in a way that no other member of the cabinet was. On a personal level, I liked, respected and admired them both and, for the sake of the country, the

Government and the Party, wanted them to stick it out together. And, most importantly, I had no personal ambition to be prime minister.

Tony and Gordon did work together in the early years but tension was never far from the surface. This wasn't surprising: their personalities were so different. It is a surprise that they got on as well as they did. Gordon came from a traditional Scottish Labour, though middle-class, background and was firmly in the centre-left tradition. Tony was in no way traditional Labour and saw that as a strength. His politics were broadly social democratic and owed a lot to his Christian faith. He was in many ways more typical of a centre-left European Christian social democrat than a traditional British Labour politician.

The period until the 1997 election victory was relatively calm. I focused on the Party, in particular helping Tony to win the Clause Four vote. But in government, the tensions quickly became apparent. Tony wanted the UK to join the euro as soon as practicable. Gordon was more sceptical and wanted the right to make the decision himself. Hence the five tests were designed over which the Treasury alone would pass judgement.

Tony clearly didn't like handing the power to make such an important decision over to Gordon but he had little choice. This part of Granita – that Gordon would have control of economic policy – was unchallengeable and Tony had to give way.

Gordon jealously guarded his position as chancellor. For instance, he rarely took Tony fully into his confidence as he was preparing Budgets. But then again, he complained that Tony never consulted him on reshuffles.

Co-operation between them was vital during elections. Every year had some election – European, local government, devolved assemblies, mayors – each required a campaign team and Tony always wanted Gordon to lead them. Most of the time this worked well but tensions were always at their highest in the run-up to general elections. The June 2001 election was already fraught because the foot-and-mouth outbreak meant it was delayed. But Tony and Gordon argued about the basis of the campaign. Gordon wanted to fight on Labour's economic record; Tony wanted a much stronger emphasis on public-service reform. In the end, they compromised. Economic stability was prominent but the manifesto began with a significant section on public-service reform.

It was this commitment to public-service reform that saw most of the bitter arguments in the second term. Tony wanted to move fast on foundation hospitals and academies, bringing in private investment with less control from the Treasury, but Gordon was more cautious. I broadly sided with Gordon because I thought it important to take the Party with us. Relations were a bit fraught between them on these two issues. With the academies, I was worried about private business people in organisations having control of schools and admission policy.

Whatever Tony actually said at Granita, Gordon *believed* he had made a commitment to go in the middle of the second term. I can see the logic in him saying that. In 1994, ten years seemed a long way off. Their overwhelming joint desire was to win a second term with a viable majority. The thought of winning a third was beyond anyone's wildest dreams. So in 1994 I could have understood why Tony might think that the best way for Labour to stand a chance of a third term would be with Gordon as leader.

But as we made our way through the second term, a lot changed. It would be a mistake to underestimate the effect of 9/11 on the psychology of the Government or Tony Blair. The immediate aftermath – Afghanistan and the ultimatum to Saddam – all demanded leadership, and Tony felt strongly that he had a responsibility to lead Britain in the War on Terror. After the 2001 election, I had become deputy prime minister in No. 10 as I had discussed before the 1997 election. Particularly following 9/11, I found myself spending much more time in ensuring that agreements on policy were reached between departments, freeing up Tony to focus on the constant demands of foreign policy.

Tony loved the role he was required to play on the world stage, which must have made him reluctant to give up. But I also think he was of the opinion that he had wasted the first term and wanted the second to bring about fundamental changes in the delivery of public services. There was also the human factor. He was enjoying it and felt that, at a relatively young age, he still had much to contribute. In particular, he began to believe he could win an historic third term.

As time went on, Gordon realised that Tony wasn't going to go any time soon and became less willing to go along with him on issues where he disagreed, including student tuition top-up fees in 2004. I worked very hard to broker an agreement between them. But Gordon was not in a particularly co-operative mood and it was clear that we

could lose the vote on this in the Commons. A lot of
Gordon's allies opposed the proposal. I spent days seeing
sceptical Labour MPs to persuade them to support the
policy. At the very last minute Gordon, too, urged MPs to
vote in favour and we won with a majority of five.

During that second term, more and more of my time was
taken up acting as conciliator. When I consult my notes
from that period, I see there must have been hundreds of
phone calls, meetings, pre-summits, summits and dinners
on various Blair–Brown issues. We met in Downing Street,
at Chequers, Admiralty House, Dorneywood, Edinburgh,
Sedgefield, Scotch Corner, even a restaurant beside a
Scottish loch and once in Hull. They would row; they
would seek my support. I would try to get them to see the
other's point of view and eventually arrange a dinner.
Peace would be restored for a while and then something
else would flare up.

The tensions were real but they stemmed from a deep
and personal connection they had, with shared analysis
and political insights. I remember once being at a meeting
with them and Peter Mandelson. What struck me was
how those three behaved like robots in a science-fiction
movie in which they needed to download from each other.

I desperately wanted to keep them together for the sake
of the country and the Party. Neither wanted to take the
final step. Tony found Gordon frustrating, annoying,
bewildering and prickly, but also brilliant, innovative and
highly effective as chancellor. Gordon brooded about
Tony's breezy style, his refusal to consult him on reshuffles
and his sometimes cavalier approach to policy. But he also
respected his abilities as prime minister.

I had my disagreements with both. I never liked the way they courted the newspaper people – Rupert Murdoch, Paul Dacre and the like. Tabloid editors were not averse to stirring things between them. The *Sun*'s editor would repeat to Tony something Gordon had said, or vice versa, and they would both come to me with complaints, based on editorial chit chat.

Nor did I like the way both men sometimes treated the cabinet and cabinet committees. But all three of us shared an important view of history: every Labour government in the past had been brought down by division and bickering at the top. I saw my job as ensuring that, infuriating as each might find the other, they understood it was in the interests of the country, the Government and the Party for them to stick together.

I had so many discussions with Gordon in which the same subject came up: when exactly is Tony going? Which, of course, he was saying to Tony too. Probably just as bluntly. And getting nowhere.

But as we got nearer the possible time for an official announcement, things always seemed to come up to make Tony delay. It was vital to win the next election, then he would announce it. Gordon would complain, refuse to co-operate. Tony would give Gordon charge of our election strategy, on the understanding that he would keep supporting him till after the election. Then, after it, he'd promise to go. Only he didn't.

I had been through all this enough times in my union life. A general secretary takes over, says it will just be for a certain time. Everyone says, 'Oh, good, that's agreed, then.' When the time comes, he can't do it. Events have happened that he has to see out, that only he can deal with. Sometimes it's because, he announces, 'all the members want me here, so I'm being forced to stay on longer, for the good of the union'. It's always the same. Only the excuses change. Once people have power, they rarely want to hand it over. Churchill did it with Eden – told him about ten times he was going.

It used to make me laugh, when this happened in my union days, but it's not funny if it happens to you. It unsettles you as you see time ticking by, which was what happened to Gordon.

As well as giving Gordon power and position to ensure his support, Tony's other technique was to persuade him to back him on certain matters about which Gordon might have his own opinions – Europe, academies, foundation hospitals and future manifestos – and in return Tony would come out with the same old promise. He was definitely going in, er, six months, perhaps a year, certainly before the next election. When it never happened, Gordon was furious – and the whole cycle began again.

Each of them tried to get me on his side, complaining about the other. Tony would say that Gordon wasn't co-operating with him at all. Gordon would say he'd been cheated again.

On one occasion Gordon wouldn't let Tony see what was in his preparatory Budget proposals. He even banned the Treasury from telling him. That was totally against tradition. The prime minister is always told in advance. The cabinet knows most of it as well. I did feel sympathy for Tony on that occasion. I think Gordon was wrong in how he handled that.

But I also felt for Gordon every time Tony went back on his promise, or half-promise. Gordon would then withdraw co-operation and I'd have to talk to him. I'd say, 'The Party needs you, we want you both working together. You are the two most important engines of power. You have to work together or we are lost. The Party will collapse down the middle, as it did in the past.'

Tony was not helped by Cherie. I think she saw Gordon as causing trouble and making Tony unhappy, which, of course, she could witness at first hand. She probably had him moaning about Gordon all the time. Perhaps she personally didn't want Tony to go anyway – but as the Blair–Brown relationship got worse, she certainly didn't want Gordon to be the one to benefit.

Tony was also influenced by President Clinton. He used to talk about what had happened to Al Gore, who had been his vice president. It had been assumed he would beat Bush in the next presidential election – which, technically, he did, except he didn't and the Democrats were out. Clinton regretted not intervening enough. He told Tony that you had to see through all the things you wanted to do when you were in power. Don't expect or hope that your policies will be carried on after you've gone. Tony began to worry that if he went too early, his work would be undone. It became an issue of legacy.

When Gordon complained to me about Tony's behaviour, I used to say to him, 'What's the problem? When you take over, you can change what you don't like.'

Once, when he was even more furious than usual with

Tony, I said to him, 'If this is how you feel, that you've been misled once again, resign.' I think he thought about it, but it never came to that. He was aware of the possible consequences – and the damage to his own chances.

With Tony, when he was moaning on about Gordon's behaviour, I'd say, 'Sack him. Find a new chancellor, if that's how you really feel.'

But neither could take the final step. They were caught in their own trap. Tony knew that sacking Gordon would tear the Party apart and we would be back to the old days of splits. He also knew, despite their differences, that they were in this together. They had created New Labour. They had made Labour electable and successful. It had been a joint venture.

I also think Tony was scared of Gordon. He didn't want to take him on. Gordon is a very tough negotiator, doesn't let things drop, keeps at something till he forces you into his point of view. That's not Tony's style.

Gordon is a difficult character, but sometimes Tony exaggerated how difficult he had been, just to get sympathy.

Tony often thought I was on Gordon's side, but I always said I was only on the side of the Party. I saw my job as keeping the confidence of both men, never revealing to others what was really going on, least of all to the press, in order to keep the Party together.

But I have no doubt that Tony was most to blame. He broke his agreement with Gordon, not once but several times. However, in Tony's defence, most of his promises were ambiguous and on condition anyway.

I remember once discussing Tony with David Miliband.

He said that you always leave Tony convinced that you've convinced him, that he agrees with you. Meanwhile he has been convinced that he's convinced you. It was all to do with Tony's charm and manner. Gordon was always tough, brutal, to the point. Tony never was. He wanted to be liked. And he was very effective in making sure he was.

I would often go in to see Tony, annoyed about something he'd done, and after a while I would say, 'Christ, Tony, I came in here disagreeing with you – and now we're in agreement.' It was a good trick.

He was brilliant at persuading people, but I don't think he was Machiavellian. He wasn't deliberately conning you, scheming or knowingly lying. It was just his way. He hated to say, 'No, we can't do that,' or 'I'm ordering you to do this.' He preferred to talk you round slowly. He'd do it so well you'd find you were beginning to agree with him. Then, of course, he believed you'd come round to his point of view. You left feeling you'd got across your position. It was always amicable. No screaming and shouting.

If, now and again, I continued to oppose what he was saying, he would always calm me down, take my sleeve. 'Don't worry, John,' he'd say. 'If you're definitely against it, I won't do it.' Then he'd get people to come and see me, try to turn me round.

Sometimes he didn't tell the whole story, but we all do that sometimes. With the Dome, for example, I never knew he was in private discussions about it with Michael Heseltine, long after Heseltine had left office. I would have been furious about that. From Alastair's *Diaries*, I discovered that he was friendly with Alan Clark, the Tory MP, who came to Alastair's house and had meals. He was

311

even friendly with the awful Nicholas Soames. That would have well pissed me off. I had no truck ever with Tories. Especially socially.

But, of course, I was always far more upset about the rows between Tony and Gordon, worried about what they might do to the Party. 'You two are the architects of New Labour, you've made it happen,' I'd say to each of them. 'I've gone along with it all – despite my original misgivings. But now it's you two doing all the arguing, so just stop it. You don't own the Labour Party. You're part of it – just like me.'

Tony used to threaten that if the rows were made public, everyone would see that it was Gordon holding back reform. This annoyed Gordon: he thought he was all for reform – but on his own terms, in his own way. Me, I always sought to fashion reform according to Rodney Bickerstaffe's phrase which held true to me: 'traditional values in a modern setting'.

Tony did tend to be in a big hurry with his reforms, such as the city academies. I was never totally convinced about them, but I was willing to give them a chance. I wanted twelve or so to be set up, then we'd think about it, see how they went, but Tony wanted four hundred established, all at once. Gordon, like me, thought this was too many too quickly. That happened on other policies as well – which made Tony even more convinced that he should hang on to see his measures through.

Foundation hospitals were another example. Alan Milburn was all for them, wanting to take control of their finances away from the Treasury. Gordon was against this as, of course, it would remove power from his department.

And while the two sides argued, the Parliamentary Labour Party was often kept totally in the dark. That was what I really objected to.

The bad feeling between Tony and Gordon was worsened by Peter Mandelson. He would stir things up, or complain that any good things he was doing were not being recognised enough. Gordon never trusted Mandelson after he had deserted him for Tony in the leadership election.

I suppose you could describe what was going on during those years as creative tension. It always happens at the top in political parties, or anywhere else. It's not necessarily a bad thing. But the longer it went on with Tony and Gordon, the more it polarised the Party. Everyone got to know that two of the Big Beasts – as Mandelson called them and me – were at loggerheads, so each attracted his own supporters, and those supporters would leak stories, spread rumours, reveal Tony's latest alleged lies or Gordon's lack of co-operation to the media.

I kept secret what I knew and witnessed. But I warned them, 'If it all ends in tears, and the Party is affected, I will not keep quiet.' And I would make it clear who I felt was most at fault – that Tony had betrayed Gordon. I often did tell Tony privately that I believed he had broken his word. But, of course, his defence was that Gordon had broken his promises on co-operation. Each believed the other was in the wrong.

When things got really bad, and they weren't talking to each other, I would try to arrange a private meeting, just for the three of us, no other ministers or staff, either at Dorneywood or at my Admiralty House apartment. It always took some arranging, as it was usually after a big row and they were still furious. I'd have to persuade them that the sensible thing to do was meet on neutral territory, unseen. Once there, I tried to calm them down. It was like trying to get a marriage back on track. I feared if I didn't, it might end in divorce.

The first time I managed to get them together was at Dorneywood, on 24 February 2002. I know the date because I got them to sign the visitors' book. On that occasion the meeting had actually come at their suggestion. They'd been arguing about academies and foundation hospitals and not speaking. Each asked independently if I could fix it, as neither wanted to be seen to make the first move.

The minute they arrived they were arguing about policy disagreements. Gordon was there first, sitting simmering, but as soon as Tony walked in, Gordon shouted at him. Tony shouted back and so it went on. Oh, the usual accusations – what the other had said or not said. Just like husbands and wives rowing.

In the middle of it, Tony turned to me and said, 'John, now you see what the problem is. I get assaulted by him all the time.'

The tragic thing was that neither could quite trust the word of the other, not the way it had been in the old days. The best I could do was not take sides and try to get them to work on going forward, not back.

In November 2003 they both arrived at Admiralty House for a secret peace and reconciliation meeting, after some scene, and they seemed fairly calm for once. As I was getting them seated, Gordon said his chair was too low and uncomfortable. I fetched a more upright one.

I said to Tony, 'Do you want another chair as well?'

'No, it's all right,' replied Tony. 'I'm used to Gordon looking down on me.'

It was at that meeting that Tony promised to go by the next election. That's definitely how I took it and how Gordon took it – as did all the Brownites because he must have told them afterwards. But Tony maintained later that he hadn't said it. As far as I'm concerned, he did. Tony reneged on his promise.

Throughout all this, the original relationship of teacher and pupil was still there, even though Tony had been PM for so many years. That was how Gordon saw it. He considered he was basically the senior person, the cleverer one. And Tony went along with that. He bowed to Gordon's superior strategic powers, but he knew he himself was better on presentation and because of that was more fitted to being PM than Gordon. Gordon's behaviour had shown him that. Tony had the feel of the electorate. Gordon was the organiser.

As PM, Tony became surrounded by people who wanted him to continue, who told him how good he was. Some tried to talk up possible heirs apparent other than Gordon, just to annoy Gordon. I suspect Tony went along with some of this. Alan Milburn was being touted at one time, then even David Blunkett, Charles Clarke and John Reid. Tony would give them more powers – especially Milburn, who he put in charge of election strategy. Gordon then downed tools, refusing to do anything, until Tony was forced to change his plans and make Gordon totally in charge.

I don't think Tony ever really saw Milburn, or anyone

else, as an heir apparent. But it got Gordon worried. Tony always accepted that Gordon would be our next leader. But at the same time he wanted someone to stand up to Gordon, keep him in his place, make it easier for him – Tony – to be PM. He didn't want to leave the Party divided, which he knew would happen if he encouraged anyone other than Gordon to be the next leader.

Gordon was relentless. He kept up the pressure, battering Tony all the time. It did get very exhausting. Gordon would go on till I could hardly take any more. Tony was always more reasonable and would at least listen to your arguments and opinions.

Deep down, Gordon is a Labour man, much more so than Tony. He honestly wouldn't do anything that might damage the Party, or consider outside options that might be offered to him, so at the last moment, he always held back from resigning. Tony's ideology was based on faith, not Labour traditions. His beliefs had convinced him that he knew what he wanted to do and that what he wanted was right. Nothing to do with Labour policy or even focus groups. He knew what was right with faith as his guide. He didn't go on about God in any meeting, but you knew that his religion was vital to him.

Tony always said to me, 'You are the only one who can exercise any influence over Gordon.' Gordon said much the same thing to me about Tony. Each was hoping I would influence the other to his own point of view.

I like to think I got on OK with both of them. I hadn't at first with Gordon, but we became able to work together. He was grateful for my part in the air-traffic-control sale and other things. He always knew I was true Labour and could be trusted, but at the same time I'd always give an honest opinion.

I also made it clear to Gordon that if there was any attempt to force Tony out I would fully support Tony and if he or his people were involved I would not support him for leader. He knew then that that would be it – he wouldn't have a chance, if neither of us supported him for leader. The two of us could swing the Party against him. When I first said this to him, he saw the logic in it, and for a time he co-operated, for which Tony was grateful. Till it all started again.

In September 2004 Tony finally told us he was going to make it public that he would serve a third but not a fourth term. Gordon happened not to be there that day, having left for a Washington meeting, so he didn't know. We all assumed Tony would tell him himself – but he didn't. He just shrugged and said Gordon would find out, which was very petty. I rang Gordon after he'd landed, and he was furious, of course. Said it was typical, doing things behind his back.

From then on, it became less of a personality clash and more a matter of legacy versus inheritance.

Tony's legacy obsessed him: he wanted to get done the things he really believed in, for which he would be remembered and could be proud of. He wanted them in place, so they couldn't be altered. This obviously took time, so he couldn't be hurried into naming the final date.

Meanwhile Gordon became obsessed by his inheritance. Would he get lumbered with things he didn't approve of? Naturally he became obstructive. He didn't want to spend too much now, as less money would be available to him when he was prime minister.

Once we realised the tectonic plates were moving at long last, and this term would be Tony's final one, ministers started manoeuvring – Jack Straw was one – taking advantage of the situation to keep in with Gordon.

That didn't matter to me. I had already decided that when Tony went I would go as well, on the same day.

CHAPTER TWENTY-FIVE

2007

End of Government

Was it my own threat to resign that finally did it? By the time I got round to it, I was well and truly sick and tired of all this messing around, promising and then going back.

It was in April 2004 that Tony spoke to me and said he'd had enough, that he'd be gone by that June. This was more than a year before our third general election, in May 2005. He in effect reinforced what I believed he said to Gordon and me at Admiralty House the previous November.

He was exhausted, by politics and by the wear and tear on his family, who had taken a bit of a battering. That incident when his son Euan was found a little worse for wear in the street had affected him more than people realised. He managed to smile it off in the end, but when he first heard the news, which broke when Cherie was away, he was devastated. I thought he appeared near to tears.

I tried to cheer him up. As a joke, I bought him a silly fish thing called Harry Haddock: when you pressed a button, it lit up and said, 'Don't worry, be happy.' He hung it behind his desk. Leo, his youngest child, loved it. He would toddle into Tony's office when Tony was working, just to press it and see it light up. Tony has always had a very close family. I'm sure it helped keep him sane in the difficult times.

I believe that Tony saw he was facing a further cycle of elections, personal disagreements and animosity stoked by the 'friends of both'. Inevitably this must have had a depressing effect on him. But a number of Tony's supporters, advisers and cabinet members, led by John Reid, convinced Tony to fight the 2005 election and pledge to serve a full term if elected. Then came Alan Milburn's selection by Tony as election supremo. For many Brownites, this decision followed hot on the heels of Tony not appointing Gordon to the National Executive in 2003 – passions were inflamed and further fears and suspicions introduced about Tony's real intentions regarding the supposed third but not fourth term. However, an uneasy working relationship was re-established when Gordon replaced Alan Milburn to head up our election strategy.

We won the general election, though not with such a

large majority. It's been argued that Tony was hoping for a bigger majority that would give him the power and confidence he needed to sack Gordon, or at least split up the Treasury. I'd told him myself several times, when he was driving me mad, going on about Gordon, that if he felt as PM he should do it, then go ahead, but I don't think he ever seriously meant it or would have done it.

These stories came from his advisers, the beautiful wonks, and MP colleagues, who press for certain things to be done and get convinced when they happen that it's thanks to their clever arguments and advice. But if it doesn't happen, they would anonymously say the prime minister or the chancellor bottled it.

I noticed that Anthony Seldon's 2007 book on Blair, one of the many he's produced in recent years, relies heavily on people close to the prime minister, most of whom are quoted but not named. You have to be careful when relying on advisers for their version of events. They don't know everything. Nor did I, but I knew a great deal, having had to deal personally and privately with Gordon and Tony for so many years.

At the first PLP meeting following the 2005 election, Tony talked about Labour's fourth term being about preparing the economy for the future and continuing the programme of public sector reform. He also told the PLP that it was his intention that he would ensure a stable and orderly transition of the premiership.

In the PLP meeting the following May, in 2006, after the poor local election results, Tony came under intensive questioning about a date for when he was going to leave.

He once again reassured the PLP that there would be a stable and orderly transition and said that his successor as leader would have ample time to prepare for a fourth general election. But no actual timetable was given.

Then, in the cabinet reshuffle in May 2006, Hazel Blears replaced Ian McCartney as Chair of the Party. This was against Gordon's request to have Douglas Alexander appointed to the role, and was seen as a less than friendly move by the Brownites.

It was just such important issues and decisions, dealt with like this, that used to prey on Gordon's mind, creating doubts about Tony's plans. The varying levels of co-operation and agreement often became particularly acute around the time of major elections, when Tony would want a campaign set up to focus on specific issues.

Each time Tony would ask Gordon to spearhead the campaign and fully support what he saw as the key message. I would then say to Gordon that if he did this, I believed that Tony would give him a date. I would reassure him, 'Don't worry Gordon, he'll do it.' But then Tony would find a reason not to. So the next time I would say to Gordon, 'Do it this time and if Tony breaks it again I will announce it publicly that he broke the agreement.' Gordon would then come on board again. And so it would go on. But the time had at last come when it was clear something had to change.

I'm not saying that my threat to resign was what did the trick, as other things would have been happening and taken into account, but I always had it in my mind that this would be the best way to bring things to a head, if I had to.

My resignation as deputy prime minister wouldn't matter too much. Tony could appoint another DPM, or just do without one. But if I resigned as deputy leader it would trigger a Labour Party election, which would make people take sides. Tony and Gordon would probably want different people to take over from me. Factions could arise, trade-offs be made, splits would appear, all the stuff that had ruined the Party in the days of Wilson and Callaghan. We were not divided on anything serious. It wasn't policies causing the problems but personalities – Tony versus Gordon. So, if I resigned as deputy leader, it could be serious. Tony himself might find he was forced to stand for re-election.

It was 11 November 2005 when I first mentioned to some of the National Executive that I might resign to trigger an election, and I discussed a possible timetable that would be good for the Government and the Party and fair to both Tony and Gordon. I then continued my discussions on the timings with both of them.

There was growing pressure for Tony to make a statement at the 2006 Party Conference on the timetable for the change over. The formula I'd discussed with all parties recognised that Tony would want to be prime minister at both the G8 summit and the European Council concerning treaty changes. But the timeframe also recognised the importance of leaving sufficient time for someone to be elected and confirmed before the 2007 Conference. Tony did not want a public announcement before these important international negotiations as he believed it would undermine his authority. I fully agreed. However, it meant that a statement would not be made until after those dates, which fuelled suspicion that there could be further delays and no Conference announcement would happen.

I realised something had to be done so I decided in April 2006, after discussions with Peter Watt, the Labour Party general secretary, that I would hand to him my letter of resignation, which he would keep confidential. Although the Party Conference was still some months in the future, I also made it clear that if for one reason or another agreement wasn't arrived at and Tony did not make an announcement on the Tuesday at Conference, then on the Thursday I would announce my resignation in my speech. And I would make clear the circumstances surrounding it. I did not tell Tony or Gordon about the letter.

Tony then told me that he was quite prepared to announce the date of his leaving at the pre-conference NEC meeting in September and at the political cabinet (which discusses Party tactics rather than solely matters of government) which was to take place on the same day. I have no doubt in my mind that that was exactly the timetable arrived at by Tony, but a public announcement would not be made until that time.

Then, at the beginning of September 2006, we had what I dubbed the Corporals' Revolt, a whispering campaign by some Labour back-benchers, ministers and PPSs, saying they were sending round a petition calling for Tony to go. I was on holiday at the time and one of my close friends was asked if I would come in with it and, without consulting me, told them definitely not. I only learned of this after it happened. I never saw the petition, but I'm sure that it existed and played a part in making

Tony realise he had to name the date before he'd planned to. But, of course, he couldn't do it immediately, as it would seem he was bowing to back-bench pressure. He managed to ignore it for a bit, carry on as usual, and it fizzled away. Some Blairites in the press speculated that Gordon was behind it. I've seen no evidence for that, but I'm sure his supporters were and many MPs believed it.

Was he forced? In one sense, no, he wasn't. For a long time, he'd told us he was going, so it was a voluntary decision. All he hadn't done was give a date. So the claim made by the corporals and others that Tony was forced out is wrong as the formula had been agreed and was to be announced at the NEC and political cabinet later in September. However, it is true to say that he was forced to bring forward a statement that he was already intending to make. Tony chose to make his announcement at a visit to a school with Alan Johnson: 'The next Party Conference in a couple of weeks will be my last Party Conference as Party leader.' So sure, the Corporals' Revolt brought the announcement forward, but the timetable had already been agreed.

It's unusual for British prime ministers not to be forced out, by circumstances, mistakes, ill-health or their own colleagues conspiring against them. It was quite a triumph for Tony to have gone on his own terms. He didn't leave in tears or with a knife in his back.

At the Labour Party Conference in 2006 we both made it clear that we would not be addressing the delegates in 2007. On 10 May 2007 we officially resigned, triggering a leadership election. The NEC decided that the result of the leadership election would be announced on 24 June 2007 in Manchester. At last we had completed the stable and orderly transition of our Party. And my letter of resignation was never required.

The Blair–Brown political partnership was unprecedented and successful. Each in his own way contributed to the enormous successes of the Labour government. And while there are differences of emphasis and language, Gordon is largely continuing the policies of the previous ten years. For his part, Tony is still a relatively young man. I used to goad him about what he would do next. President of Europe; UN secretary general. In his role as UN Middle East envoy, he is doing an important job in trying to achieve a settlement between Israel and Palestine. But I think Tony still has his sights on a more permanent statesman role, such as EU President.

I honestly think he will be looked upon as a good prime minister. He has many achievements of which he can be proud, at home and abroad, especially in brokering stability and power-sharing in Northern Ireland. And as leader of the Labour Party, I think you'd have to say he was the most successful ever. Winning three successive general elections with large majorities was an astonishing achievement. Hard to see that happening again in the near future.

I don't think Tony was personally weakened by his relationship with Gordon and all their rows, as some people assume he was. It was time-consuming and depressing for the rest of us – and him – but it certainly didn't stop him doing the things he wanted to do.

The most the rest of us did was try to slow him down, for instance allowing only fourteen foundation hospitals at first, rather than the hundred or so that he wanted. That led to complaints from our MPs when they weren't getting one in their constituency, while the next one was.

My main worry was that we would end up with first- and second-class hospitals. My other worry was that once you get the private sector involved, they want more and more public money. It never stops.

In cabinet meetings we would all agree that we wanted a more efficient NHS. How do we do that? It needs more money. We'd agree on that as well. But then came the problem of how to do it. People like me and Gordon accepted it as probably the *only* way we could do it – but Tony actually believed it was the *better* way. Privately funded hospitals, like privately funded academies, was the way to go, so he believed.

He could have carried on, acting in the same old way, making promises and breaking them. In an ideal world, I suspect he would have preferred to remain in place for another year, till he had established his legacy. And I think Cherie would not have objected. She did enjoy being the first lady. But, more importantly, I think she disliked Gordon, so she probably felt the longer he suffered the better – and Tony's staying on might lessen his chances of a smooth takeover.

There was, of course, no vote for our new leader. Gordon got in unopposed, fully endorsed by the Party, and became prime minister. But there was an election for deputy leader. I voted for Alan Johnson. I wish he'd got it – and I think he would have done, if he'd run a stronger campaign. Harriet Harman got it and I certainly would never have voted for her. I did find it amusing, however,

327

when in a passing comment she said to me, 'John, you know where all the bodies are buried. Perhaps we could have a word some time?' I just smiled. That's for me to know, I thought, and you to find out.

The election had been for deputy leader, not DPM. Gordon left the position empty. Perhaps there will never be another. It might mean I'll end up with the honour of having been the longest-serving deputy prime minister ever. One of my research staff, before I left, did some digging.

As with so much of the British constitution, the office of deputy prime minister has never been properly formalised. Its existence depends on whether or not the prime minister of the time recognises that he or she has a deputy.

So, working on that definition, the role first came into existence during the war when Attlee served as Churchill's deputy in the coalition cabinet. He held that post for three years, 1942–5. Herbert Morrison did it for six years, 1945–51. Anthony Eden, my old friend from my stewarding days, did it for only four, 1951–5, and Rab Butler only managed it for one, 1962–3. In the sixties, under Harold Wilson, George Brown and Barbara Castle held the title first secretary of state, but were never formally recognised as deputy prime minister. But Willie Whitelaw had the position officially for more than eight years, under Margaret Thatcher, 1979–88. Geoffrey Howe lasted only one year, 1989–90. Michael Heseltine had his base in the Cabinet Office, and made quite a bit of noise as deputy prime minister, but only for two years.

When I resigned at the end of June 2007, I'd held the

position for ten years and two months – an all-time, all-comers world record.

Over those ten years in a Labour government, there are lots of things I'm proud that we did. Creating full employment, with two million more employed than had been in 1997, plus low inflation and a sound, growing economy.

On a personal note, Kyoto was a high point for me. And the China Task Force. Back in 1997, I was banging on about green issues and carbon emissions when everyone was either not bothered or saying, 'Boring, boring.' Now that's changed, fortunately for us all. The whole world is trying to be eco-friendly, build eco-houses and live eco-lives.

The Channel Tunnel link has been a huge success. In my Transport days I was pilloried by many people for the congestion charge and other things, but now I find myself at dinners in my honour given by the transport industry. *Transport Times* has just done a big feature on me, saying I was ahead of my time. 'Remember the glory belongs to the man in the ring, not the critics on the side-line carping. Thanks for everything, John.' So that's been nice.

There was one relatively minor change I brought about, which I'm sure most people are not aware of. When the high-speed 125 trains first came in, it was possible for the doors to open while the train was still travelling. This led to several deaths every year because people had fallen out. I complained about it to the railway authorities, when I saw the figures, but they said, 'Oh, it's nothing to worry about, just drunken squaddies, playing around with the doors.' Malcolm Rifkind, then Tory Transport secretary, refused to take any action.

And then a little girl fell out, aged about eight. That showed me something was wrong. She couldn't have opened the door herself. They still said it would be too expensive to make all the doors secure, but I insisted they had to. With the child's mother, I arranged a London press conference about the incident. Rifkind then found it was possible to put these locks on the doors.

Today, on the mainline trains, you have to wait for the light to go on when the train has stopped. It's only then that you can open the door. You never read about people falling from trains now. When I go on the 125s today, and note the locking light is working, I think of the twelve to fifteen people each year who might have died but for this simple electronic device.

On the countryside, I am very pleased it was under Labour that open access came in, plus new National Parks, thanks to my legislation. And on shipping, changing the flags of convenience and bringing in a tonnage tax brought huge benefits – I'm quite proud of that.

One result was the new *Queen Mary 2*, which still flies the Red Ensign. It was a shame it was built in France. I did ring Cammell Laird in Merseyside when they estimated £100 million more than the French. I asked them to consider it – and over the weekend they said, 'OK, it's now £100 million less.' That showed me they had no chance and Cunard wouldn't accept it. You can't just lose £100 million in a weekend.

At one stage the ship's name caused a problem. The Royal Household expressed concern about the use of Queen Mary the Second. I said, 'If this ship sails under the Panama flag, the owners can call it anything they bloody like.' So that's why it's called *QM2* not *QMII*, using the figure not the Latin numeral, to keep the Royal Household happy. The Queen herself launched it.

I suppose my biggest disappointment was in regional government, though my legislation did lead the way to the Scottish Parliament and the Welsh Assembly, after their rejection in the first referendum, and also the London Assembly. I had hoped for more assemblies in the English regions, but we lost the vital referendum in the North-east. I still think regional assemblies are a good idea and they'll be introduced one day.

There was one real cock-up, during the North-east referendum. They got me to record a telephone message, to go out to all homes in the area. The phone would ring, you'd pick it up, and you'd hear me saying, 'This is John Prescott, I hope you'll be voting for a regional assembly tomorrow . . .'

Unfortunately, someone forgot to program the computer and the message went out to the North-west and Yorkshire too, not just the North-east. Even worse, it went out at five in the morning.

A woman rang me up absolutely furious. She'd been sitting by her phone all night, waiting to hear about her husband who had been taken to hospital. So she rushed when her phone rings – only to hear me talking: 'I'm John Prescott . . .' That referendum must have caused thousands of phones to be pulled from their sockets. But we made personal apologies to all those who complained.

The regional assemblies may not have worked as I'd hoped, but we did have some considerable success in that policy area. One of our first acts of government was to set up the Regional Development Agencies, which I did with Dick Caborn. Everyone agrees they've really worked in reducing unemployment, increasing prosperity and reducing the economy differential between the North and South.

All parties are now fully committed to retaining them and increasing their powers and resources. Alongside this, working with the RDAs, came the New Deal for Communities and the National Coalfields Programme.

In both these areas there was high unemployment, low educational attainment and deprivation of the worst kind. In the case of the coalfield communities, their collapse arose directly out of the savage policy of the Thatcher government in destroying the mining industry.

Two months into government I recall attending a film called *Brassed Off*. The film struck a chord, confirming what I already knew about the terrible plight of these areas. I got increasingly angry at what had happened and decided something had to be done. I set about establishing a policy for the coalfield communities. Indeed, I announced it at the Durham Miners rally in June 1997, saying that this Government would respond and do all that it could to improve the communities and reduce the damage they had suffered under the Thatcher government.

I got together with an excellent agency of the department, English Partnerships, who set up a £500 million programme for the coalfield communities along with a £2 billion programme under the New Deal for Communities initiative, investing in thirty-nine of the country's most deprived areas. Both policies, according to independent bodies, have been a huge success. Working with the RDAs, the local authorities and the communities themselves the programmes have reduced unemployment, poverty and deprivation and brought back greater pride. I am very proud of the difference that the Labour government has made in these areas.

Looking back, I can't remember a really serious row with Tony. That Harriet Harman incident was about the most heated, from his point of view, and it was piddling. I did give him more serious cause for complaint, yet despite what the papers wrote at the time, such as over the punch-up, I was never given a bollocking, or in the slightest danger of the sack.

I suppose the worst thing I did was say, 'President Bush is crap.' This happened during my summer watch of 2006 when the police raided the London home of some people who were allegedly plotting a terrorist outrage. I'd been told it was going to happen for fear of a chemical bomb. I rang Tony and John Reid, the home secretary, and expressed my concern. The police argued that it was an operational matter, but I thought they overreacted, sending in hundreds of armed cops, closing off the streets, preparing to move people out of their homes in the middle of the night – and in the end they found nothing. The Asian community was up in arms, and so were our Labour MPs, particularly the Asian ones.

I held a private meeting with a group of MPs to try and calm them. I said I thought the police had acted deplorably. They made critical remarks about President Bush, expressing their constituents' views, blaming him for causing all this, and that's when I found myself saying, 'Look, many of us in the Party feel President Bush is crap, but we must concentrate on our priorities.' It got leaked by one MP, not an Asian, to the *Independent*, which did a big story that everyone followed up – saying I would now be for the chop.

It was a private meeting. None of it should have come out. I know who did it, oh yes. And he is well aware of what I think of him.

I rang Tony in Barbados and told him the circumstance. I said, 'Yes, I admit it, I did say the words "President Bush is crap".'

He thought for a minute, then said, 'Oh, well, your standing in the Party will go up ten points.'

His people tried to put it about that he was really upset with me, but he wasn't. Tony was never a bayonet guy.

The time when the papers said I'd been demoted, after my department was broken up, they got that all wrong. I had been planning for the changes that were made, and had agreed it with Tony long beforehand, as early as 1997.

People always thought I might have got into trouble for giving the V sign to the press. It happened when I was walking to a cabinet meeting in Downing Street. As usual, the photographers and TV people were there, shouting at me, trying to get a reaction, or at least get me to turn my head. Some of it is pretty abusive, and personal, which, of course, you don't hear on TV or read about in the papers.

On that particular day, some TV guy shouted, 'When are you going to resign, John?' I just ignored him, didn't look in his direction, but as I entered No. 10, I gave him a V sign with my fingers behind my back. I hadn't realised some of the press would get a photograph of this, though I should have.

Joan Hammell then got lots of phone calls, asking her about what I had done and why. She didn't know what they were on about. She had been walking ahead of me, into No. 10, so hadn't seen what I'd done.

Next day the *Sun* had the photo on its front page with the caption 'Same to you Prescott'.

Tony never said a word to me. I did try to say arthritic fingers had caused it, but nobody believed me. After that, Joan always walked behind me when we went into No. 10, to obscure the photographers' view.

Did I have a major effect on his policy and thinking? I'm not going to claim I did. Lots of people have thought, and written, that they had great influence over him. I think they overestimated that.

I confess to having my own agenda in attempting to find a solution to certain policy issues which Tony and Gordon disagreed on. I played some part in getting a final solution, on hospitals, on academies, for instance, which was as near as possible to the values which would be acceptable to the Party.

My opposition to Paddy Ashdown right at the beginning of the Labour government, I'm sure that did affect Tony's decision. There were also occasions when he would have been in trouble if I hadn't backed him. I saw my job as supporting him while trying to get government policy through. As for keeping the peace between him and Gordon when they were at each other's throats, I did that for the good of the Party.

Despite all those rows with Gordon, Tony in fact got stronger as the years went on, which is unusual. Prime ministers usually fade, after an initial surge. I think it was because he was hesitant at first, never having had any experience of government, or even of being a junior minister. He had to find his way, work out how to do the job, and in the first year, he was lumbered in his cabinet with people he had inherited. Tony got better at governing as he learned on the job how to do it.

I was very lucky to be Tony's deputy prime minister and proud to have achieved with him the best record of any government, Labour or Tory, on economic prosperity and social justice. I was also proud to have worked with Gordon Brown, whose support was essential for a number of my achievements in office.

Without Tony, we would not have won those three elections. He was a New Man: he appealed to the public who clearly liked him as a person. We needed a change of leader, and he was the right man for the time, a brilliant, exceptional politician. I don't think people at home ever realised just how much he was admired in Europe.

But, of course, we were also lucky to have Gordon, in charge of the economy, which he looked after magnificently. Yes, our opponents will always say the economy would have done well anyway, but I disagree. Anyway, Gordon did it. They didn't.

So, what we had was a combination of economic prosperity and social justice, which is very rare in a country's history, plus a brilliant leader. And that's why we won those three elections.

If we failed for all those years earlier because we were

seen to have heart but no head – then at last we had turned things around. For once, Labour was seen as having both heart *and* head. That was Gordon's contribution, without which we would not have won those three elections. And I now believe Gordon will go on and win a fourth.

On 3 July 2007 when me and Tony had been out of office for a week, I got a very nice letter from him. Handwritten, as he doesn't type or even use a computer – at least, he didn't used to:

Dear John,

I was really proud to have worked with you as the DPM over our 10 years together. The Channel Tunnel Rail Link, the renaissance of shipping in Britain, inner city regeneration, the China Task Force and much more all contributed hugely to the record of our Government. But quite apart from the specific achievements, your role as DPM in smoothing out problems, sorting out colleagues and trouble shooting were an integral part of getting things done. The completely unique Prescott blend of charm and brutality – made always more effective by the unpredictability of which would be predominant – got you through the decade, kept the Government together and above all, gave me a lot of fun.

I was lucky to have you as my deputy. Thank you.

Yours ever,

Tony

CHAPTER TWENTY-SIX

2008

Today
Early Summer

Now, almost a year since I left office, things have settled down and I feel much better physically and mentally. I've got new routines, some new positions, which keep me busy.

We found a place to live in London, in a newish block, with lots of glass, just across the river, ten minutes from Parliament. The views are brilliant, right across to Big Ben. We don't need a clock in our apartment any more as we always know the time. I hadn't realised there's so much action on the Thames. I can watch the boats all day long, or look down from our big picture window and see the people below, bustling over Lambeth Bridge like little Lowry figures. I keep thinking it's a film set. The flat has just two bedrooms, but enough for me and Pauline when we are in London.

I walk to the House most days, to keep fit, and there's also a gym in the block, which I try to use every day.

I haven't been in touch much with Tony, not socially, though we have met a few times at Labour Party things. But why should I? We weren't personal or social friends, just good colleagues.

In the ten years Tony was PM and I was his deputy, I can think of only two occasions when I was invited to Chequers. Pauline often used to say, 'When are we going? Why haven't we been invited?' There was one occasion when Al Gore wanted to see me, and had asked if I would be at the dinner at Chequers. The other time was early on, a proper invitation, personal, for me and Pauline. You could say that was the only proper invite we had in ten years. Yet when Tony left, it emerged after, I think some Liberal MP forced it out of No. 10, that there had been endless dinner parties for celebs – pop stars, sports stars, writers, the odd cabinet member – of the New Labour variety. I read the lists with amazement – because I was looking for Labour people. And there were hardly any.

At the grand opening of St Pancras station in November 2007, a bloke came up to me who said he had done the sculpture of John Betjeman that stands there, with a bag, looking up, holding his hat on. He said he wanted to sculpt me. My head was made for sculpting, he said.

'People usually want my head on a plate,' I replied, 'not on a pedestal.'

I don't think I'll agree to do it. I can't be bothered. Though I got thinking that there's no painting (except that one where I was 'removed' from the front bench), photograph or statue of me anywhere in the House of Commons, despite all those years in office and serving as DPM, yet lots of ministers get remembered in some form.

But I have got a nice photograph, which Pauline took when they were putting up the statue of Margaret Thatcher. It wasn't ready, but they had the plinth, waiting for the statue to arrive. Pauline got me to stand on it – then took my photograph. It makes me smile. That's how I'd like to remember my time in the Commons. I worked hard, got a lot done, but I also enjoyed it and had some laughs.

I've also got some nice letters from Prince Charles, from my years as DPM; many of them handwritten, or bits handwritten. They were mainly about his various interests and charities, like the Prince's Trust, telling me what they were doing. He would often send me copies of speeches he had recently made on, say, climate change, in case I'd missed them. He usually added a few personal touches: 'I hope there will be a chance of seeing you again in the not too distant future. Meanwhile, this comes with my warmest good wishes to Pauline and yourself.'

One handwritten note was about something I might buy. 'I saw recently in a Christie's catalogue that an unusual full-length portrait of Oliver Cromwell had come up for sale and wondered if you had been tempted to add it to the collection of pictures in your office . . . !'

341

He always signed himself, 'Yours ever, Charles'. I never quite knew how to write back. I felt 'Dear Charles' was a bit familiar, yet 'Your Royal Highness' seemed a bit flunky-like. So I stuck to 'Dear Prince Charles'.

Now I'm taking lots of exercise, trying to eat sensibly, not over-indulge or overdo things, I'm very much back to form. I'm at home more often now, as I don't work such long hours and rush all over the place, so I'm seeing more of Pauline and the boys.

Johnathan is married, lives in Beverley, near Hull, and will be forty-five this year. When he left school he did a number of jobs before leaving the UK to live in Boston, Massachusetts, where he worked for a large franchising company. After returning home, he entered the retail sector and became property director for a UK clothing company. Following this, he joined a housing-regeneration company where he became project manager. Today, he runs his own property company with a London-based business partner. They source and structure land and property investment deals in the UK and Europe. He's very busy and travels a lot.

Johnathan has had a rough time with the press, mainly because he is involved with the property sector. He has always respected my position in government and has never discussed his business with me. However, even though the press have always known this, they have not stopped pursuing the Prescott agenda by trying to get at me through him, which was deeply regrettable. But he's a strong character and we are proud of him and his wife, Ashley.

David, now thirty-seven, played in a pop group for a while, when he left his comprehensive, around the North. Then he became a journalist, working locally. In one of his earliest jobs he had to ring up his mother and get a quote. He's married to Rozlynn and they live in London. He's also worked in TV, travelling the world as a producer and reporter for GMTV until he came back to launch local TV in Hull, before becoming a home-news editor for BBC Network News. He's now a director at the UK's number-one consumer PR agency and a local Party activist in London.

What most people don't know is that David had been an unpaid researcher and adviser to me for more than twenty years – even briefing me in No. 10 for PMQs and providing some of my best lines of attack. He never asked for a penny. He just wanted to help his father and the Party in any way he could.

He did try on three occasions to work for Labour. I kept telling him, 'You're wasting your time – they can't stand one Prescott in this Party, let alone two!'

David made the very brave decision of standing, unsuccessfuly, to become the next Labour candidate for Hull East. It was the hardest seat he could ever go for but he was passionate that he wanted to represent his home town. The name probably did count against him but he's a real fighter, has a lot to give and I'm very proud of him as well.

After his second marriage collapsed, my father, Bert, did meet another woman, quite a wealthy one, but never married her. My mother married again, to Ron Swales, a civil servant. He became my stepfather and I got on with him OK.

My father lived till he was ninety-two. On his ninetieth

birthday, he announced he was giving up buying LP records. After he died, we scattered his ashes on Chester racecourse, beside the winning post, which is about the nearest he got to it in real life. There was me and Pauline and a few close friends. We had a bottle of champagne with us, in a bucket. While one of our friends, Gordon Vickers, was reading a poem for Bert, which he'd specially composed, the cork popped out of the champagne bottle, all on its own. 'Typical Bert,' we all said. 'Even now, he can't wait to have a drink.'

My brothers and sisters got married and are still alive. Ray went into the RAF and became a flight engineer, then worked for various airlines, such as BA, but is now retired. Dawn also went into the RAF. Viv lives in North Wales. Adrian, the youngest of our family, is a church worker in Liverpool, married with two kids.

When Raphael Samuel, my old tutor at Ruskin, died in 1996, the *Guardian* asked me to write his obituary. He had such an influence on my early life, and was such a wonderful man, I agreed to do something. I made notes then dictated it over the phone. They typed it out and corrected any grammatical mistakes.

I can write things when I have to, despite what people might say, but after all these years it still doesn't come easily. I prefer talking, making speeches.

While I was looking through my papers, documents and scraps for this book, I found a union notice I'd got printed when I was on board one of the Cunard liners. There were two versions – the one the captain printed for me and the other my rough handwritten one, which I'd given him to print. The printed version has a grammatical mistake – 'it's' instead of 'its' – but the funny thing is, I hadn't made that mistake in my original copy. The captain or his staff had made it, not me. Just shows you. If I take time, I can usually get things right. Well, sometimes.

The other day I wrote an introduction for a book on the history of Cunard stewards. I did it in longhand, as I can't type, but I got my secretary to type it out and correct any obvious grammatical mistakes. But there weren't any.

All the same, I am still embarrassed by my use of English. It did upset me all those years when I got mocked for it, even though I tried hard to brush it off. A few years ago I had a dental plate put in my mouth, and that made speaking more difficult. I still maintain I always got across my message. But, of course, it can take the gloss off a message if someone takes the piss out of how it is delivered.

It probably explains why today I get no pleasure from reading, not novels and suchlike. Never have done. I got put off all that at school, or I should say I put myself off by not being interested. Today, when my son David says something is not very well written, I don't know what he's on about. I can't tell so-called good writing from bad. All I'm interested in is getting information. That's the only reason I ever do any reading. I'm gobbling up facts. When it comes to style, or literary qualities, I'm just not aware of it. It goes over my head.

Another thing that's hardly changed, despite all these years of having to appear in public, is that I always feel self-conscious – not in a big public gathering or event: I can address an audience of thousands without any worries or embarrassment. But I can't go into a restaurant on my own, or a hotel. I have to be with Pauline or my sons. And

I usually let them go in first, so I can slip in after them, unnoticed. I can't even ring a hotel or restaurant – I have to get others to do it for me.

I don't quite understand it. I feel as though everyone is looking at me, and have done since long before I went into politics. You could say, I suppose, it's a form of vanity, thinking people are looking at you when they're not. But I think it's probably a sign of insecurity. If I'd gone to Eton, I probably wouldn't have felt it. Joke. I know it happens to people from all walks of life, but the upper classes seem able to cope with it better. Confidence is built into their system whereas working-class people are plagued with doubts the further they progress in their working life.

I also hate waiting. I just can't do it, whether I'm in a queue for the cinema or at a restaurant for a table. I can't do it. I'd rather leave. And I don't like being told what to do or that I've done something wrong.

I hardly ever go into shops. I don't like buying things and I really detest the idea of bargaining. I just accept whatever I'm told. My son Johnathan will always try to get a deal, find out about a bargain, but I'm not bothered, though I do like to pay the lower price.

I suppose it's because I'm not interested in money – and never have been. When I left the Government and had to buy somewhere in London, I couldn't believe the prices of flats. Just as well Johnathan did all the work for me.

I was also embarrassed when that rubbish came out about this American billionaire, Philip Anschutz, I visited in America, the one who had bought the Dome and was looking at ways to develop it. I was already in the US, on political business, when I went to see him, to look at the sports and recreational facilities he had, with a view to what might be possible for the Dome and possibly the Olympics. He then invited me to have a look at his ranch because he knew I'd be interested. And I was. In fact, it was the second ranch I'd been to on my trip. Anyway, I stayed there two nights. We went out riding and it was fascinating and enjoyable. End of story.

The press made a huge fuss about the fact he gave me some riding gear – jeans, boots, a hat, a shirt etc. – the working clothes I'd been out riding in. I was pleased with the outfit. I've always loved cowboys, since I was a kid. They made out it was the most enormous bribe and I was therefore going to do him a favour over the Dome – which was press prattle. At the time, talk of 'super casinos' was generally in the air and the press tried to make a link – as if I was going to help the bloke get a casino licensed at the Dome. Total rubbish. We didn't discuss casinos at all – and why would we? I had nothing to do with the decisions being taken over the casinos. In the end it was never turned into a casino anyway. I was always an advocate for Blackpool as the place for a super casino, to help turn it into a modern conference centre. And just to clear things up finally about my stay on the ranch – I offered to pay for the two nights but was refused. Instead, I came to an arrangement – which was cleared officially by the Government – that an appropriate payment would be made to charity.

I was amused recently when the papers dug out a list of presents Tony received as prime minister – which included a pair of cowboy boots from President Bush. That's what Americans do, it's part of their culture. But he didn't get criticised as I did because no one found out at the time.

It has been hard, in my political life, having to put up with stories of freeloading, two Jags and all that, when I know money has never mattered to me. It's almost as if they did it deliberately, knowing that money has never been my vice, just to hurt me. As for something I did do wrong, well, I had to pay very heavily for that one, and always will.

CHAPTER TWENTY-SEVEN

2008–

Tomorrow

I'm still an MP, and will be till the next general election, whenever that takes place. I'm also a delegate to the Council of Europe, a job I used to do almost forty years ago, and a delegate to the Western European Union Defence Assembly. I was elected to both positions by the PLP after I resigned as DPM. I was initially leader of the Labour group in the Council of Europe but now I am leader of the whole UK delegation (likewise for the WEU assembly), made up of MPs and peers from all parties.

There are 450 or so members and we meet in full assembly in Strasbourg and Paris once or twice a year. It's a bigger, older body than the European Parliament but, of course, doesn't have the same powers. It's more of a discussion forum, but has a monitory and enforcement role in the Human Rights Act.

The Parliamentary Assembly of the Council of Europe is the institution which aims to maintain and further human rights and fundamental freedoms and facilitate social and economic progress. The assembly also monitors the member states' commitment to the two hundred plus Council of Europe treaties. As leader of the British delegation to the assembly, I get the use of a car while the Council is in session four weeks of the year, and expenses, but the position is unpaid. Committee work within the Council means I am in Europe two weeks out of four.

In early 2008, I went three times to Armenia to oversee the fairness of their elections, leading a delegation of thirty MPs from all over Europe, on behalf of the Council. It took a lot more time than I expected as a result of post-election protests. These led to the death of eight people and hundreds injured. An emergency order was imposed and I was sent by the president of the Council to try and assist. I was able to help formulate an agreement to restore normality.

I'm also hoping to be involved more in China. I've made so many contacts there over the years and I'm fascinated by the country. Its power and importance are growing all the time, and its status, with the Olympics in 2008, then Expo 2010 in Shanghai. I'm no longer joint chairman of the China Task Force, as that was a government appointment.

Tony, of course, as an ex-prime minister and world statesman, has a big role to play, and he can also earn a lot of money. He's supposed to have got £250,000 for giving one speech to some property developers in China. I don't know if that's true, it's only what I've read, but I taunted him when I met him recently, at a Labour Party function in the North. 'I spoke to the same people as you, Tony, three bloody times – and I wasn't paid a penny!'

The reason of course was that I was a government minister at the time, so it was part of my job.

This do was to thank us, me and Tony, for our ten years as prime minister and deputy. In his twenty-minute speech, Tony spoke about me, praising my work, thanking me and cracking a few jokes.

He told a story about me and this very important person whom he was trying to get rid of. He called him into his office, while I was there, and started twittering on to this bloke, going round the houses, trying to work himself up to telling him he wasn't doing a very good job.

According to Tony, I suddenly interrupted and said: 'Listen, Tony thinks you're crap – you'll have to go.'

Everyone laughed when Tony told this story, nodding at me. It was true – but what Tony didn't know was that I had already done a deal with this feller. He knew he was for the chop, but I'd met him privately beforehand and fixed a deal. So before Tony started on him, he knew what was coming. He got what he wanted. And Tony got the person in his place he wanted.

But during Tony's talk, I did learn something I didn't know, which happened at a cabinet meeting. It was when I was secretary of state for the Environment and was about to give them a long, detailed report on some environmental issue. I was in the middle of it, when Patricia Hewitt interrupted to ask me about women and the environment. I went mad, telling her she was absolutely wrong, it wasn't just a women's issue, what was she on about, typical of the Sisters . . .

What I didn't know was that it was a put-up job. Tony had suggested she asked the question, just so the rest of the cabinet could enjoy my reaction, watch the steam coming out of my ears. I do have a reputation as a male chauvinist pig, which I don't think is correct, as I've done a lot for the cause of women, such as implementing the women's lists in the Party, but it's true I was always suspecting the Sisters' increasing demands.

I fell for it. And I had never realised, until now, that it was a joke at my expense. I don't think we would have pulled the same stunt on Tony. You don't do that to a prime minister. But he wasn't that sort of person anyway. He was always relaxed. He didn't get worked up, not the way I did when it was an issue I really cared about.

While we were at that event, Tony asked me how my book was going. He is doing his own, for some supposedly large amount, and I'm sure it'll be much bigger and more important than mine. 'You'll be launching your book in Waterstone's,' I said to him. 'I'll be launching mine in the supermarkets.'

He laughed, and then he said, 'I hope you'll be kind to me.'

'Tony,' I said, 'I'll just be telling the truth. You wouldn't want me to do otherwise, would you? But don't worry, the full political story will await more reflection.'

I'll be making a few speeches in future, on the lecture circuit. I've only done one so far, addressing some of the UK's mortgage lenders at their big dinner in Monaco. Funny that, how they tend to pick such pleasant places. Pauline came with me, so it was nice for her as well. I found it a bit nerve-racking, wondering how to pitch it – did they want serious economics or just jokes? I did both.

Since the time of Keynes, I told them, economists and the financial world generally have been able to blame the Government when things have gone wrong – often with good reason. But the present instability in the financial markets, the problems with Northern Rock and other institutions, is in fact their fault, not the Government's. We've given them ten years of a strong, solid economy, two million more in work, lowest inflation for decades, growth all round, but their greed has got them into trouble. All these huge City bonuses, lending to dodgy people, giving millions to the sub-prime market, has led them to take risks they should not have done – and it's backfired. So I fairly hammered them.

I also told some old jokes. I said my wife had recently lost her credit card. I didn't report it. Whoever has stolen it has been spending less than she has . . .

Then I told the one about the woman in a bank who's trying to get some money out of her account. She's asked if she has further proof of her own identity. So she opens her handbag, takes a mirror and looks into it. 'Yes, that's me . . .'

My fee was quite modest, I'm told, compared with what some speakers get, but it was an interesting experience. I hope to do a few every year, depending on the organisations that might ask me.

So, yes, I've now just broken my forty-year rule of not taking money for any outside work. Now I'm no longer a minister, and about to stop being an MP, I feel I should be trying to earn some money for my retirement.

I'm also planning to work on a two-part TV series this year. The subject is class. They think I'm an expert. I dunno why.

I've taken on one unpaid job in Hull, as a director of Hull Kingston Rovers. Now that I'm out of office, I'll be able to do a bit more for my constituency than I was able to as a minister. I can't say I'm a huge rugby league fan, but I've always supported them and often been to watch them play. They have future plans I may be able to help them with from my parliamentary experience.

Will I go to the Lords? I know that previous deputy prime ministers, like Willie Whitelaw and Michael Heseltine, went straight there. Pauline would like me to, but I'm not thinking about it at the moment. I've always been against too much flunkery and titles and all that. I'm quite happy for now to be a back-bench MP, till this Parliament finishes. We'll see what happens.

Looking back over almost forty years in Parliament, one of the biggest changes has been in the media. We now have twenty-four-hour, round-the-clock news. There are so many papers, TV and radio stations and blogs that you can't keep up with them all, or their demands. In the old days, I might have been asked once a week to comment on some topic of the moment, now it's on the hour. Nobody can have a scoop any more, even though they boast about breaking news. It's all so fast, with so many outlets.

Nobody has any real news so what we have is the cult of celebrity. Which includes politicians. Every titbit gets reported, and if there are no titbits, they make one up – 'inside gossip', as it's called. When they write about celebrities, they don't worry about accuracy. They just shuffle the gossip around, repeating the same old stuff that someone has already shuffled, by which time nobody knows or cares what was true. In showbusiness, they've long been used to this, and I suppose most of them don't care. They see it as good publicity. In politics, we now get the same treatment. The Press Complaints Council should be dealing with it, but they don't. They're useless.

The general public is now supposed to have a low estimation of politicians. But I don't believe it. It's just what the newspapers like to peddle. When I meet people in the street, they're still as pleased to see me as they were forty years ago. I don't get booed or hissed at, just because I'm an MP. Which is the image the press likes to give. Since leaving the Government, I've been getting an even nicer reception, to my surprise. In fact, I hardly dare say it, but everywhere I go these days I seem to be met with affection. It must be lack of power.

I have to admit the culture of spin might have got worse over the years. And I suppose it is partly thanks to the School of Mandelson.

When we were in the shadow cabinet, we were worried by the Tory press continually suggesting we had fallen out among ourselves. They would jump on one word that was different, then hammer us. This has become the main object of people like John Humphrys and Jeremy Paxman: to catch you out. If they do, they think they've got a news story, or 'set the agenda', as they like to call it. Other media will do follow-ups and they'll feel dead clever and smart.

I was once being interviewed by David Frost. I think he might be getting a bit deaf, because I could hear what was being said into his earphones while he was asking me questions. The voice of Tony Blair seemed to be coming from David Frost, and I realised his producer was feeding into his ears the exact words of some statement Tony had made earlier – hoping to catch me out by getting me to say something marginally different. Luckily Frosty was getting so annoyed and confused by the noise in his ear that he pulled out his earpiece. We were then able to have a proper conversation. I much prefer, when being interviewed, to live on my wits, and have the other person do the same.

Anyway, once the shadow cabinet realised that this was what so many in the media were after, to catch you out on some word, Mandelson made sure all ministers worked to a brief, stuck to the prepared position. You can call that spin, if you like, but it was our defence against what was happening. It was brilliant and it worked. All ministers, from all sides, now do this. They get told the awkward questions they might be asked, and the replies to give.

So it was funny, I suppose, when Lord West, the retired admiral who'd suddenly become security minister in 2007, came a cropper. On the *Today* programme, he said he wasn't convinced about the need for a fifty-six-day detention period for suspected terrorists – then had to recant two hours later after No. 10 had got on to him. A prime minister might like the idea of having outside experts in government, but they have to learn to dance the right steps. They think they can speak their minds. They can't. The bloody press will crucify you.

I might have gone on a bit saying, 'I dislike the media,' or 'I dislike the Tories.' I have always tended to view politics in black and white. I saw Tories and Liberal Democrats as the enemy, just as I used to see employers as the enemy. I never mixed with them, never socialised. I'm sure my attitude wasn't right. A lot of them were probably good people, but that's how I grew up, that's what I thought.

And, yes, I know, I have complained about journalists stigmatising and pigeonholing me, making generalisations about me, when I do much the same when it comes to Tories. If that's a contradiction, then that's me, a mass of contradictions. My life has been full of them.

I notice that the whole problem of phone-tapping and buggings, the so-called 'Wilson Doctrine', has recently come up again, in relation to the bugging of an MP. The Wilson Doctrine originally just referred to phone-tapping but it now applies to all forms of interceptions and to bugging by the security and intelligence agencies.

I did at one time go to see Tony about this issue and followed that up with a further discussion with the Speaker, thinking we can't hold back, we've got to have a new ruling. I was also worried about the police habit of photographing demonstrators during marches or demonstrations, which I knew all about from my days at seamen's strikes.

Ministers from all parties have for a long time often

made it clear that they didn't want to know about such things. 'Don't tell me,' they'd say to the security forces, so they could always deny any knowledge. The whole subject is a Pandora's box. Once you open it up, God knows what you'll find. But I think the most important thing with security is that you must always keep control of the people ordering, or actually doing, the tapping and bugging.

Another issue is party political finances. I was staggered to hear that deputy leadership campaigns were costing over £100,000. I spent only £10,000 on mine – and that was mainly on leaflets. I got a personal loan from the bank, which I had to pay back, and the rest came from donations, in sums of fifty or a hundred pounds from my personal supporters.

Cash for honours has always been a bit of a mess, and a grey area. It goes back to Lloyd George. Obviously, the vast majority of the people in the Lords never paid a penny for their peerages, but you hear these stories, none of which ever gets proved. I'm sure it has gone on, though I never had any personal knowledge of it.

Under Old Labour, it was known we got money from the trade unions, which was honest, if you like, as it was open and above board, and union members could vote against it. With New Labour, and the weakening of the union links, we had to rely on business donations, and that's where it got dodgy. I hated all the gala dinners where we invited wealthy people to donate money. I went to one and found myself seated next to Owen Oyston, who later went to prison. There was a book auction, signed books or something, with the money going to the Party. Next day, I read in the papers that I had spent three thousand pounds on books. Me? Buying books? What a laugh. I hadn't, of course. It was just a way of some wealthy bloke giving money to the Party.

Labour has always had trouble raising money. In the old days, we would spend the first half of a new parliament paying off the debts we had incurred for the last election. Then halfway through we would be solvent again, and start saving for the next election. In recent elections, we've spent the whole five years in debt, permanently forced to borrow from the Co-op bank and others.

I always wanted all political donations to be recorded, and I got that passed, and also a limit set, but that never happened, because of the Tories. In Labour Party Executive meetings, I would try before each election to agree a limit on our expenses.

I was especially against last-minute expenses. They were usually on advertisements, when they'd say, 'Oh, we've got to do it. The Tories are doing it.' I thought the adverts were a bloody waste of money, and said so, but No. 10 would take no notice. At the last moment, you'd find they were spending money we hadn't got. I'd complain and they'd say, 'Don't worry, John, the money is guaranteed.' So, after each election, we'd end up with an even bigger headache. Hence all the fuss about third-party donations – given through other people.

Jack Dromey, the Party treasurer, says he never knew about these donations, which I could believe, but I think he should have done. I also believe his press statement, made against NEC advice, helped damage the Party's image and to my mind led to the unfair treatment of the general secretary of the Party. And that, along with other matters, has led to a kind of blame culture within the Party, which is not healthy.

I think what will happen in the future is two things. First, all parties will have to agree on a limit on election expenses, which will mean getting the Tories to agree. Secondly, there will have to be state funding. It's the only way if you want to stop talk of political parties being involved in dodgy deals and suggestions of sleaze. It's not generally recognised that opposition parties receive millions of pounds of state funds.

As I have said often enough, the politics of organisation are equally as important as the politics of ideas. We will have to do a great deal more to improve relations between the Party and Government if we are to get to our full campaigning and recruiting capacity. At the moment we are some way away from this and the mood in the Party and amongst its officers is not as good as it needs to be, and should be, to win the next election.

So who are the government stars of the future? I've read that I'm supposed to hate Ed Balls, who became Gordon's Education minister. But it's not true. I can only assume that it's another example of unnamed advisers telling stories. This is why there are going to be so many differing accounts of Blair's premiership – because, hell, we've had so many advisers. Where do they all come from? And what can they advise on when many have done nothing in their lives?

As for Ed Balls, I always admired his abilities when it came to economics. He is clearly highly intelligent. But I can't say I always agreed with his political judgement. He was part of the Gordon group, running around, spreading stories. Tony had his little gang of cronies doing the same. When I used to confront Tony or Gordon, about leaks or whatever, they would always deny it had anything to do with them. 'So you can't control your own fucking team,' I'd say to them.

The other young minister tipped for glory is, of course, David Miliband, who got promoted to foreign secretary. I always called him one of the No. 10 Mekons. He told a story about me at one of my farewell parties. He said when he became one of my ministers at the Department of the Environment, I took him round on his first day and introduced him to the senior civil servants by saying, 'The Mekons have landed.' I don't remember that, but I probably did.

He's good and clever, a high flyer. Like Ed Balls, he will develop. But they both need experience. And they need toughening up a bit. But it will happen. They should go far.

But I do worry that in the future we won't have many politicians, in any party, who have come from my sort of background, people who have had experience of real, ordinary working life. They'll all be lawyers or people who have gone straight from university into the political world in some form – working in think tanks, as researchers or advisers. I'm not saying lawyers don't work hard, because they do, but they've not had 'worker experience' as I understand the term.

What you do in your life before you become a politician affects your life and attitudes as a politician. That's not to say someone who has only been a graduate will make a bad politician. It's just that their experience of life will be limited.

The channels I came through, doing an ordinary working job and then with the union, tended to produce a person who was used to fighting the bosses. You were naturally hostile to a lot of what the authorities were doing or telling you. You had a subordinate role in the hierarchy, often at the bottom of the pile, but you prided yourself on being independent. You would kick out, even though you knew it might lead to losing your job or getting marked in your industry. That's what toughened you up, made you think about what you really believe in. You worked on a gut feeling, on what you believed right or wrong. Lawyers don't and never have come through all that. They go by what's already been written or done.

The modern politician works on focus groups and polls – that's what decides his or her actions, not their gut feelings. There's been a sea change. The result is that all modern politicians are likely to be the same. All from the same cloth, with the wrinkles ironed out.

By 'gut feeling', I don't mean just a knee-jerk emotional reaction. Knowing something in your guts is partly common sense, from long experience of what should and can't be done, without the need for spreadsheets. Lawyers know about the law and logic but they often don't have common sense.

The other element in a gut feeling is courage. They don't teach you that at law school – or in think tanks. You get that from living – and working – in the real world.

To succeed as a trade-union official you had, of course,

to know when to compromise, when to save bullets for the targets that really mattered. That's a useful skill for any politician. In the union movement we learned that – the hard way.

These changes are all to do with changes in society at large. And we can't go back. So many of the traditional industries have gone, with their factories, mines, docks and mills, and so have the huge unions that once produced all-powerful leaders.

But it will be a loss, I think, when people like me totally disappear from the cabinet. Parliament should reflect society. There should always be a place for people with what I call basic common sense and courage, even if they haven't been to a good school or Oxbridge. They can come from any walk of life, you know, and at any time in their life.

Most of all, I can't see a place in future for the awkward buggers. Where are they going to come from?

Appendices

Appendix 1
Election Results in my Constituencies 1964–2005

My first involvement in general elections was as a Labour Party agent in the 1964 general election in Chester, trying but failing to get the Labour candidate, Anthony Blond, elected.

In 1966, I stood as the Labour candidate in Southport – but didn't get in.

I was first elected to Parliament in 1970 for Hull East.

	Party	Votes	(%)
1964 *Chester*			
Labour Party agent			
J. M. Temple	*Conservative*	23,172	(48.82%)
A. B. Blond	*Labour*	16,708	(35.20%)
P. J. Samuel	*Liberal*	7,583	(15.98%)
Electorate: 59,654; turnout: 79.56%; Majority: 6,464 (13.62%)			

	Party	Votes	(%)
1966 *Southport*			
W. I. Percival	*Conservative*	22,324	(51.02%)
J. L. Prescott	*Labour*	12,798	(29.25%)
C. J. Coleman	*Liberal*	8,630	(19.72%)
Electorate: 60,218; turnout: 72.66%; Majority: 9,526 (21.77%)			
1970 *Hull East*			
J. L. Prescott	*Labour*	36,859	(71.44%)
N. S. H. Lamont	*Conservative*	14,736	(28.56%)
Electorate: 75,678; turnout: 68.18%; Majority: 22,123 (42.88%)			
1974 (February) *Hull East*			
J. L. Prescott	*Labour*	41,300	(69.99%)
E. D. M. Todd	*Conservative*	17,707	(30.01%)
Electorate: 80,681; turnout: 73.14%; Majority: 23,593 (39.98%)			
1974 (October) *Hull East*			
J. L. Prescott	*Labour*	34,190	(62.41%)
S. Dorrell	*Conservative*	10,397	(18.98%)
J. Adamson	*Liberal*	10,196	(18.61%)
Electorate: 81,624; turnout: 67.12%; Majority: 23,793 (43.43%)			
1979 *Hull East*			
J. L. Prescott	*Labour*	39,411	(62.51%)
M. M. Beam	*Conservative*	15,719	(24.93%)
M. J. Horne	*Liberal*	7,543	(11.96%)
D. J. Matson	*Nat. Front*	374	(0.59%)
Electorate: 89,023; turnout: 70.82%; Majority: 23,692 (37,58%)			
1983 *Hull East*			
J. L. Prescott	*Labour*	23,615	(49.90%)
D. Leng	*Conservative*	13,541	(28.61%)
C. Grurevitch	*Alliance* [*Lib*]	10,172	(21.49%)
Electorate: 70,037; turnout: 67.58%; Majority: 10,074 (21.29%)			
1987 *Hull East*			
J. L. Prescott	*Labour*	27,287	(56.31%)
P. Jackson	*Conservative*	12,598	(26.00%)
T. Wright	*Alliance* [*Lib*]	8,572	(17.69%)
Electorate: 68,657; turnout: 70.58%; Majority: 14,689 (30.31%)			

	Party	Votes	(%)
1992 *Hull East*			
J. L. Prescott	*Labour*	30,092	(62.90%)
J. L. Fareham	*Conservative*	11,373	(23.77%)
J. Wastling	*LibDem*	6,050	(12.65%)
C. Kinzell	*Natural Law*	323	(0.68%)

Electorate: 69,036; turnout: 69.29%; Majority: 18,719 (39.13%)

	Party	Votes	(%)
1997 *Hull East*			
J. L. Prescott	*Labour*	28,870	(71.31%)
A. West	*Conservative*	5,552	(13.71%)
J. Wastling	*LibDem*	3,965	(9.79%)
G. Rogers	*Referendum*	1,788	(4.42%)
M. Nolan	*ProLife*	190	(0.47%)
D. Whitley	*Natural Law*	121	(0.30%)

Electorate: 68,400; turnout: 59.19%; Majority: 23,318 (57.60%)

	Party	Votes	(%)
2001 *Hull East*			
J. L. Prescott	*Labour*	19,938	(64.58%)
J. Swinson	*LibDem*	4,613	(14.94%)
S. Verma	*Conservative*	4,276	(13.85%)
J. Jenkinson	*UKIP*	1,218	(3.94%)
L. Muir	*Socialist Labour*	830	(2.69%)

Electorate: 66,397; turnout: 46.50%; Majority: 15,325 (49.63%)

	Party	Votes	(%)
2005 *Hull East*			
J. L. Prescott	*Labour*	17,609	(56.58%)
A. S. Sloan	*LibDem*	5,862	(18.84%)
K. A. Lindsay	*Conservative*	4,138	(13.30%)
A. Siddle	*BNP*	1,022	(3.28%)
J. H. Toker	*Liberal*	1,018	(3.27%)
G. E. Morris	*Veritas*	750	(2.41%)
R. E. Noon	*Independent*	334	(1.07%)
L. Muir	*Socialist Labour*	207	(0.67%)
C. A. Wagner	*Legalise Cannabis All.*	182	(0.58%)

Electorate: 65,407; turnout: 47.58%; Majority: 11,747 (37.74%)

Appendix 2
General Elections 1964–2005

	Party	Seats	% Seats	% Votes	Party leaders
15 October 1964					
Labour	*Lab*	317	50.3	44.1	H. Wilson
	Con+UU	303	48.1	43.3	A. Home
					E. Heath
Turnout = 77.1%	*Lib*	9	1.4	11.2	J. Grimond
31 March 1966					
Labour	*Lab*	363	57.6	47.9	H. Wilson
	Con+UU	253	40.2	41.9	E. Heath
Turnout = 75.8%	*Lib*	12	1.9	8.5	J. Grimond
					J. Thorpe
18 June 1970					
Conservative	*Con+UU*	330	52.4	46.4	E. Heath
	Lab	287	45.6	43.0	H. Wilson
Turnout = 72.0%	*Lib*	6	1.0	7.5	J. Thorpe

	Party	Seats	% Seats	% Votes	Party leaders
28 February 1974					
Labour	Lab	301	47.4	37.2	H. Wilson
	Con	297	46.8	37.8	E. Heath
Turnout = 78.8%	Lib	14	2.2	19.3	J. Thorpe
10 October 1974					
Labour	Lab	319	50.2	39.3	H. Wilson
					J. Callaghan
	Con	276	43.5	35.7	E. Heath
					M. Thatcher
Turnout = 72.8%	Lib	13	2.1	18.3	J. Thorpe
					J. Grimond
					D. Steel
3 May 1979					
Conservative	Con	339	53.4	43.9	M. Thatcher
	Lab	268	42.2	36.9	J. Callaghan
					M. Foot
Turnout = 76.0%	Lib	11	1.7	13.8	D. Steel
9 June 1983					
Conservative	Con	397	61.1	42.4	M. Thatcher
	Lab	209	32.2	27.6	M. Foot
					N. Kinnock
Turnout = 72.7%	All.	23	3.5	25.4	D. Owen/
					D. Steel
11 June 1987					
Conservative	Con	375	57.7	42.2	M. Thatcher
					J. Major
	Lab	229	35.2	30.8	N. Kinnock
Turnout = 75.3%	All.	22	3.4	22.5	D. Steel
					P. Ashdown

	Party	Seats	% Seats	% Votes	Party leaders
9 April 1992					
Conservative	Con	336	51.6	41.9	J. Major
	Lab	271	41.6	34.4	N. Kinnock
					J. Smith
					M. Beckett
					T. Blair
Turnout = 77.7%	LibDem	20	3.1	17.8	P. Ashdown
1 May 1997					
Labour	Lab	418	63.4	43.2	T. Blair
	Con	165	25.0	30.7	J. Major
					W. Hague
Turnout = 71.4%	LibDem	46	7.0	16.8	P. Ashdown
7 June 2001					
Labour	Lab	412	62.5	40.7	T. Blair
	Con	166	25.2	31.7	W. Hague
					I. Duncan Smith
					M. Howard
Turnout = 59.4%	LibDem	52	7.9	18.3	C. Kennedy
5 May 2005					
Labour	Lab	355	55.0	35.2	T. Blair
					G. Brown
	Con	198	30.7	32.4	M. Howard
					D. Cameron
Turnout = 61.4%	LibDem	62	9.6	22.0	C. Kennedy
					M. Campbell
					N. Clegg

Appendix 3
My Parliamentary Career
1970–2008

PPS to Peter Shore, secretary of state for Trade, 1974–6;
    Shadow spokesman for:
        Transport, 1979–81
        Regional Affairs and Devolution, 1981–3

Member of shadow cabinet, 1983–97

    Shadow minister for:
        Transport, 1983–84
        Employment, 1984–7
        Energy, 1987–8
        Transport, 1988–93
        Employment, 1993–4
Deputy prime minister, 1997–2007
Secretary of state for the Environment, Transport and the
Regions, 1997–2001

First secretary of state, 1997–2007

Commons back-bench committees
Member, Labour Party Departmental Committee for
Environment, Transport and the Regions, 1997–2001

Party groups
Deputy leader:
    Labour Party, 1994–2007
    Labour Party National Executive Committee, 1997–2007

International bodies
Member, Council of Europe, 1972–5
Delegate, European Parliament, 1975
Leader:
    Labour Party delegation to European Parliament, 1976–9
    UK delegation to Parliamentary Assembly of the Council of
    Europe, 2007–
Western European Union Defence Assembly, 2007–

Appendix 4
Pamphlets, Papers and Policies

Over the years I have been responsible for producing many pamphlets and policy papers. The first, *Not Wanted on Voyage – The Seaman's Reply*, was done before I became an MP. Others were done in that period and once I became an MP. Many of the key ones were produced when I was on the front bench, in opposition. When we came to power in 1997, many of these pamphlets and papers were implemented and became policy. The work in opposition was not in vain.

Below I have listed some of the key pamphlets I produced and the policies and papers that they turned into, once Labour was in government.

Economy

Opposition Papers

1982   Alternative Regional Strategy (setting out the case for decentralisation)
1985   Planning for Full Employment
1987   Real Needs – Local Jobs
1994   Financing Infrastructure Investment (private sector working with the public sector to increase investment – such as the Channel Tunnel Rail Link)
1994   Jobs and Social Justice (achieving economic prosperity and social justice)
1994   Policies into Action (my manifesto to become deputy leader – implementing the policies and ideas in previous pamphlets)

Government Policy Papers, actions and initiatives

1997   Regional Development Agencies
2002   State of English Regions
2004   Regional Assemblies
2004   Northern Way (driving sustainable economic growth in the North)
2004   Jobs, Enterprise and Deprivation

Transport

Opposition Papers

1989   Moving Britain into the 1990s (huge increase in investment in our transport services)
1991   Moving Britain into Europe (high-speed European rail link)
1993   Full Steam Ahead (shipping tonnage tax)

Government Policy Papers, actions and initiatives

1997   Channel Tunnel Rail Link
1998   New Deal for Transport – 10 Year Transport Plan
1999   British Shipping – New Course Tonnage Tax

1999   Re-opening enquiries into the loss of the *Derbyshire*, *Gaul* and *Marchioness*

Sustainable Communities

Government Policy Papers, actions and initiatives

1997   Regional Development Agencies established
1999   Urban Renaissance White Paper
1999   New Deal for Communities
1999   Coalfield Community Programme
1999   Urban Regeneration Companies
2001   Neighbourhood Renewal
2001   Millennium Community Programme
2002   Core City Programme
2002   Urban Summits
2002   Living Places, Powers and Responsibilities White Paper
2002   Homeless Act
2003   Sustainable Communities
2003   Fire Services reform
2004   State of English Cities
2004   Northern Way Strategy
2005   Design for Manufacture Competition (£60k houses)
2005   Homes for All

Appendix 5
Fact File and Q & A

Basics

Born: Prestatyn, Wales; 31 May 1938. Father Bert, railway worker; mother, Phyllis; two younger brothers, two younger sisters.

Married: Pauline Tilston, 11 November 1961; two sons, Johnathan, born 1963 and David 1970.

Education: Grange Secondary Modern, Ellesmere Port, 1949–53; Ruskin College, Oxford, 1963–5; Hull University, 1965–8.

Employment: Commis chef and hotel porter, 1953–5; ship's steward, 1955–63.

Height: 5'9", but I was taller, till I broke my back in a car accident.

Weight: 15 stone 5 pounds (96 kilos). It has been up to 16 stone 5 pounds, but I now do forty-five minutes in the gym every morning.

Personal

House: I've only ever owned one house at a time and have lived in our house in Hull since 1965. I now also have a flat in London near Westminster, bought 2007.

Car: I always have Jaguars, and always second hand. For some time I've had an XJS Sports, fourteen years old, which cost me £7,000. I've recently bought a Sovereign saloon, as well, ten years old, as it's got more space. So, it's come true at last – I do own two Jags . . .

Newspapers: I read the *Guardian* and the *Independent*. Pauline gets the *Daily Mirror*.

Hobbies: I don't really have any. I used to do quite a bit of diving and swimming, but not in recent years. I love the cinema and usually go once a week.

Drink: I don't normally drink. I never have wine with a meal – though Pauline usually has a glass of white wine – or drink beer. I have rarely used the Members' bars in the House of Commons. Perhaps a couple of times a year I might have a glass of champagne at a wedding or a shandy at a party. I prefer water or soft drinks. When I was at sea, I would go drinking with my mates at the end of each voyage, but I never drank during a voyage. I have been drunk, a few times in my life, when I've stupidly found myself drinking brandy, such as watching the England–Scotland football game with Gordon Brown.

Smoking: I have never smoked, except the odd Churchill cigar when I was at sea. But, no, I didn't inhale.

Clothes: Not really interested, but I like to be smart. I usually wear suits, have done since I became an MP in 1970. I used to get them from Hepworths. Now I use a shop in Hull, James Wright's, for my Pal Zileri top suits and shirts for my working suits, but always off the peg. Pauline chooses my shirts and ties.

Religion: Agnostic, though I was brought up Church of England. I refused to have my sons christened, which upset Pauline. I wanted them to make up their own mind about religion when they got older. David, in fact, has chosen to become a Roman Catholic – just like someone else we know . . .

Cooking: I can do a bit, because I trained as a chef, but I leave it all to Pauline, though I have done the Christmas dinner, and when we have company, I usually clear up.

Favourites

TV: I like the History channel best. I can watch anything about the Second World War or any diving programmes.

Films: The last one I saw was *Atonement*, which I went to because I thought Pauline might like it. Neither of us did. My favourite is *West Side Story*. I saw that eight times. I also liked *Billy Elliot*, the film and the stage version in which a Hull lad played the lead.

Music: Jazz, especially Duke Ellington, Sarah Vaughan and the late Marion Montgomery; she was a great friend of ours and her husband Laurie Holloway still is. I often go to Ronnie Scott's. I love the National Youth Jazz Orchestra, run by the wonderful Bill Ashton, MBE.

Food: I can eat anything. I like it all – as long as it's plain and simple, such as fish and chips. My favourite restaurant is Jack Chu's in Hull and the Gran Paradiso in Victoria, London.

Q & A

A common misconception about me is . . .
That I'm a lager lout. That came from *Spitting Image*.

The most surprising thing that ever happened to me was . . .
Marrying the most beautiful girl in the world. Well, in Chester, anyway. Becoming an MP, that was a surprise. I never planned to be one.

I'm good at . . .
Swimming, diving and boxing. I'm still working on the croquet . . .

I'm bad at . . .
Keeping my temper. I let 'em have it. I do tend to blow up, but then it's over quickly. There are people I will never speak to again, because of something they have done or said.

What irritates you about your wife?
When she walks in front of the telly as a goal's about to be scored, or a boxer's about to be knocked out, or says something to me when she can see I'm working.

What does she find irritating about you?
That I'm irritable and aggressive.

In moments of weakness, I can . . .
Scoff a whole packet of digestive biscuits, or loads of Marks &
Spencer trifles, one after the other. I love them.

What's your earliest political memory?
Delivering Labour Party leaflets for my dad when I was eight or
nine. He was a local councillor.

Who were the biggest influences in your life?
Mr George, a teacher at my secondary modern in Ellesmere Port;
Raphael Samuel and John Hughes at Ruskin College, also his wife
Vi; then John Saville at Hull University.

Who were or are your heroes?
In politics, I'd have to say Ernie Bevin and Clement Attlee. Attlee
was a hero in our house when I was growing up, while Churchill
was seen as a baddy for shooting at the miners in Wales. As for
other heroes, William Wilberforce. He was an MP for Hull, and I
was active in the anniversary celebrations for the abolition of
slavery. For an all-time hero, it's got to be Mandela.

Why did you want to go into politics?
I didn't. I wanted to be a trade-union official.

So why did you do it?
Well, it's better than working. Joke. No, I consider it a privilege.
I don't think I could have been as happy in any other job. I can't
think of another occupation in which my quirks would have
been tolerated. You don't have a boss. Only the electorate can
sack you. And I've been fortunate to represent Hull for many
years.

So what are the pleasures?
Being able to help at local level and solve people's problems,
especially when I was standing in for Tony and the total
government machinery was available. People usually come to see
their MP because they're in real trouble, suffering poverty or
deprivation. On a national scale, being able now and again to
change laws. Introducing £60,000 sustainable houses – only a
national government could have made that happen.

What's the worst?
The press. I hate nearly all of them. Bastards. I don't speak to them. Over the last forty years, personalities have begun to matter more than policies, which I think is sad. There's also too much cynicism, a lot of it spread by journalists, at the behest of their editors.

What does it take to be a successful politician – ability, hard work, luck, able to manoeuvre and intrigue?
I'd put luck first – you have to be in the right place at the right time – followed by hard work. In my case, I didn't do any manoeuvring. When I arrived, I owed nothing to anybody and I had no patrons.

You've had several nicknames – Thumper, Two Jags, the Mouth of the Humber, Prezza. Do any upset you?
No. I've called other people lots of names. I gave Tony Blair the nickname Bambi. That came out of me being called Thumper. I was trying to think of other Disney characters I could call people.

When were you happiest?
At Ruskin. But I've enjoyed all the stages of my life.

As a politician, what would you say were your strengths?
Sensitivity – I do like to think I care for and understand ordinary people, especially those in trouble; ability; aggression.

And your weaknesses?
Quick-tempered; too trusting – I tend to trust people till I have reason not to; my use of English grammar. I've suffered a lot for that, having to put up with jokes, but I think good judgement is more useful than good grammar. I said that once to William Hague, after he was mocking something I'd said. In his judgement, Jeffrey Archer, whom he was backing as Mayor of London, was a good man . . .

When did you last punch someone?
Ha-ha. That's what President Clinton always asks me when we meet. The point about hitting that man who threw an egg at me was that it was in self-defence. I've never actually physically attacked anyone. Only when they've hit me. Or emptied a bucket of water over me.

What was your best speech?
There was one I gave when I was in my early twenties, to an

385

open-air rally in Liverpool of striking seamen. Many people, including my dad, said I shouldn't do it. I was too young and inexperienced. But I did and it worked. As a politician, I suppose my best was the One Member, One Vote speech at the Labour Party Conference in 1993, when it looked as if John Smith, our leader, would have to resign.

In all your years in the House, who have been the best speakers?
I'm not sure what you mean by best, but I think the most effective was Robin Cook. I also like Dennis Skinner. On the other side, among the Tories, the best in my time was probably William Hague. But I don't actually rate being a good performer in Parliament. I was never a chamber man. I think in fact it's a bit of a circus. But it's the best one we've got.

Who, in your time, was the best Labour leader?
Harold Wilson. He had a much harder job than Tony Blair, keeping the Party together. The Labour Party was going through a very difficult period when Wilson was in charge. Tony had it easier as we were united. But I don't think actually that Tony was Labour like Harold.

The best prime minister?
In my lifetime, undoubtedly Attlee. In my time in Parliament, Tony Blair – ahead of Margaret Thatcher. She just bulldozed her way. Tony was the best politician I ever came across in deploying his case. He didn't try to dominate but to persuade, which he did very well. He was a great performer, a great presenter. He was also a Teflon man – usually managing to slide away with no damage.

Tories, are there any you have a soft spot for?
I think a lot of Labour people liked Ted Heath. He created the most warmth on our side. I think we saw him as more of an old-type caring Tory, a dying breed. He believed in fairness, which was close to the heart of the trade unions.

You've been a Hull MP since 1970, yet Hull regularly features in the list of worst places to live in the UK. Why? And should you share some of the blame?
I have to admit that educationally Hull does badly, and I should know having had two sons at local comprehensives. Things have got better, but not enough. The crime figures are also poor. I think, in each case, Hull has not been helped adequately. Its location has been a handicap – it's isolated. The southern towns

are bound to come out better on all these 'best' lists, because they're richer and middle class, which means better schools, more work. On the other hand, their carbon output is worse than ours, with all their 4x4 cars, and they have a lack of community facilities, such as local halls etc. When I see these best lists, most of them pretty stupid, or those TV property programmes like *Location, Location*, I tell them to come to Hull and I'll show them round. But they never do. Hull docks now has a beautiful marina and the Deep, which is an aquarium, gets about a million visitors a year; there's a new shopping centre, and Hull University is very good. More students want to stay on in Hull after graduating than they do in almost any other university town. Now I'm a back-bench MP, I have more time to get involved in local activities, such as becoming an unpaid director of Hull Kingston Rovers. I hope to do more.

There's a general public perception that politicians are untrustworthy, obsessed by spin, on an ego trip. Any truth in this?
All politicians are involved in a bit of spin, in that you naturally want to see the best interpretation of your policies. I like to think I told things as they were. As for trust, the media is always trying to catch you out for having changed your views, which they then say proves you can't be trusted. But circumstances change. Things don't sit still. The press are always trying to create dramas, often out of their own imagination, but that's the price you pay for a free press. As in any other walk of life, there are good and bad politicians but I'd say the vast majority are genuinely trying to do their best for the country.

I don't think I've been obsessed by my ego. I never saw myself as a career politician, planning the next stage. I just did each job as well as I could. But I have pride in what I did, which I suppose you could say is a form of ego.

What have you learned during your years in politics?
Michael Heseltine gave me some advice when I first became a minister – listen to your civil servants, then make your own judgements. It was good advice. Things always take longer than you expect – that's been a hard lesson to learn. Projects I worked on in the 1970s took thirty years to succeed. Also, you never know when something will be successful. The Dome is now, but it was rubbished for years. Always have in mind the big picture, the long-term, not the short-term, view. Don't worry if you don't

accept the conventional view and have to accept temporary unpopularity. That happened to me during the Cod War, but my strategy was proved right.

What would you say have been your main successes?
Locally, being a good constituency MP, looking after local needs. Nationally, helping to bring about full employment. Internationally, negotiating the first Kyoto agreement, when all seemed lost.

Your biggest disappointment?
That I didn't succeed in establishing elected regional assemblies – but I know they will come, as in Scotland, Wales and London.

How would you like to be remembered?
As good-looking, dashing and intelligent, speaking perfect English. As that's not likely to happen now, I'd settle for someone who tried to do his best and gave his all.

Index

Note: Subheadings are in chronological order. 'JP' stands for John Prescott. Page numbers in *italic* denote Appendix entries.

389

Picture Credits

Credits are listed according to the order the pictures appear on the page, left to right, top to bottom.

'JP' denotes photographs that are courtesy of John Prescott and his family.

Section 1
Page 1: Daily Herald, JP, JP, JP; page 2: all JP; page 3: JP, JP, JP, Mirrorpix, JP; page 4: all JP; page 5: Gillman and Soame Photographers; page 6: JP; page 7: all JP; page 8: JP, Mail News & Media Ltd, JP

Section 2
Page 1: Southern News Pictures, JP, Mail News & Media Ltd; page 2: Mail News & Media Ltd, JP; page 3: John Harris/International Freelance Library Ltd, JP, JP, Andrew Wiard/Report Photos, JP, Adam Butler/TopFoto; page 4: JP, PA Photos, JP, JP, JP; page 5: PA Photos, John Frost Newspapers, Rex Features, TopFoto, isfphotos; page 6: Matthew Polak/Corbis, JP, PA Photos; page 7: PA Photos, PA Photos, Rex Features, Joan Hammell; page 8: Express Newspapers, JP, JP, JP

Inside front cover: JP

Inside back cover: H P Merten/Robert Harding World Imagery/Corbis